CYCLING THE BUSH
100 Rides in Tasmania

By the same author
CYCLING THE BUSH: 100 Rides in New South Wales
CYCLING THE BUSH: 100 Rides in Victoria

CYCLING THE BUSH
100 Rides in Tasmania

Sven Klinge

HILL OF CONTENT
MELBOURNE

First published in Australia 1993
by Hill of Content Publishing Co. Pty Ltd
86 Bourke Street, Melbourne 3000, Australia

Copyright © Sven Klinge, 1993
Cover photo: Forth River (Ride 72)
Typeset in Australia by Midland Typesetters, Maryborough,
Victoria
Printed and bound in Singapore by Kyodo Printing Co.
(Singapore) Pte Ltd

National Library of Australia
Cataloguing-in-Publication data

Klinge, Sven, 1969–
    Cycling the bush

    ISBN 0 85572 223 1.

    1. Bicycle touring- Tasmania- Guide-books. 2.
    Tasmania-Guide-books. I. Title

796.6409946

Please note: The author and publisher can accept no
responsibility for accident, injury, or misadventure incurred
in attempting any of the suggested rides. Tasmania has some
very remote areas, inclement weather, and localised
infestations of venomous snakes. It is the cyclist's
responsibility to ensure self-sufficiency regarding overnight
rides.

CONTENTS

ACKNOWLEDGMENTS

I would like to thank Tim O'Loughlin, Wilderness Recreation Officer at the Department of Parks, Wildlife and Heritage, for advice on the legality of mountain biking in national parks.

I'd also like to acknowledge the following people and companies for their interest and support in building up this series of guides: Russell Spence at the Repco Cycle Co. Huw Kingston at Paddy Pallin Pty Ltd, John Rae and Martin Hanley at Hanley Trading, Alan Malone (Eureka Tents), Noel McFarlane at Bunyip Bags, Terry Townsend from Bicycles Incorporated, Hanimex in Hobart, and Robert Avery at TASMAP. All photographs including the cover were shot on Fujichrome *Velvia* 50 ASA 35mm film.

I'm also grateful to Frank Bichler, my cycling companion, Linda Rodriguez for the illustrations reproduced within, and to my parents, without whose support this guide would not have been possible.

FOREWORD

Tasmania, the mountain island, was made for the mountain bike. National Parks and other reserves comprise a relatively high percentage of the state's land area. The state's rich pioneering history has left a legacy of wild trails along which the cyclist can explore a diversity of spectacular landforms: jagged mountain ranges, pristine rivers, alpine plateaus, mossy rainforests, glacial lakes, and dramatic seascapes.

This guide suggests rides representative of all these types of terrain and more. Due to the high proportion of both international and interstate visitors who fly down with their bikes, ride descriptions have been constructed so that the bus network can be used to access staging areas. Many overseas visitors tour the periphery of the island, staying at youth hostels, and many rides start and end from the main perimeter roads, thus serving as interesting one or multi-day diversions. This is also useful for local cyclists who have the opportunity to drive to these staging areas. Occasionally, where appropriate, walking tracknotes are included.

Yet cycling is recognised as perhaps the best value method of seeing this island. Tasmania has no passenger trains (except for the tourist vintage-train at Devonport) and limited public transport and since it costs about $1000 to take a car to Tasmania from the mainland, cycling provides an economical way of touring. Many trails are closed to four-wheel-drives, either seasonally or permanently, while others are simply too rough for any motor vehicle but present no challenge to the adventurous mountain biker. A cyclist can carry over twice as much luggage as a walker, covering nearly four times the distance in the same amount of time while still possessing the flexibility of leaving their bike and proceeding on foot. Tasmania is relatively small, less than one per cent of the land area of Australia. Accordingly distances between any two points can be covered in less than a week.

The mountain bike has the versatility to cruise along highways and backroads at high speeds due to high gear ratios as well as being able to tackle rough rocky muddy trails because of knobbly tyres. However, as its popularity grows, it will no doubt come under the scrutiny of the recreational policy developers in the Department of Conservation and Environment. Already attention is being directed to their impact on the bush that they're designed to traverse. Erosion is a serious problem in Tasmania due to the soft soils, high rainfall, and frequency of visitors. It is essential that care must be taken to ensure that mountain bike users are not categorised with four-wheel-drivers as being a high impact recreational activity, resulting in limited access to Tasmania's scenic lands.

While there are only fourteen National Parks, they make up a large area totalling some 2,000,000 hectares. But this figure is tripled by the inclusion of dozens of protected areas, state reserves, conservation areas, and forest preserves. In addition there are state forests and vacant unallocated crown land. Thus the total non-rural/non-urban land area exceeds a third of the state – a vast playground through which the mountain cyclist can exercise, explore, photograph, and fish. With much of the scenery being of World Heritage status, and the drinking water and air among the purest in the world, the visitor can cleanse both body and mind.

Sven Klinge

RIDE LOCATIONS

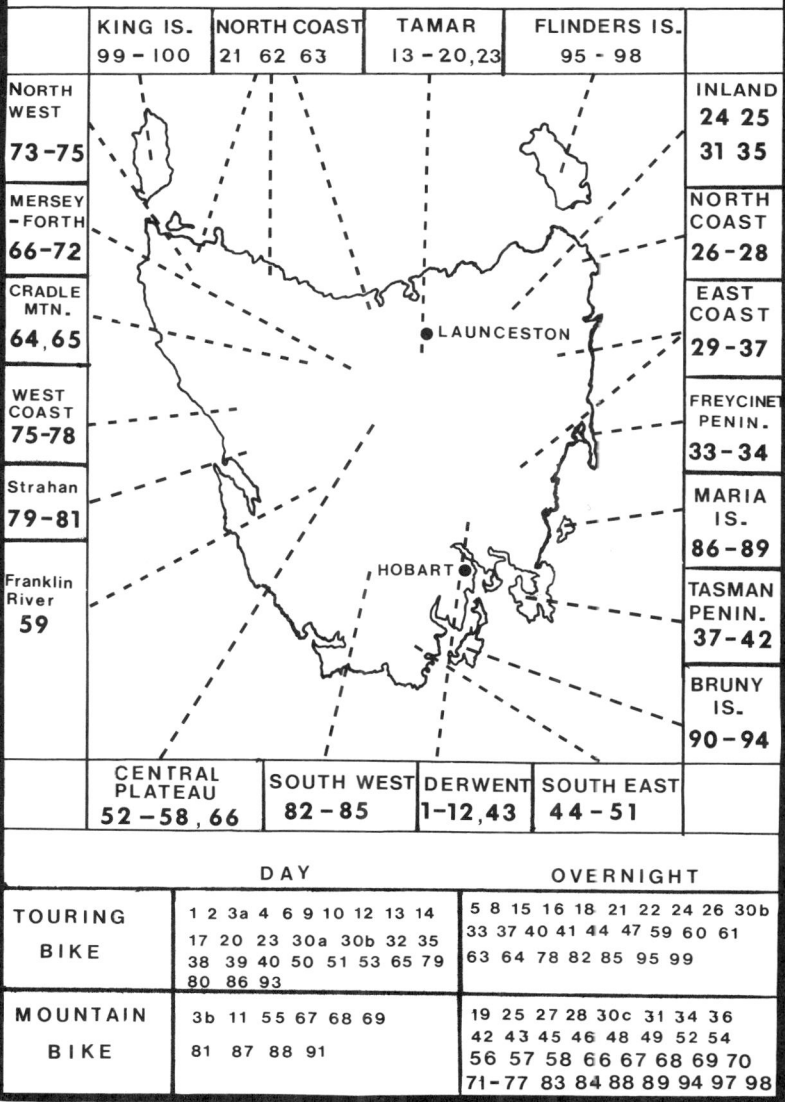

	KING IS. 99 – 100	NORTH COAST 21 62 63	TAMAR 13 – 20,23	FLINDERS IS. 95 – 98	

NORTH WEST 73 – 75

MERSEY – FORTH 66 – 72

CRADLE MTN. 64,65

WEST COAST 75 – 78

Strahan 79 – 81

Franklin River 59

●LAUNCESTON

●HOBART

INLAND 24 25 31 35

NORTH COAST 26 – 28

EAST COAST 29 – 37

FREYCINET PENIN. 33 – 34

MARIA IS. 86 – 89

TASMAN PENIN. 37 – 42

BRUNY IS. 90 – 94

	CENTRAL PLATEAU 52 – 58, 66	SOUTH WEST 82 – 85	DERWENT 1-12,43	SOUTH EAST 44 – 51	

	DAY	OVERNIGHT
TOURING BIKE	1 2 3a 4 6 9 10 12 13 14 17 20 23 30a 30b 32 35 38 39 40 50 51 53 65 79 80 86 93	5 8 15 16 18 21 22 24 26 30b 33 37 40 41 44 47 59 60 61 63 64 78 82 85 95 99
MOUNTAIN BIKE	3b 11 55 67 68 69 81 87 88 91	19 25 27 28 30c 31 34 36 42 43 45 46 48 49 52 54 56 57 58 66 67 68 69 70 71 77 83 84 88 89 94 97 98

KEY TO RESERVE CLASSIFICATIONS

WORLD HERITAGE AREAS: Areas of outstanding and cultural significance registered with Unesco in Paris. Tasmania has 20 per cent of its area (equivalent to 1.38 million ha) classified as world heritage. Land tenure is determined by state legislation, but international agreements and commonwealth legislation regulate management frameworks. A related reservation status is the Unesco Biosphere Reserve which act as a control against which human impact on pristine areas is monitored and recorded.

NATIONAL PARKS: Reserves having high conservation, scenic and recreational values and usually larger than 4000 ha.

STATE RESERVES: Generally less than 4000 ha and preserve a particular feature or site. An example is Hastings Caves.

NATURE RESERVES: Essentially for the conservation of a particular flora or fauna habitat which is unique, rare, or important. Occasionally recreation facilities are provided.

GAME RESERVES: Areas where habitats and animals are protected to the same level as in state reserves but where certain species may be hunted by permit. An example is Bruny Island Neck.

CONSERVATION AREAS: These provide protection from the actions of the public but not from actions undertaken in pursuance of a right granted under other legislation. The level of protection of a conservation area can be expanded by the implementation of a statutory management plan of the area. Examples are the Central Plateau and Cape Direction.

PROTECTED AREAS: Similar degree of protection to conservation areas allowing a controlled use of resources but reserved under the Crown Lands Act (Tas) 1976. An example is Mount Roland.

FOREST RESERVES: Declared by the Tasmanian Forestry Commission under the Forestry Act 1920 for several purposes: preservation of flora and fauna, aesthetic values, recreation, and sites of scientific interest. Mining is permitted, but forestry operations are not. The total area of the 45 reserves is almost 20,000 ha. Examples are Sandspit and Fortescue.

STATE RECREATION AREAS: Areas managed to provide for community recreation with some controlled commercial use of resources while protecting the natural environment. Usually contain a range of picnic facilities. Examples are the Meehan Range and Snug Falls.

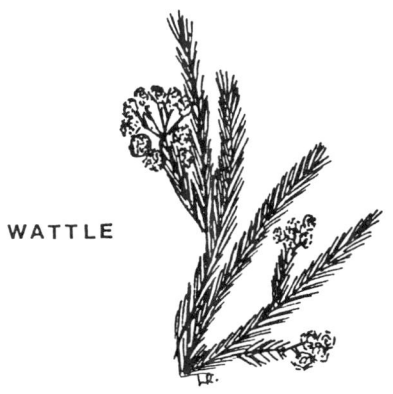

WATTLE

COASTAL RESERVES: Because of the popularity of water, these and Lakeside Reserves are managed on a multi-utilitarian basis where the aquatic and marine natural environment is protected as well as access and facilities provided for public enjoyment. Examples are Adventure Bay and Coles Bay.

HISTORIC SITES: Areas of significance in terms of European exploration or settlement with provision for public access. Examples are Port Arthur and Oyster Cove.

11

STATE FORESTS: Multi-use areas of forest production, protection, and recreation. Visitor conditions are relaxed, although some restrictions concerning hunting, fires, and camping apply. An example is Wielangta south of Orford.

TIMBER RESERVES: Same as state forests but without a recreational emphasis. Similar public restrictions apply.

OTHERS: Small miscellaneous areas include Muttonbird Reserves, Wildlife Sanctuaries, Aboriginal Sites, Archaeological Sites, River Reserves, Crown Reserves, and Non-Allocated Crown Land. The Hydro-Electric Commission (HEC) also owns land that is open to the public. Lastly the Commonwealth Government owns some land in Tasmania such as military training areas, quarantine stations, and lighthouses.

Please note when area sizes are given throughout text:

1 hectare = 2.471 acres.

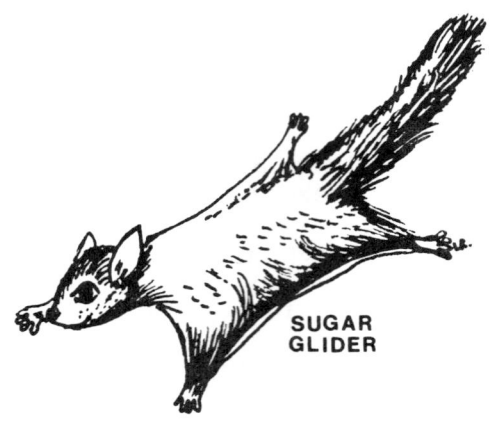

SUGAR GLIDER

TASMANIAN FORESTRY COMMISSION
(DISTRICT OFFICES)

HEAD OFFICE
   199 Macquarie St, Hobart (002) 30-8142

Geeveston (southern state forests)
   Main Road, Geeveston (002) 97-1501

Triabunna (south-eastern state forests)
   Victoria Street, Triabunna (002) 57-3243

Norfolk (Forentine concession)
   Royden House, 30 Patrick St, Hobart
   (002) 30-7450

Launceston (Wesley Vale reserve area)
   Prospect House, Bass Hwy, Launceston
   (003) 41-5356

Scottsdale (North-east state forests)
   Ellenor St, Scottsdale (003) 52-2466

Deloraine (Wesley Vale Pulpwood Area)
   Emu Bay Road, Deloraine (003) 62-2388

Devonport (south Asbestos Range area)
   Stoney Rise, Tugrah Rd, Devonport
   (004) 24-8388

Burnie (North-west state forests)
   Reece House, Mount & Cattley St.
   (004) 30-2234

Smithton (North-west forest reserves) (003) 52-1317

A KEY TO RIDE AND TRACK GRADES

GRADING OF RIDES

The difficulty of each ride is assessed from a fitness point of view. From this one can determine what the rate of progress will be. Please note these are only averages and approximations and are very subjective. They are included to give a more specific differentiation between rides than the traditional 'easy—medium—hard' classifications contained within many cycling guides. A ride will vary in its difficulty due to equipment, weather, fitness, hours of daylight, and track quality. Rides will naturally take longer to perform if they augment a full Tasmanian tour and the cyclist has to use his/her own power to travel to the staging area. All distances given are return. Some variations may vary slightly as I have sometimes taken distances from the nearest Youth Hostel which is not always in the centre of town. To give an appreciation of vertical variations spot heights are also given.

1. Downhill coasting; some pedalling required.
2. Level; easy pedalling.
3. Undulating.
4. Gentle uphills.
5. Short steep gradients.
6. Long steep gradients.
7. Some degree of fitness necessary to enjoy ride.
8. Challenging.
9. Experienced or fit cyclists only.
10. Masochism.

GRADING OF TRACKS

For each ride, the quality of the track will be graded on a scale of 1-10. The higher the number, the better tyres one will need, the slower one will have to travel, and the more challenging the ride. Where different types of tracks are encountered, the grading refers to the *worst* one. For all tracks rated at 3 or less, a conventional touring bike can be used.

1. Intercontinental expressway.
2. Country road, sealed.
3. Country road, unsealed.
4. Rough dirt road.
5. Roughest 2WD road.
6. 4WD track.
7. Abandoned fire trail.
8. Overgrown track: rocks, corrugation, erosion gullies, fallen trees, sand, washouts, and potholes.
9. Walking track: narrow, overgrown, steps, and roots.
10. What track?

Due to Tasmania's wet climate, many of the rougher tracks in the south and west can turn to mud. A mountain bike is recommended for all rides rated 3 and higher, and is essential for grades 5 and above. Fit wide knobblies and carry a pump so you can deflate and inflate pressures in accordance with terrain. Tracks along quartzite and dolerite mountain ranges are very rocky and kevlar belted tyres and thornproof or anti-crevaison tubes are recommended.

1
THE BIKE

An Introduction

Today mountain bikes are big business. Spearheading a new bicycle boom, they are capturing an ever increasing slice of the market. Even racers have mountain bikes as their second bikes. Young teenagers responsible for the BMX craze want a larger bike, but just as tough. Cycling magazines are full of articles, reviews, and advertisements for mountain bikes, and sponsorship of mountain bike racing has already entered the Australian scene in a big way.

Also known as All-Terrain Bicycles (ATBs), they are at the spearhead of rapid technological development. Aluminium, titanium, magnesium, and carbon fibre are replacing steel and chrome-moly traditionally used for constructing the frame and forks. These materials are lighter, stronger, and ultimately have the potential to be cheaper. High technology has also played the primary role in the rapid evolution of mountain bike components, with more efficient gear selection systems, and greater reliability in braking.

This development and level of popularity has ensured that competing manufacturers specialise their bikes to suit a variety of riders' needs. Accordingly, there is a tremendous range to choose from. Today one can pick up an imitation mountain bike with ten gears with the groceries at a supermarket for little over $100. The more enthusiastic can blow $10,500 for a top American 24-speed titanium competition model with shock-absorbers, up-turned racing bars, handle-grip gear selection, leather seat, kevlar tyres, and spokeless wheels. In Europe there are schools that teach the paying customer how to ride ATBs. Subjects include obstacle clearance, controlling descents, maintenance, falling, and navigation.

A BRIEF HISTORY

Although the mountain bike boom in Australia began in the early 1980s, its origins can be traced to the inter-war years. It was in 1933 that Ignaz Schwinn introduced his Excelsior, the bicycle equivalent of the tank, to the US. It was the first production bike to come with balloon tyres, coaster-hub brakes, only one gear, and wide backswept handlebars. It was constructed from twenty kilos of carbon steel. But unfortunately at the time, few saw its merits and its use was confined to newspaper delivery and other similar utilitarian duties.

Its potential was only discovered after groups of local teenagers 'terrorised' the country backroads with motorised trail bikes. The problem became so serious that environmental damage was being caused by the hundreds of motorbike wheels spinning in soft ground. Restrictions were consequently enforced.

Legend has it that in one particular region near San Francisco where this erosion problem and complaints by rural residents were particularly severe, the young enthusiasts looked for an alternative means of descending steep hills as fast as possible. It had to be on wheels, and noiseless, and incredibly strong. After many spectacular and often 'unhealthy' experiments with various types of bikes, the old Schwinn Excelsior, a motorbike lookalike, made a comeback and remaining models in the locality were quickly bought up for as little as $5.00 each. It was one of the few bikes on which riders had a fairly good chance of reaching the bottom without their relatives making a life insurance claim.

But it wasn't without its faults. On one famous stretch in Marin County on the slopes of Tamalpais, the Cascades Fire Trail was so steep (total drop:

800m) that continual use of the brakes was needed during the 'bombing'. The coaster hub the Excelsior was equipped with had a tendency to overheat, to the extent that the grease was boiled right out of the bearings and had to be repacked before the next descent. Old footage of this was seen in the BBC documentary series on the bicycle screened in Australia in 1992.

This hill, now named Repack Hill, is considered the birthplace of the mountain bike, for it was here that new equipment was tested. By the process of natural selection, the bike evolved to its present form. Gary Fisher, a racer, added derailleur gears, thumb shifters, and a quick-release mechanism on the seat-post of his Schwinn so that riding *up* the hill was now possible, and indeed he was first man to demonstrate this feat.

The maturing of the mountain bike was facilitated by two men: Jow Breeze and Tim Neenan. They developed the frame geometry and, with California businessman Mike Synyard, they sold the first production mountain bike, the Specialised Stumpjumper, for $750.

Even with a huge advertising budget, the Japanese manufactured bike had only moderate success, and it wasn't until Tom Ritchey and Charles Kelly teamed up with Gary Fisher that mountain biking came into its own. The conservative European manufacturers initially lagged behind America, Taiwan, and Japan, but soon caught up and introduced a whole series of high quality frames and innovations. By manufacturing aluminium rims and nylon gumwall tyres, four kilograms can be shaved off. By the late 1970s, this constant refining led to standards required by serious competitors. But perhaps more importantly, they gave it the status that's now taken for granted: the mountain bike was no longer a device whereby some offbeat suicidal daredevils got their thrills, but a respectable machine that everyone from businessmen to bushwalkers could use.

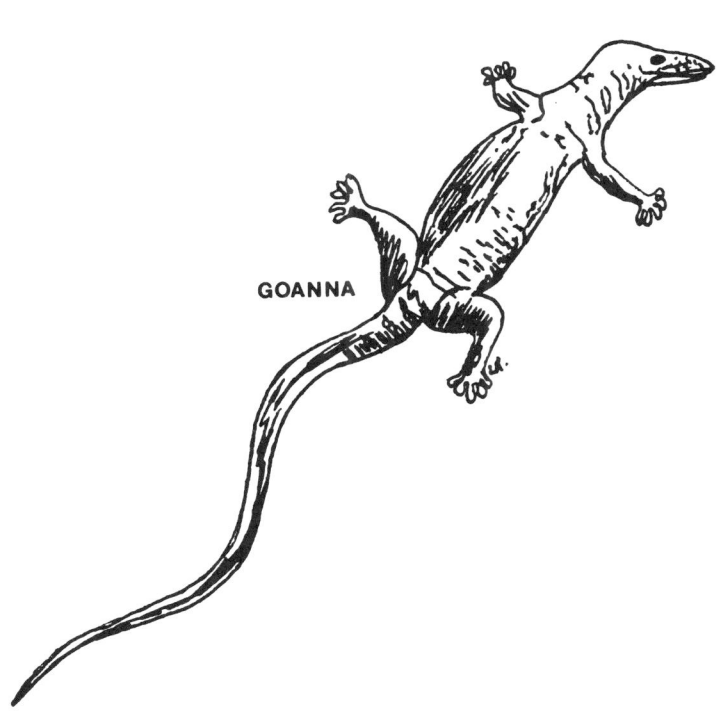

GOANNA

STEEL HORSES
The Bicycle in the Australian Bush

What more hallowed turf than the MCG could hold Australia's first bicycle race in 1889? While early models were built with the aid of Americans and Europeans, it wasn't until 1875 that importation of mass produced bicycles began, and the Tasmanian bicycle club became established in 1880. Newsletters were written, rallies and exhibitions were held, and distance records were established between capital cities. The Australian capital of cycling was undoubtedly Melbourne—the focus of the golden age of bicycles in the 1890s when significant improvements and price reductions meant thousands could afford this easy to use, cheap, efficient form of transport.

The Dux Cycle Co* in Melbourne employed up to 150 labourers who constructed bikes for domestic and even international markets. Around the turn of century there were dozens of brands (from Acme to Zimmy) on the market, selling tens of thousands, first costing around £35 each then dramatically dropping to between £4 and £10. It sounds cheap but this was the equivalent of several weeks' wages.

Bush bikes were advertised as having superior clearance, thornproof tyres, greater strength, and were 'designed to suit the rough roads of Australia'. Tall tales abounded as to the feats people had performed riding the first bicycles in the Australia bush. For example, adding springs to jump post-and-rail fences, kangaroo shooting, and chains made from bullock hide, and races with horses, and luggage of forty kilos for trans-continental treks. As it infiltrated the bush, the bicycle was

---

* A Dux bike was first used to cycle from Perth to Brisbane in 1897, a distance of 6000 km.

used increasingly for rural tasks, until observers were predicting the extinction of the horse. In Tasmania, for example, a farmer carried cans of cream on the crossbar on a 12 km route, while others converted their early treadlies to haul vegetables and coal.

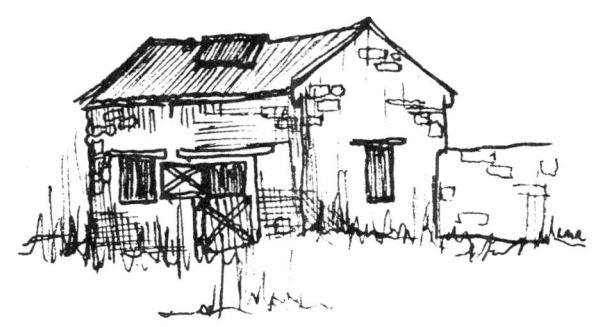

Cycle touring grew in popularity—because of the rough nature of early roads and the virtual non-existence of motor vehicles, bush cycles were the ideal way to travel. However, the pastime was not without fatalities. Thirst, break-down, lack of efficient brakes, being chased by dogs were all causes of death. In Tasmania, track conditions were especially bad with over two-thirds of roads graded as natural surface or cleared only. Punctures were numerous and average speeds were far less than on equivalent country roads in the States and Canada.

Early cycling gazettes and magazines are full of colourful accounts of the hazards early bush cyclists had to go through. One adventurer complained of the continual loss of spokes due to sticks being flipped into the wheels, while others encountered fencing wire in the cogs, stumps, anthills, salt lakes, mud, logs, and plagues of prickly *Emex australis*. Cyclists went out of their way to travel on anything but the appalling roads—even to the extent of travelling in between railway lines and on camel pads. The latter was claimed to be the best cycling surface and camel tracks were used extensively in the West Australian gold fields. It was here that official bicycle paths were formed with the levying on a bicycle tax.

Mountain cycling was first recorded in the late nineteenth century. Excursions to the Victorian Alps began as early as 1896, the rugged Budawangs in NSW were crossed in 1889 and the summit of Kosciusko attained by bike in 1898. The first guide for mountain cycling was written in 1897 and published as the *Austral Wheel Guide to the Victorian Alps*. Tracknotes included alpine settlements, touring routes, road conditions, food, and accommodation. Mountain touring was a great contrast to cycling conditions experienced normally: there was abundant fresh water, little dust, shade, exciting downhills, little headwinds, and spectacular views. Ronnie Smith and his friend, the legendary Gustav Weindorfer of Cradle Mountain, used to ride bicycles over some atrocious old tracks in accessing the rugged Tasmanian highlands.

Constant improvements in the standard of bicycles broadened the spectrum whereby ordinary workers of both sexes could enjoy a ride in the country just as much as the more athletic pioneers and hermits. Pneumatic tyres, freewheeling hubs, universal wheel sizes, steel rims, front and rear brakes all were standard by the early twentieth century.

These developments were augmented by improvements in mapping and road conditions, reductions in working hours, and higher disposable incomes. The Jenolan Caves in NSW were just one popular tourist attraction visited by touring clubs on weekends around the turn of the century.

Throughout the next seventy years the basic design of the bushbike didn't change. Interest grew in the motor car, and to a lesser extent the motorcycle. Speedwells and Raleighs became dominant leaders in the touring market: thicker tyres, strong construction, and room for saddle bags. It was only in the late 1970s that the mountain bikes that had evolved on Repack Hill started to be exported to Australia. The first of these were called 'Cruisers', the evolutionary link between the BMX of the early 1980s and the modern All-Terrain Bike with 26-inch wheels and gears.

The late 1980s saw a revival of the BMX, in somewhat altered form as principally a stunt bike on which a multitude of spins, leaps, and other acrobatics could be performed. However this fad was shortlived, being replaced by mountain bike fashion and accelerated technological improvements. Today we see Australian companies such as Apollo and Repco competing with cheaper Taiwanese models. There are annual national competitions, the most important being the MTB Titles, regularly attracting hundreds of competitors, many from overseas. Australia's performance in international events is improving too, after early disappointments due to the lack of any factory-sponsored professional athletes.

Still in its infancy, mountain biking has become an economic miracle for manufacturers faced with poor 10-speed racer sales and a dying BMX fad. The market in Australia has more than doubled in the last five years from 70,000 units in 1988 to approximately 150,000 in 1992, accounting for nearly half of all bicycle sales. A quarter of these are in Victoria and Tasmania.

The next ten years promise even greater heights of technology—lighter components, lower costs, and a greater range of Australian bikes built for our unique conditions. A young Australian, Glen Sharrock, built a 2WD mountain bike with its own front wheel gear and derailleur assembly. While definitely increasing handling performance, this might be offset by the added weight of the additional crankset and derailleur. But new models are coming onto the market made of lighter, stronger metals, front and rear shock absorption, through-the-tube cable housings, wider and knobbier tyres, puncture-proof tubes, and even in-built computers. The distant future has further innovations in store for us: solar powered bicycles with disc-wheels, hubless wheels, and drag-reducing fairings. Accessories are equally innovative: smaller double-action light-weight pumps, compact tool kits that fit in a drink-bottle lid, altimeters, double-sided clipless pedals, mountain bike shoes, push-button gear selection, handlegrip gear selection, and gel seats.

Initially new bike models are expensive, but like personal computers, mass production has ensured dramatic price reductions less than three years after first release. In the late 1980s, 21-speeds were upwards of $1500, now they're $500. Aluminium frames are falling under $1000 and it won't be long before carbon-fibre follows. The average retail price is in the $299–$350 price range, and this is the fastest growth bracket as quality parts move down the range: cantilever brakes, index gearing, alloy rims, off-road tyres, and oversized tubing.

A little patience will see today's top-priced bikes become affordable as later models come onto the market. While this seems good for the consumer, there is a drawback: once purchased, they don't keep their price on the secondhand market. But then again, regular maintenance should ensure that these new generation bikes will last for years.

BUYING A MOUNTAIN BIKE

Obviously, those satisfied with their bike can skip this section. For those looking for their dream machine, there is no simple answer. A bike requires a lot of interaction between rider and machine, and that's where things get complicated.

For the novice, selecting a mountain bike will prove a confusing experience. You will inevitably be confronted with technical jargon by the salesman about frame metallurgy and components. The following is a brief glossary of technical terms associated with the industry.

Chrome molybdenum tubing: Don't let the salesman lose you by telling you that the bike is made from Cro-Mo: they all are. Cro-Mo stands for chrome-molybdenum steel: an alloy of chrome, molybdenum, manganese, carbon, silicon, sulfur, and phosphorus. This is the most common type of steel alloy in the frame and is responsible for most of the bike's cost. In general, the thinner the grade, the higher the cost. But not all the bike will necessarily be made from chrome-moly: for the down-market models the forks and rear triangle are sometimes made from high-tensile steel as a sneaky cost-cutting measure.

New materials include carbon fibre, titanium, magnesium,* metal matrix, and plastic. These are the bikes of the future.

Indexed gears: Users of the old 'guess-what-gear' system will know how frustrating the hit and miss process of selecting a gear can be, especially when concentration is needed elsewhere such as negotiating a difficult corner. What indexing basically entails is an accurate and reliable means of changing gears as each setting is represented by a click and a stop. Pushing the shifter one click

* Extracted from sea water in Norway.

up changes gear one gear lower. It's as simple as that! Top models include the Shimano Deore XTR 24-speed and the Suntour XC 9000 and XCD 4050 components. A recent fad has been the introduction of Rapidfire 'push-button' gears. Despite their name however, gear change is slower and consequently professional competitors still use the traditional lever. Furthermore they have a relatively fast wear-out rate, due to the inclusion of a complicated system of springs, and consequently are difficult to repair.

Cantilever brakes: A very efficient braking system whereby two brake pads are mounted by pivots to the frame and contracted by means of an anchor plate connected to a centre-pull cable. Campagnolo's Euclid and Centaur brakes are top of the line and available only at a hefty price. For value for money, it is difficult to go past the popular Shimano Deore system. The Suntour XC 9000 SE brakes are designed to give greater braking power by having the pad move in a three-dimensional arc. The energy of the rotating rim is utilised by a directional helix mechanism to enhance braking efficiency. The next revolutionary brake design coming onto the market is a hydraulically activated system which allows easy control through light pressure by the fingers but gives very strong rim pressure and consequently stopping power.

Roller-cam brakes: These have the advantage of not protruding as far, therefore causing less damage if the bike accidentally falls over. They work by having the cantilever arms separated at the top end by means of a cam plate guided between two rollers connected to the brake arms. They cost considerably more than cantilever brakes and are recommended if you intend to ride down cliff passes at speeds that would attract police attention. If you are not a kamikaze, cantilever brakes are perfectly adequate for recreational riding in the Tasmanian highlands.

Clusters: This is the group of five to eight gears on the rear wheel. The latest on the market are Shimano's Hyperglide range which can handle changing gears even under pressure. Previously this would have meant the chain coming off or even breaking, but this remarkable gear system handles the stress considerably well, although there has been debate concerning inferior performance when caked in mud. The system is now virtually standard in mid to high price-range bikes.

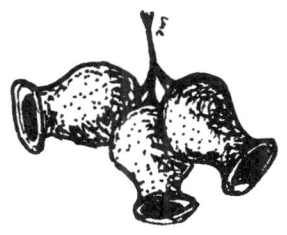

Drop-outs: This refers to the rear triangle assembly where the wheel is secured to the frame. If one has to push the wheel forward to remove it, it is called a Horizontal Drop-Out, or if the wheel can be pulled straight down after removing the nut it is a Vertical Drop-Out. The latter has the advantage of better wheel alignment, while the former allows for superior gear adjustment.

TIG welded lugless joints: The majority of mountain bike frames are made of tubes which are welded together using this method. In order to prevent corrosion, the electrical welding is conducted in an inert argon-gas atmosphere. The joints are made less abrupt by applying a polyester spackling compound.

Other joining methods include brass brazing with lugs, and fillet brazing (no lugs).

Bottom bracket: A flexible bottom bracket reduces inefficiency as pedal power is wasted in moving the bottom of the frame from side to side. The Repco Cycle Co., Australia's largest bicycle wholesaler in the dealer market, sells a wide range of mountain bikes. In particular two quality models, the Kakadu and K2, are constructed using a double-ovalised Cro-Mo frame design so that lateral movement is reduced to the rear and vertical stress is minimised in the front. The bike on the cover and featured throughout has such a frame design. Repco's latest releases are the new Maxtracks series of ATBs which take advantage of the new Shimano groupset componentry.

Kirk Precision has developed frames made of magnesium. Here the bottom bracket moves half as much as steel frames due to stiffer material.

Bottom bracket height: This is the height from the centre of the crankcase to the ground. If you intend to do a lot of offroad riding in rough conditions, you would be well advised to buy a bike that maximises this height so that the chainwheel or pedals don't scrape the ground every time you pass over a small crest or rock.

Quick-release capabilities: These have been the standard in racing bikes for years and have only recently ventured onto mountain bike frames. What is referred to is a small lever that replaces the bolt on the seat and wheels so that they can be easily removed. This means that changing a tyre can be done in less time, as can changing seat height for differences in gradients. Testing has apparently confirmed there is no loss of safety when riding offroad. The disadvantage is that theft of the wheels and seat is made easier. Some of the up-market brakes also have quick-release capabilities, so that tubes do not have to be deflated to remove the wheel. The angle of the seat can be adjusted with a special quick release clamp on top of the seat post.

When first selecting a mountain bike, size is of crucial importance. A good bike store will let you test ride the bike. Make sure that you don't have to stretch to reach the pedals, and that you can straddle the top tube with at least 50 mm of crotch clearance with both feet flat on the ground. If not, get the salesman to adjust the seat, or try another frame size.

Mountain bike frames come in four common sizes:

Rider Leg Length	Frame Size
28-31"	43cm (17")
32-34"	48cm (19")
34-36"	53cm (21")
35-37"	58cm (23")

The next most important item to consider is brakes. Make absolutely sure the bike cannot be moved forward when the brakes are applied. The same should apply if only the front is applied. The back brake should skid when applied separately.

If you plan to tour extensively with your new bike, you need to carry panniers for extra storage space. Accordingly, select a bike with a strong frame and adequate provisions (eyelets and lugs) to attach front and rear panniers. There's nothing worse than having one break during your trip.

Choose tyres according to what terrain and climate you will be riding in. For the central highlands, knobbly tyres are recommended due to the soft nature of the soils, and the high annual rainfall. Many of the trails are close to lake shores, and many actually go *through* semi-dry lakes. For the south-west, there are many steep descents due to the extremely rugged terrain and knobblies such as Panaracer Smokes ($35) provide that extra braking power. They are also ideal for sandy trails near the coast. Their multi-faceted knobs give better cornering on loose surfaces. However, if the majority of cycling is along sealed roads, I recommend Avocet Cross K tyres which are a good compromise having some grip and yet being smooth enough to average 10 km/h faster than knobblies on tar. They permit sharper banking angles on sealed surfaces and contain an interwoven kevlar composite shield for puncture resistance. They have a very low hysteresis (measure of memory time) and therefore can rebound very quickly after being compressed or deformed. The result is longer life expectancy, and less rolling resistance. For complete off-road usage through the disused state forest trails of the Southport hinterland, west coast, and Eastern Tiers, Hutchinson's new On the Rocks are perfect. They come with sexy black sidewalls and a kevlar interwoven belt. They retail for about $35.

Insist on thorn-proof tubes (26″ x 2.125″) once you make your final decision. Any good bike store will fit them straight away. They cost approximately $12.00 each but they are worth it. Ensure that they either give you the original tubes as spares or deduct them from the cost.

Skellerup has introduced a tube that never goes flat. It is made of natural rubber and weighs about 740 grams. As spokes need to be re-tensioned, they're a bit of a hassle to fit and well cycling, give a harder ride than normally inflated tubes— about 65–90 psi (448–620 kilopascals). Nails, sharp rocks, etc can all penetrate but will have no effect on performance as the tubes are not pressurised. The disadvantage is that they're not adjustable for different riding conditions, and they weigh substantially more. An alternative is tyre liners that fit between the tube and the inside of the tyre.

A very dangerous feature on some cheaper mountain bikes is foam sponge handle grips that slide off when wet. This can result in a very serious accident. Beware!

Finally, if all this sounds daunting, a simple

checklist will prevent the most inexperienced novice from getting 'ripped off', either in the bikestore or buying second hand:

1. When looking from the front, with the bike vertical, the back wheel shouldn't be visible. If it is, the wheels are out of line. Either demand a lower price or go to someone else.

2. Check each wheel for sidewards movement. If there is any play, follow the same procedure as above.

3. Hold each wheel up and spin it. It should look like it will spin for three or four minutes. If it stops straight away, it's good for scrap.

4. Try to rattle the crankcase. It should be impossible.

5. Apply the brakes and try to push forwards. If there is movement in the handlebars, the headset in the neck is loose or worn. If the seller can't rectify it, leave.

6. Test-ride it while changing gears and using brakes. Does the chain stay on at extreme settings? Is the rear brake alone sufficient to stop you on short notice? If the answer to these questions is no, offer him loose change or go home.

All in all, be prepared to spend at least $400 for a good bike that will be reliable if you intend to do any of the longer or more difficult rides suggested in this book. Any less, and you will be sacrificing safety and risking a long walk.

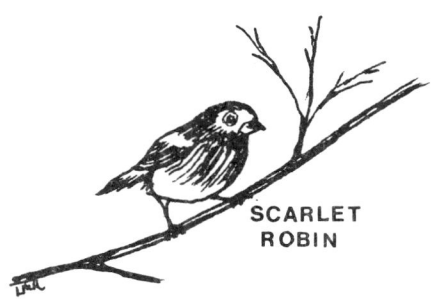

SCARLET
ROBIN

ACCESSORIES

One can spend more on accessories than the cost of the bike itself. Many are necessary for long distance touring, most are not. National Parks can be inhospitable places at times. The extreme isolation in some regions of Tasmania requires good preparation, and tough equipment. In order of priority, the following accessories are recommended.

Essentials

1. *Air-pump:* Unless you're the world's slowest rider, chances are you will get a flat in the bush sometime in your life. Since it's a long way to the nearest petrol station, a portable pump is a necessity. They are lightweight, small, and can be attached almost anywhere on the frame, the most popular place being on the upright tube below the seat. Make sure the attachment fits your valve. If not, another hose can be bought for around $2. New pumps, such as the Blackburn MP-1 Minipump, need no hoses and fit both Schraeder and presta valves. Despite being only 29 cm long they're rated up to 180 psi and can inflate an average mountain bike tyre in a minute. Cost is about $35.00. Its hardy aluminium construction will ensure it lasts many years. An alternative to manually pumping up the tube is to carry small pressurised air cylinders. These work by screwing a plastic attachment onto your valve and then screwing the air cylinder onto the attachment. These can be obtained separately or in Rema Tip Top Mountain Bike ATB Puncture Repair Kits.

2. *Tool kit:* It is also inevitable that you will have to make some minor adjustments or repairs to the bike while on the go. Although somewhat heavy, a toolkit doesn't need to be bulky and can be permanently stored in a bag under the seat or in

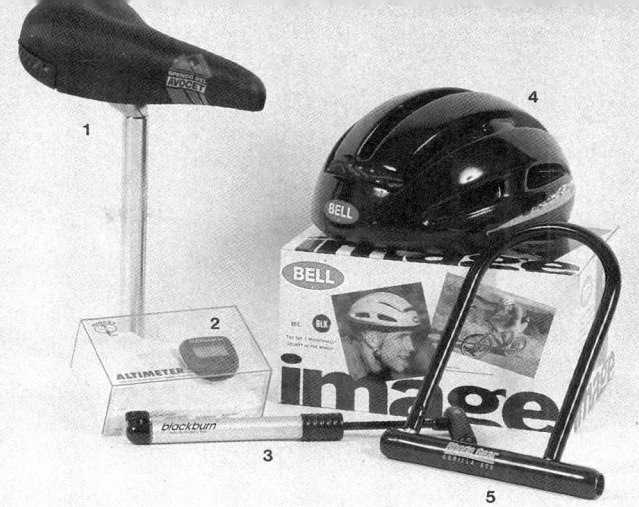

Accessories: (1) Avocet Gelflex mountain bike saddle, (2) Avocet 50 Altimeter computer, (3) Blackburn Mini-Pump, (4) Bell Image II helmet, and (5) Rhode Gear Gorilla ATB U-Lock

Repair kits: (1) A complete socket and allen key set that fits into the base of a spare-tube container, (2) The Rema Tip-Top MTB puncture repair kit, (3) The Beta repair kit fits neatly into the bottom of the bidon

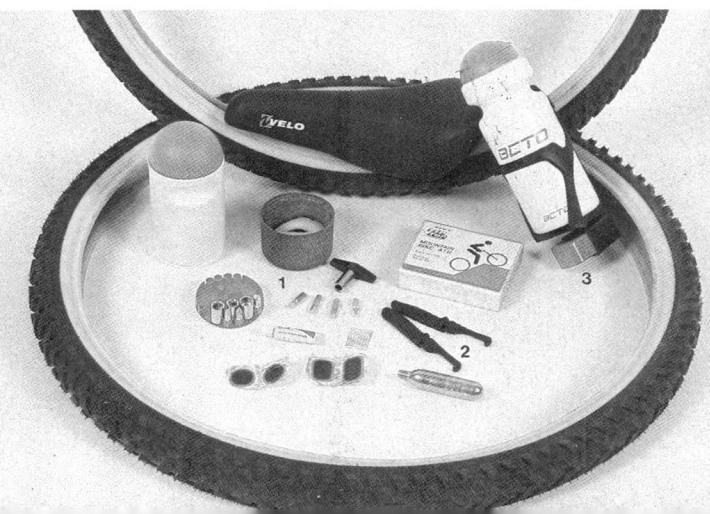

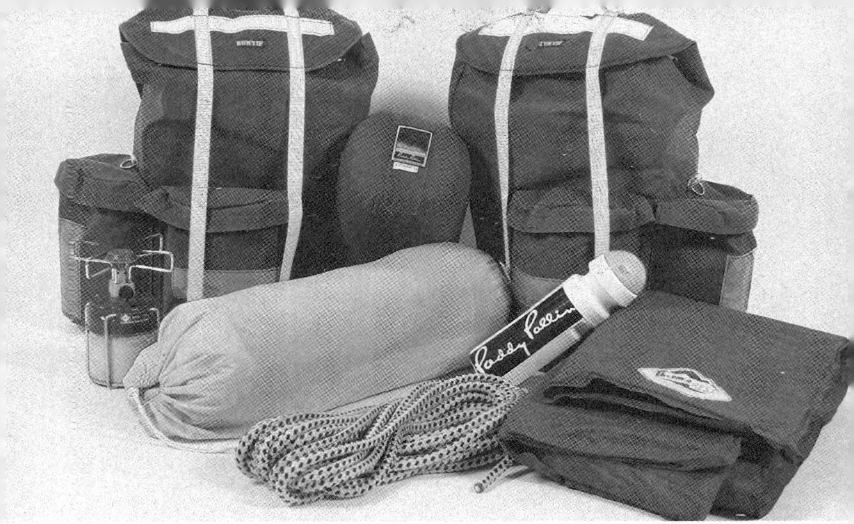

Bunyip panniers are extremely durable and have a large capacity for storing touring gear

A selection of mountain bike tyres available:
(1) Chen-sung 60 psi MTB tyre, (2) Tioga Farmer John's Cousin, (3) Panaracer Smoke, (4) Chen-sung 40 psi all-round tyre, (5) Hutchinson On the Rocks kevlar, and (6) Avocet Cross K

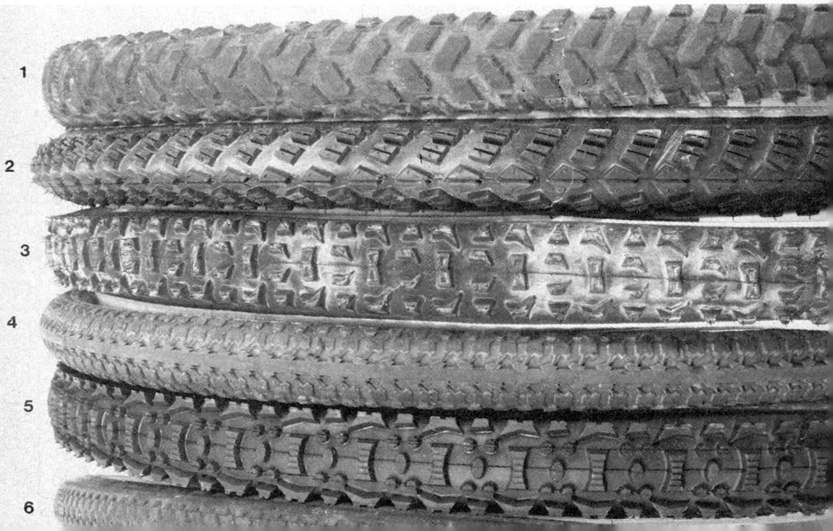

the back pocket of one of the panniers. Standard equipment includes: puncture repair kit, tyre levers, allen key set, small 5–10 cm shifter, 32 cm shifter, multi-faceted bone, pliers, screwdriver, 15 mm phillips head screwdriver, and spare tube. Some companies sell complete compact tool sets that are designed to minimise weight. These can also save on cost.

On longer trips, one should expand this to include spare spokes, spoke tightening key, chain link remover, spare links, grease, small lubricating oil flask (dry molybdenum or lithium based), and valve tightener. But above all, no matter how long the ride is, ensure that you have the right tools to repair a flat and tighten the brakes.

A spare tube will prevent mucking around with patches and glue. The new Hutchinson Anti-Crevaison tube contains a self-sealing liquid for automatic repair of small punctures.

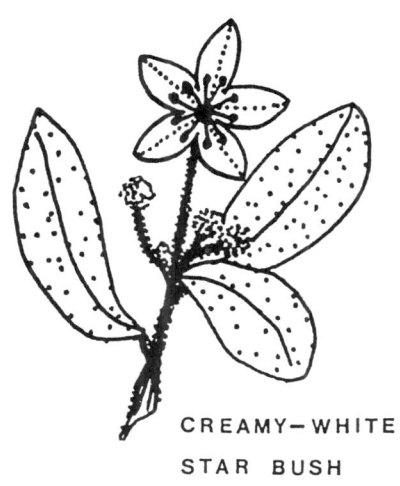

CREAMY–WHITE
STAR BUSH

3. *Water bottle:* I've seen water bottles for $32. Mine cost $4.98 and hasn't leaked a drop. They can be attached via bosses to any of the three major tubes of the frame, or even to the handlebars. You can then use them as drink bottles on any walks you may do away from the bike. Don't fill them with anything but water as heat and time will make a mess of other solutions. Some have tyre repair kits attached to them while others can be used as containers for a spare tube or snacks. Some models have a specially designed spill-free pull top valve so they can be opened without using your other hand.

4. *Panniers:* Panniers come in a variety of shapes, sizes, and prices. What type you buy will depend on what length excursions you intend to go on and/or what degree of luxury you intend to travel in. Whether you carry food, clothes, camera gear, stereo, or the wine cellar, panniers should be strong and the racks likewise. People who make their decision solely on whether it matches their bike colour are asking for trouble. Remember that if your rack hooks break, you could be forced to leave your valuables behind. Other considerations besides strength are the size of zippers and the number of compartments. The more the better, as gear can be classified into areas for ease of access. Straps at the top for a sleeping mat are convenient as are little pockets at the back where the day's snacks and repair kit can be stored.

The premier Australian brand is undoubtedly Bunyip. Although they aren't available in the wide range of fluorescent colours that imported panniers come in, experience has proved that their nearly unbreakable reputation is well founded. Designed in Australia and manufactured in Tasmania, Bunyip panniers are made from thick waterproof cotton stiffened by high density polythene. The Rear Touring models have two sizeable external pockets to store tool kits, snacks, etc. in, stainless steel rack hooks that fit 8mm aluminium alloy carriers, and four locking straps and adjustable shockcords that prevent the panniers from jumping off. Large 3M reflective strips ensure safety for night riding. They're adjustable, quickly detachable, portable, and give easy access to a large storage area; just one pannier can hold a sleeping bag and tent in the main compartment. There are various models in different shapes and sizes including a handbar mounted bag. Colours are either green or black. Distribution is limited and they are available from only large specialist bike stores, or one can write to the Bike Warehouse, P.O. Box 156, Summer Hill NSW 2130.

Before going on a major trip with any new panniers, test them first. Put some lead ballast or bricks in them and ride up and down a few gutters. Many Tasmanian fire trails and 4WD tracks are very rough in places and consequently rocks and corrugation will cause loosely secured panniers to jump off. If they pass this, spray them down to simulate rain. Check inside for leakage. Remember your clothes and sleeping bag will be in there. If they do leak, and most cheaper ones will, one can spray them with a waterproofing compound. A more reliable method is to simply wrap up your gear in plastic bags. Pack so that the items you need *during* your trip are on the top.

It needs to be said that there are also disadvantages with panniers: (1) It is more difficult to ford deep rivers, (2) there is more hassle when lowering the bike down cliffs, (3) a fully laden bike becomes quite strenuous to push up steep hills, and (4) panniers reduce the room available on bike racks if they are to be transported by car. There are two ways around all but one of these problems: purchase panniers that are easily detachable so they can be separately carried across rivers or down cliffs. During transit they can be simply stored in the boot. The other way is to use a backpack.

Despite what one might think there aren't any major stability problems and you will find that pushing up hills is much easier. Backpacks also have the advantage of being able to take your gear down to a campsite by the river where access is often only on foot necessitating leaving the bike at the ridge-top for the night. Some tri-compartment pannier models can be unzipped to reveal straps converting the top compartment into a detachable day-pack large enough for maps, snacks, waterbottle, and a camera.

Non-essentials

1. *Gauge:* One can accurately measure air pressure to adjust for different riding conditions. In muddy conditions, hot weather, and sand, it would be wise to *lower* pressure somewhat to maximise traction and minimise the risk of a puncture.

2. *Mudguards:* Usually more of a hindrance than anything else as they can get in the way of brakes and pannier tie-downs, not to mention clogging up with mud. In any case, tri-compartment panniers act as pretty good mudguards.

3. *Computers:* The Japanese have shrunk everything from cameras to cars, and cycling computers are no exception. Ever since the Cateye Velo CC-1000 set the standard for such features as digital readouts and average speed calculations, the trend has been more features in a smaller unit. Indeed, today's computers, such as the Cateye Vectra, are about half the size of the original, yet retails for about twice as much, $65-$70.

Wheel circumferences can be accurately entered to take into account tyre sizes and rider's weight. Regular functions include speed in kilometres or miles, trip distance and time, as well as overall distance, maximum speeds, a clock, and calculation of average speeds.

All are water-resistant, and should work even

when the sensor is caked in mud. Battery life expectancy is about two years, the accuracy is astounding, and most can be easily detached when locking the bike up in public. Another advantage is a motivational one: when you have a constant reminder about your average speed, you are more likely to expend extra energy when climbing in order to maintain the figure.

One of the top units on the market at the moment is the Avocet 50 Altimeter. Apart from having the standard functions of speed and distance calculations, it has an inbuilt barometer that converts air pressure into altitude readouts. Even when ascending small hills, the readout updates altitude changes every second. Furthermore it records accumulated height gained over a longer trip and can even be useful for predicting weather. For example if one has set up camp and the readout is steadily increasing, air pressure is falling, indicating a possible front approaching. It automatically compensates for temperature differentials and wind doesn't affect its accuracy. Another advantage is that it's easily detachable and still operates in your pocket when walking. This can aid in navigational queries as one can reconcile one's altitude with topographical information on maps so as to locate your position.

New models come with cadence readout and even heart rate monitor! Who knows what the future will hold? Thermometer? Compass? Databank? Mobile phone? Satellite navigation?

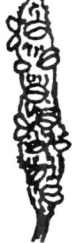

COAST

BANKSIA

FRUIT

4. *Lock:* While in Tasmania's National Parks, you will almost definitely have to leave your bike behind as many areas such as lookouts can only be visited on foot. Since the Tasmanian wilderness is so vast, an infinite number of hiding places exist where the bike can be stored for a few hours or a few days. Obviously locks are unnecessary here as the most likely being to stumble across your bike is a devil. However, if passing through a township in order to resupply, or in the more popular tourist areas, it would be advisable to carry a lock.

A U-Lock or thick chain is most effective. For example the Rhode Gear Gorilla ATB lock is specially designed for mountain bikes, being longer so that it can encompass the wider tyres. It's made of high-tensile molychrome, has a ball bearing behind the lock that prevents drilling, and over 700,000 combinations ensures excellent security.

Another design is the rear-wheel lock used in China that fits permanently onto the bike. With a small bar that fastens through the spokes, it prevents those daring thieves who steal your bike from under your nose while you're in a shop. There is a slight risk that the lock can occasionally snap shut when the bike is in motion—that's why it's fortunately placed over the *rear* wheel.

Lastly, those small plastic covered four-digit combination locks on sale in supermarkets are useless and can be easily pulled apart by stepping on one end and pulling. Owners of bikes with quick release wheels are at a disadvantage and would have to disassemble the bike every time they wanted to leave it alone. Another risk experienced by cyclists is expensive accessories that aren't lockable: leather or gel seats on a quick-release post, computers, halogen lamps, pumps, bidons, frame-repair kits, etc. This is an issue manufacturers will have to address.

5. *Bike rack:* For transporting your bike to staging

areas. Many of the rides described in this book are in National Parks out of reach by coach. Good racks are about $100 and accommodate 3 bikes. They are secured to the rack by a plate which fastens on using two winged nuts. However, the gradual introduction of red light cameras and speed cameras have caused police to enforce licence-plate obstruction laws and consequently new racks have entered the market that have provisions to mount the licence-plate on the back. This is not a hassle if the rack is installed permanently but for hatchback, utility, and station wagon owners, racks would need to be detachable. This necessitates continually changing the location of your licence-plate. Alternative bike rack designs, such as the Thule 549, can mount your treadly securely on the car roof. This is also a good option for four-wheel-drivers who damage their pushbikes along rough trails, but has the disadvantage of susceptibility to overhanging branches. Another alternative is the Ark bike carrier that tilts downwards thus allowing hatchbacks, utes, and wagons to open.

6. *Lights:* Cycling in the bush at night, while cooler, is a little dangerous. If it's a necessity, lights will be more of a hindrance because you will be travelling too slow for a dynamo to work effectively and it is better to let your eyes adjust to available light. An alternative is batteries, but these are of course expensive. Models such as the Cateye Halogen are relatively efficient. But for the specialised mountain bike market, OK Electrical has released a set of Soubitez 6 volt, 9 watt, 2.1 amp halogen lamp and battery set. Rechargeable batteries give 4-5 hours performance, up to 1200 times.

7. *Mirror:* Useless. If you already have one and you're male, take it along so you can shave.

8. *Toe-straps:* These increase cycling efficiency as one can pull through the zero-torque point (when the pedals are in 6 o'clock position) as well as push down. They are a bit of a hassle to enter and have

to be manually tightened to optimise efficiency. Furthermore they can prevent a quick escape during an accident as one needs more than a split-second to release if they are tight. Despite these drawbacks, they are making their way down the range of mountain bikes.

9. *Clipless Pedals:* Competition has developed clipless pedals where the sole of your mountain bike shoe clicks into a specially designed pedal. There are a number of different systems on the market and one must buy the right shoe compatible with the right pedal. Shimano has developed a system called SPD (Shimano Pedalling Dynamics) specifically for the mountain bike market. They have a recessed cleat in the shoe to enable you to go walking. Formerly, this was not possible. The SH-M100 shoe ($160) is a good all-round hiking/cycling shoe with Velcro straps and plenty of grip. However, it's not designed for extended bushwalks through mud, water, and boulder scrambling. The double-sided low-profile PD-M737 pedals that go with the shoe weigh 225 grams each and cost about $300. You exit by twisting your heel outwards. Both release-tension and entry-position are fully adjustable and, unlike other systems, they work well in muddy conditions.

10. *Gel Seats:* All the rage at the moment. One of the most common problems that mountain cyclists experience is a tender backside from the constant shifting in the saddle.

The Avocet Gelflex saddle manufactured with Spenco gel distributes vertical and lateral pressure more evenly over the contact area and, unlike other gel saddles, it doesn't lose its elasticity during the colder temperatures that a cyclist can experience in the Tasmanian highlands. Weight is kept to a minimum by varying the thickness of the gel in critical pressure points, and the nylon/lycra cover moves *with* the gel so that its hydrostatic properties are not diminished.

There are various models on the market with various thicknesses and shapes catering for everyone from the casual weekend recreationalist to the professional competitor. The cost of the mountain bike model is about $60.

11. *Shock absorbers:* The recent introduction of adjustable polyurethane elastopolymer and magnesium-alloy shock absorbers on the market have allowed mountain cyclists to have a smoother ride without compromising weight. There are designs also for the rear but it is through the front forks that the vast majority of vertical stresses pass.

Along rough flat roads and descents, kinetic energy expended perpendicular to the road surface is minimised with shock absorbers and forward momentum is maintained. In this respect, shock absorbers *save* energy that would normally be wasted in hitting a small obstacle such as a rock. Because the wheel moves up and over the obstacle, there is less resistance and therefore less energy loss. However during ascents, queries have been raised concerning their ability to assist as energy can be wasted as the shocks are compressed as much as 4 cm.

Depending on the model one can select the stiffness of the shock absorbers from a 'soft ride' to 'hard ride'.

Clothing

1. *Helmets:* Most cyclists rarely fall, and when they do, reflexes ensure the head is protected. But it is those lower-end statistics, those could-have-been-saved cases which make the helmet an almost essential item. The space-helmet look is no longer necessary with new energy-dispersing impact-absorbing materials such as expanded polystyrene (EPS). It works by crushing on impact, and therefore has to be just the right density in order to reduce a 400+ G shock to under 200. If the foam

is too soft, it will compress too easily, while being too hard will also damage the head during a fall or collision.

Bell are the largest manufacturer of helmets and consequently can sink a lot of time and money in research and development such as wind-tunnel testing. Their Image II weighs in at only 255 grams and has a microshell bonded to the energy absorbing liner to protect it from everyday handling abuse. It sells for around $85.

Always try on the helmet before you pay for it. Remember that any small discomfort will be multiplied many times on a long ride. Also make sure it has maximum ventilation so your head doesn't sweat too much on a hot day.

If you use soft foam adjustable fitting pads, note that the Traffic Accident Research Unit in NSW has found that the thicker these pads, the more pronounced the stress on the skull because of secondary shocks if the head bounces. Furthermore they can result in the helmet becoming dislodged.

A helmet therefore works at optimal efficiency when there is a maximum amount of surface area of the inner shell of the helmet in contact with the skull. It is important that these foam pads be kept to a minimum quantity and thickness, and where possible to match the shape of the helmet to the shape of the skull *directly* and not by the use of foam.

Legislation has made it compulsory for cyclists in Tasmania to wear an Australian Standards (No.2063.2) approved bicycle helmet. For international visitors they can be hired from outlets such as the Backpackers Barn in Devonport or the Launceston Youth Hostel.

2. *Pants:* One can enjoy the Australian country perfectly well without spending unnecessarily on cycling pants. The advantages are that they absorb perspiration and offer some protection from grazing during a fall. I have found that a pair of

ordinary corduroy beach shorts have proved themselves indestructible. Remember that if walking is on the schedule, cycling shorts will be lacerated by the bush, especially if any rock scrambling is involved.

3. *Shirt:* Special cycling shirts allow greater perspiration evaporation but for the recreational mountain biker, any T-shirt will do.

4. *Shoes:* Normal sandshoes or sneakers are perfect. If some lengthy or difficult walking is involved, a good pair of walking boots will be needed. If no walking is in store, shoes are the *least* important of all items for hopefully your feet will never touch the ground!

Recently mountain bike shoes have been marketed which are made of materials such as carbon, nylon, and glass fibre that are supposed to be 'the most efficient tool ever designed for transferring energy from the foot to the drive chain'.

5. *Gloves:* Cyclists in the Tasmanian highlands in winter and even in summer can experience freezing temperatures. Any gloves from home are adequate if cold weather and/or strong wind is expected. You might also need a pair of gloves if your handlegrips cause blisters or chafing. Specialist mountain biking gloves from Adura contain a 3 mm layer of neoprene for shock absorption and cost around $35.

6. *Glasses:* Not really necessary for the recreationalist, but if your eyes water during high speeds, in winds, or during hazy, glary days, cycling glasses definitely will be comfortable. Make sure they are shatter-proof, scratch-resistant, reduce glare, block out all UV and some blue light as well in order to improve contrast. Some of the newer mountain bike glasses come with a lycra band for retention and perspiration absorption.

7. *Wet-weather gear:* Here prices can range from as little as $5.00 for a poncho (great for those brief thunderstorms) to Gortex Thermal Ski-Jackets (for

settled-in rain and cold) for $700. Gortex has a well respected reputation in Australia for being waterproof, windproof, and breathable. This is achieved by a semi-permeable microporous membrane that lets condensation and perspiration evaporate out through the fabric but prevents moisture from entering.

Whatever you choose, make sure that it doesn't impede your knees so you can ride with it on and that it has pockets for maps, food, etc. Good value lightweight foul weather gear includes the Peter Storm 123 Cyclists Overtrouser which has greater breathing ability* than Gortex without sacrificing water-proofing. Furthermore it is approximately a third of the price of Gortex.

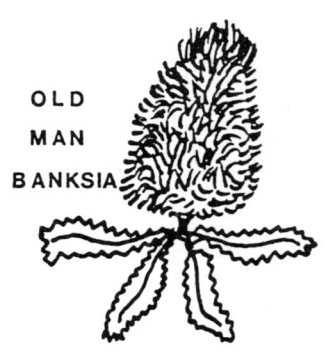

OLD MAN BANKSIA

---

* 6.2 litres of moisture vapour can be transmitted out per 24 hours.

MAINTENANCE

At home

Whether it's pumping up the tyres or reconstructing the rear wheel, some degree of technical knowledge will be called for. There are many books available which cover this subject, the definitive one being Van der Plas's *Mountain Bike Maintenance*.

Before embarking on any ride in the bush, one can quickly carry out the following four-point check:

1. *Tyres:* Ensure the tube is fully inflated: usually around 40–50 psi (276–344 kilopascals). For slicks, this can be as high as 85 psi (586 kilopascals).
2. *Brakes:* The bike should be impossible to move forwards or backwards when both brakes are applied. Remember that if you're travelling over 30 km/h, you need at least 10 m to stop. In dirt roads or wet weather or steep downhills, minimum braking distances are significantly higher.
3. *Chain:* Lubricate if dry.
4. *Wheel:* Tighten if there is lateral movement in the rim.

If planning a major ride of several days duration it would be wise to overhaul the bike by:
1. Regreasing all bearings. A lithium-based grease will provide good protection (do not use oil).
2. Lubricating all cables (with a graphite-in-solution lubricant) and moving parts such as the flywheel and derailleur pivot points. Specific ATB oils, such as Finish Line, are based on teflon, trilinium, and paraffin that not only reduces friction but gives rust protection, improves water resistance, and does not attract grime.
3. Check for even spoke tension.
4. Check for wear in the chain wheels and shifting mechanism.

5. Tighten all nuts and bolts.
6. Replace brake blocks if worn.

A bike specialist would also do the above for you, but it is better that you do it yourself in order to familiarise yourself with the componentry.

In the bush

1. *Punctures:* Locate small holes by filling tube with air and immersing in water. If there is no water, rotate the inflated tube next to your ear. Clean area around hole and rub with sandpaper to ensure adhesiveness of the patch. Wait 3–4 minutes to dry before replacing.

Always take a spare tube along in case the puncture is too big for a patch or is too close to the valve.

As a last resort, grass and normal bracken ferns can be stuffed inside the tyre. But they must be replaced every few kilometres for heat and friction quickly displaces any moisture in the plant and all that is left is brown dust. Shift weight off the wheel that has no tube.

If the tyre is slashed as well, cutting a small square off a foam sleeping mat and pressing it between the inner tyre wall and the tube will usually alleviate the problem until the nearest bike store is reached. Both Specialised (Airlock) and Hutchinson (Anti-Crevaison) have produced a tube which contains a built-in sealant that self-repairs small punctures.

2. *Squeaking brakes:* This is probably due to a dirty rim or worn pads. If not, then don't worry too much: now you've got a horn!

3. *Weak brakes:* Worry. At best, it is just due to a wet rim, or some oil that has dripped down from the cluster. Wiping the rim and block and braking hard a number of times will remove the problem. At worst it could be due to bent braze-ons which

would mean purchasing an entire new brake assembly unit. If it's the rear brake, one could probably get away with it until the next bike store. But one should *NEVER* ride in the mountains without a properly functioning front brake.

4. *Slipping chain:* This occurs when the rear derailleur is out of adjustment, usually because the bike was leaning against a tree with the gear assembly pressing against the trunk. Simply adjusting the 'high' and 'low' screws in the adjustment mechanism with a philips screwdriver will bring the chain back into line with the gears. At worst, the slipping could be due to a worn chain, or even a worn freewheel sprocket. These would need replacing. Simply remain in low gear until civilisation is reached and avoid riding up hills.

5. *Steering out of alignment:* Either you ride like a maniac or head-set bearings are loose. These can be tightened by means of a large shifter. If you don't have one, hand tighten as tight as possible and take it very easy.

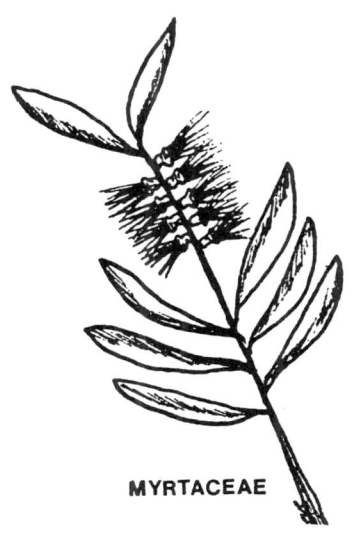

MYRTACEAE

6. *Broken spoke:* Things are starting to get serious. Replacing a broken spoke, especially in the rear wheel, is about the equivalent of a human by-pass operation. On most bikes, specialised tools are needed. And even with these, the operation takes about half an hour, because the entire hub assembly has to be taken out piece by piece, including the bearings. The new spoke then has to be inserted and tightened. Then the whole wheel needs re-adjusting so it spins without wobble.

The band-aid solution if you don't have the tools is to simply twist off the broken spoke, take as much weight off the wheel as possible by moving luggage forward or backward or giving it to your companion. Coast to the nearest bike store.

But spokes will soon be outdated with the recent development of carbon/kevlar wheels that give greater suspension, durability, energy efficiency, and less wind resistance.

The Tioga Disc Drive is manufactured from thermoplastic, alloy mesh, and kevlar cord arranged in a geodesic pattern of angular and tangential cords forming a continuous tensioned linkage between hub and rim. The trouble with disc-wheels, however, is that a strong cross-wind can cause some riding instability. Some wheels have just three aerodynamically designed blade-spokes that actually assist forward momentum in a cross-wind.

7. *Bent links:* If some of your chain's links have become twisted, it is not as bad as it looks. A small chain-breaker or chain-removing tool and some spare links will rectify the problem easily.

8. *Uneven pedalling:* A loose crankcase is usually the cause of this problem. It can be easily tightened with a shifter. If it happened just after an accident, suspect a bent chainwheel or pedal axle.

9. *Rack stay broken:* Normally caused by people overloading their panniers and riding as fast as possible over branches, rocks and ledges. Usually

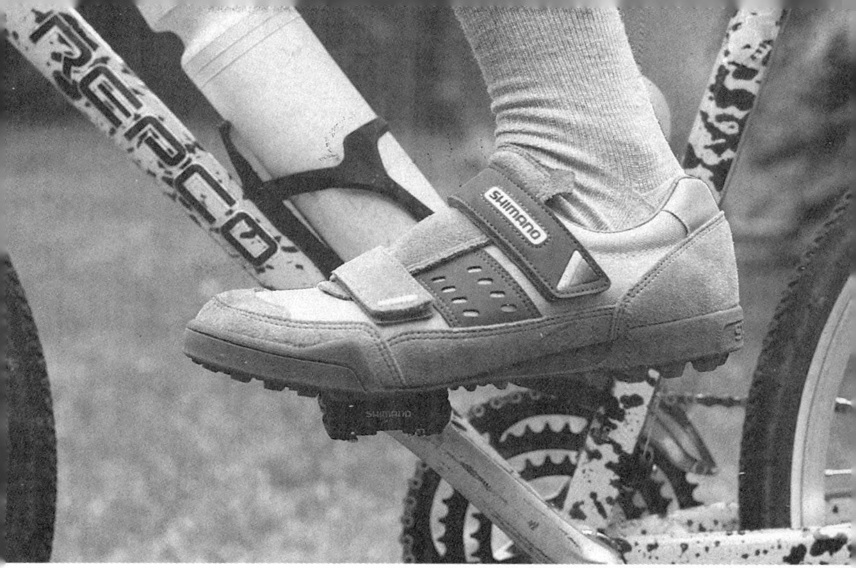

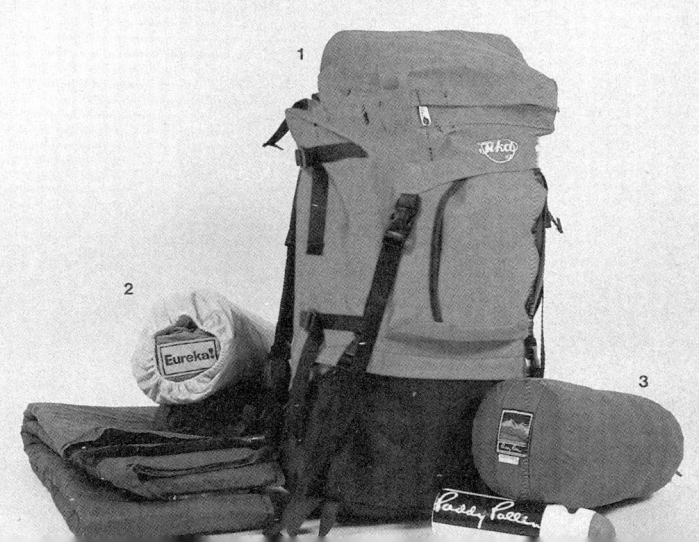

Shimano SPD-737 clipless pedal and SH-100 shoe

*(1) Tika Taranaki 80 litre backpack, (2) Eureka Bike &
Hike 2-person tent, (3) Paddy Pallin Gingera down
sleeping bag, and (4) Therma-a-rest inflatable air-mattress*

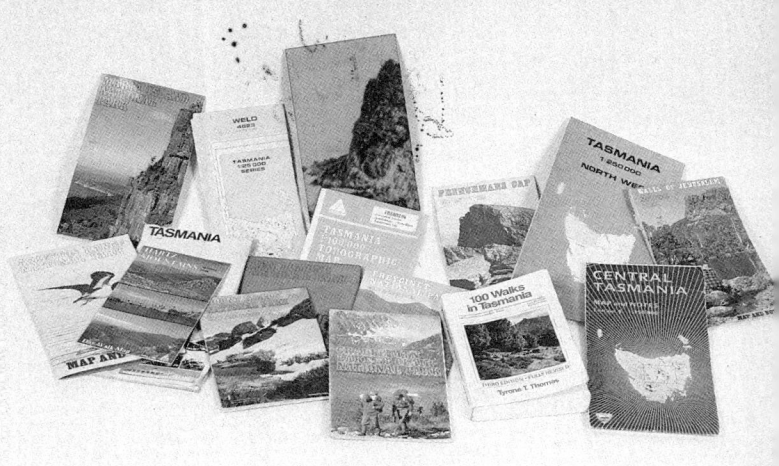

A selection of Tasmanian national park, tourist, and topographical maps produced by TASMAP

When all gear is working together, some remote areas can be accessed. Camp beneath the Walls of Jerusalem

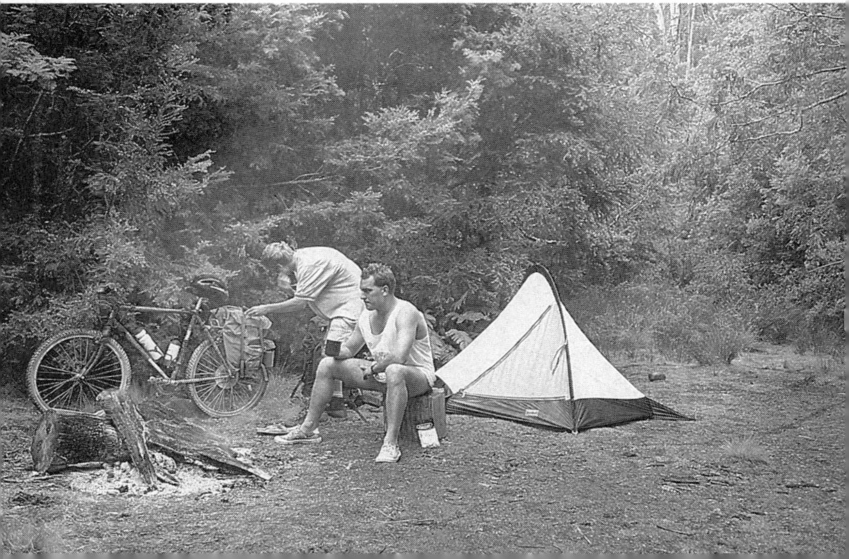

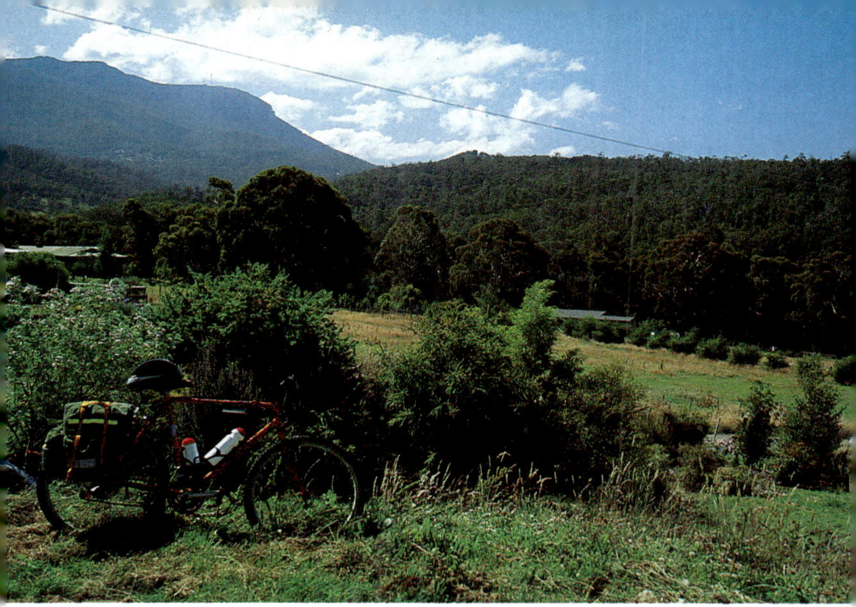

Kingston valley dominated by Mt. Wellington (Ride 5)

The oldest bridge in Australia at Richmond (Ride 10)

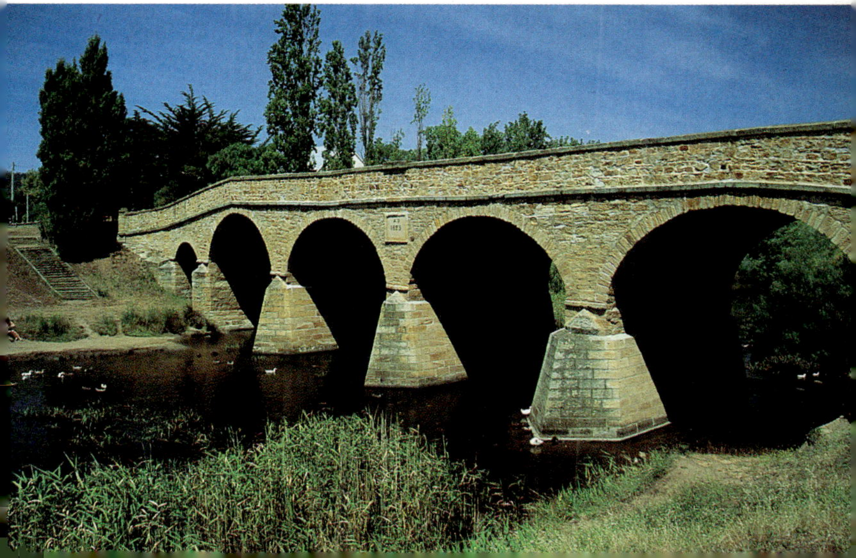

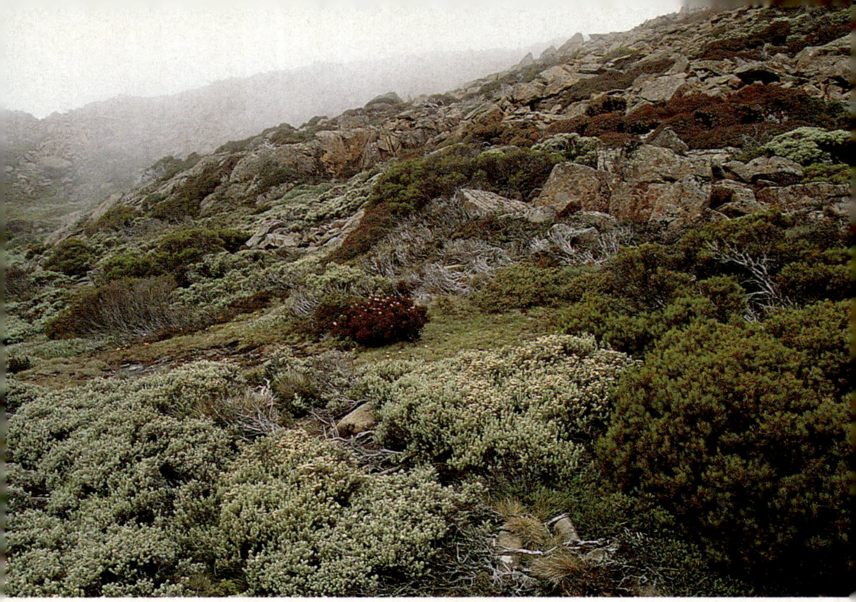

Near Legges Tor in Ben Lomond National Park (Ride 20)

The Hazards from Coles Bay (Ride 33)

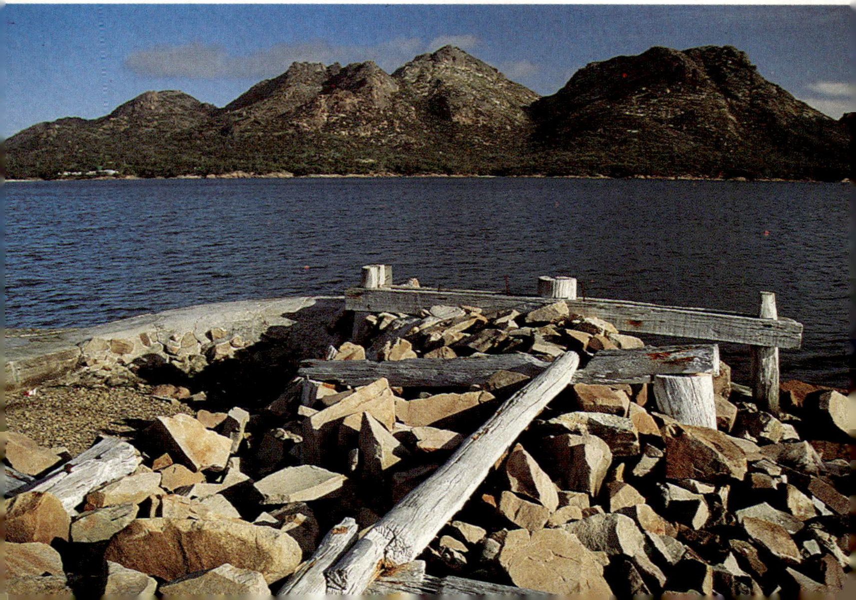

only one of the stays would have been broken. This one can be fastened up to the bottom of the seat by some strong string. Transfer as much weight as possible from the pannier to the other end of the bike, your back, or a friend.

10. *Snapped frame:* Either you bought a cheap bike or you ride a little too aggressively—something to think about while they reassemble you in hospital.

At home again

Whether you've spent an hour or a month in the bush, your bike will be dirty, either from dust or mud, usually both. Hose it down straight away and spray all moving parts with some form of WD spray to protect against rust. This is doubly important for cyclists living near the coast. Don't believe the people who tell you it's cool to have it covered in grime—unless you can afford disposable mountain bikes.

Long term

An annual service with an authorised dealer will ensure everything is tightened, greased, and oiled. He should also be able to touch-up scratched paint-work. Many components, such as derailleurs, freewheels, rapidfire gears, and the crankcase require specialised tools such as torque-meters.

RIDING TECHNIQUES

The final part in this chapter will try to relate a few handy tips that can improve cycling efficiency and enjoyment. It's better to learn it the right way first, so that in a short time the new skills will become a matter of habit.

After selecting the right bike and adjusting the handlebars and seat height for your comfort, you should be eager to try it out. People *converting* to mountain bikes from racers will immediately notice that greater effort is necessary to achieve high speeds. The reason is in the thicker tyres and in the less crouched seating position. The higher gears will also be lower ratios, while gear levers will be positioned on top of the straight handlebars. Those accustomed to lifting their bike up stairs will also find a few extra kilos of metal separate a mountain bike from a racer.

Cycling in our rugged mountains is different to all other forms of cycling. New skills are required, and concentration is directed away from long distance 'rhythm' cycling to focusing on avoiding obstacles: with continual steering, braking, and gearing changes as the cyclist negotiates his way through rough, winding, and undulating fire trails, across streams, through rivers, under overhanging branches, and down narrow cliff passes.

1. *CLIMBING:* Due to the nature of Tasmania's landscapes, staging areas are usually low. Ben Lomond and the Central Plateau Conservation Area are good examples of cycling areas over 1 km higher than the surrounding land. The southwest is similar although lower.

Therefore a lot, and I might even add, the *majority* of the time will be spent climbing, and climbing, and climbing . . . You will indeed wonder if Australia is really the flattest continent on Earth.

Three methods of climbing exist: walking, spinning, and honking.

Walking: Some mountains just can't be conquered on a bike, no matter how many gears you have. But even pushing a bike can be faster due to the fact that you can rest your upper body on the handlebars. If it's a really big slope, you can let your bike carry any pack you might have on. Experiment with different techniques: push in short bursts and rests, or one slower consistent uphill trudge. The break-even point where cycling has no energy efficiency advantage over walking is about a 1 in 5 slope. Any steeper and walking is metabolically more productive.

Spinning: Choose a very low gear and stay seated the entire length of the slope. Concentrate on maintaining your cadence (the number of pedal rotations per minute). If the rear wheel starts to spin in the dirt or mud, get up and lean back to put more pressure on it so traction increases. Although walking seems like the easier alternative, cycling up a gradual slope actually requires *less* effort but is more tiring as your muscles are required to expend much more energy per unit of time.

Honking: This method is used for steeper shorter slopes and a higher gear is selected while standing up and leaning forward. But perhaps the most efficient way is a combination of honking and spinning for the variation temporarily relieves certain muscles. But there is no substitute for fitness.

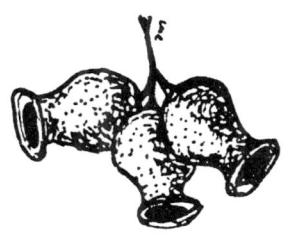

A handy water bottle is almost essential for cooling down. Expending just 74 watts of energy, a cyclist can maintain an average speed of 22 km/h on level ground and the 22 km/h headwind will ensure adequate heat dissipation. But on a 1:6 slope, only 2.4 km/h can be maintained at the same 74 watt power output, resulting in at least a doubling of energy used to remain stable. However heat dissipation without a regular drink will prevent this level of output from being maintained.

Attitude is also important. Think positively about the hill: it will be another obstacle out of the way, you will feel good about conquering it, you are nearer to your destination, there will be a good view on top, and best of all, there'll be a downhill on the other side!

2. *DESCENDING:* As always in life, the fun things are the most dangerous. Physics defines force as proportional to the square of the bicycle's velocity. This means that there will be a point where braking resistance is insufficient in stopping a fully laden bike on a steep slope if the rider allows it to accelerate too much. Always try to use constant pressure on the rear brake *alone* to slow you down. If it is not enough, lean back to put more pressure on the rear tyre. If you still accelerate, apply the front brake gradually. Never speed up and then suddenly jam the brakes at the last minute because you might fall further than you expect: six feet further.

When at the top of a steep, long descent, stop and quickly check your brakes and anything else that might be loose. Once you get going, you don't want to stop until you hit the bottom!

Jumping: Imagine you are flying down a fantastic trail, the trees a blur, adrenalin surging through your veins. Suddenly you round a corner and there's a fallen tree lying right across the track. There's not enough time to brake, so the only alternative is to harmlessly pass over the log. How? By jumping.

Begin a jump by waiting until your strongest leg is at the top. Then suddenly lean back on the handlebars, lifting the front wheel off the ground, while simultaneously pushing down the pedal. With some practice you should be able to hold a 'wheelie' for about 2-3 seconds. When you've mastered this, lift the front wheel again while standing on the pedals and throw your weight forward while raising your legs. This motion, called a bunnyhop, should raise the rear wheel off the ground (but only for a split second). This action becomes infinitely easier when one is using clipless pedals and shoes.

By co-ordinating the wheelie and the bunnyhop, one should be able to clear small objects with practice. Don't worry too much if you can't actually get the rear wheel airborne; the reduced pressure off the ground will be sufficient to tackle the majority of obstacles such as sharp rocks and small branches. Bunnyhopping cannot be done with a bike that has excessive luggage attached and descents must therefore be more controlled.

Falling: Instinct is to release your hands to protect your fall but statistics reveal that this often leads to a sprained or broken wrist, and so experts advise to keep one's hands on the bars, thus protecting your arms. Then again, who remembers statistics while soiling their breeches?

3. GENERAL

Corners: Avoid excessive leaning in on turns when the ground is loose. Rather take the corner slowly and drift from inside to outside.

Watch out for traffic the other way. Blind corners, especially when descending fast, are just as dangerous for cyclists as for cars. Be aware that the trail you are riding on could be open to four-wheel-drivers, walkers, cyclists and equestrians coming the other way. The single most important factor that parks authorities consider when assessing the impact of mountain cyclists is the conflict with walkers. If too many walkers complain of being frightened by yahoo mountain cyclists flying past with their hair on fire, it'll be the cyclists who'll have to go, not the walkers.

Loose surfaces: If approaching a sandy patch in the road ahead, accelerate and coast straight through it if it can't be skirted. Avoid steering, gear, and acceleration changes when actually in sand as they can all result in a loss of momentum. If a lot of sand is expected, deflate the tyres by 10 psi.

The same applies for mud. Don't worry too much about getting the mud off immediately afterwards. Most of it will come off by itself. The rest can be left as decoration until you reach public transport or a stream. Avoid skidding in soft wet ground as erosion is greatly accelerated. This applies to flat plateaus as well as river banks.

Watercourses: Check to make sure there are no large river rocks across the ford when crossing. Don't ride too slow as loss of momentum could be embarrassing in a strong current. Also watch out for exposed concrete mesh on fords. When riding in a group, cross large streams one at a time. If the stream is a strong one from overnight rain and debris is being washed down, it is better to walk the bike across. As a rule of thumb, any fast flowing water above 40-50 cm (especially if the bottom is uncertain) is potentially unsafe to ride across.

2

THE BUSH

Tasmania offers quite a variety of environments to cycle in: from eucalypt tall forests in the Lune River valley to the picturesque sandy coves of Maria Island, from the rugged wilderness of the south-west to the hundreds of lakes on the Central Plateau, from the windswept desolation of the Arthur Pieman Protected Area to the fishing lakes of the Mersey River valley.

Equally dynamic are the State's geological features. The cyclist can choose from the dolerite peaks that dominate skylines such as the Mt. Wellington range, Cradle Mountain and Ben Lomond or the quartzite peaks of the Sawback Range bordering Lake Gordon.

Cycling is a fantastic way to see these places. You have the advantage of not being sealed off in the cabin of a car, and you can see vastly more than the walker. It's not as tiring as walking, yet one still gets very fit. While the walker is limited to little more than a fly and a groundsheet for accommodation and freeze-dried powder for food, the cyclist can roll into the campsite, set up his waterproof tent, and start cooking dinner: french onion soup, spaghetti bolognaise, a sparkling rose, together with some tropical vegetable salad, followed by some canned pears for dessert. He can then proceed to take some photographs of the area with his 35mm camera outfit complete with collapsible tripod and zoom lens, then decide whether to proceed with the journey the next day, or just read a book by the stream.

CAMPING EQUIPMENT

After some preliminary day rides around your area or in the nearest national park you might like to try camping overnight. The times immediately before, during and after sunset really give the bush an atmosphere unparalleled anywhere in the world. The gum tree's silver leaves glow a brilliant red, the wind stops, and the only sound audible is the crackling of logs in the campfire.

As with bike equipment, only the *essential* gear should be purchased at first for camping. Cyclists will update their inventory once experience and ambition take hold.

Sleeping bag: Cyclists have the advantage that they're not restricted to expensive small lightweight models, but can choose more according to comfort and warmth rather than size and weight. Prices start at around $100 for Thermofill models that weigh close to 2 kg. These are good for all summer camping in relatively warm climates such as by the coast. Slightly upmarket are Quallofill bags that are warm even when wet. The disadvantage is that they're bulky. Expect to pay around $300. It is difficult to go past a fill that is comprised mainly of duck or goose down. Coming mostly from China, down is by far the best insulator due to its air-trapping qualities. Furthermore down bags are light (1–2kg) and can compress to incredibly small sizes. The damage? From $200 to $700 depending on the amount and ratio of the fill. The up-market models have Gore-Tex exteriors but unless you plan to cycle Antarctica or camp in rivers, they're not necessary.

Australia's leading camping equipment suppliers, Paddy Pallin, have a complete range of down sleeping bags that are treated with 3M Scotchguard which enables the down to resist the effects of condensation and moisture in general.

A light breathable fabric called Pertex is used to further protect the down from light moisture that can seep up through the tent floor. Paddy Pallin rate their bags on a scale of 1-6, with 1-3 being for mild climates, and 4-6 designed for multi-season, extreme latitudes, and high altitude use. For Tasmanian conditions, a grade 4 Gingera with 700g of down gives excellent warmth for its low weight (1.38kg). Its compactability makes it perfect for the mountain cyclist with luggage and weight constraints. Price is about $370.

Accessories also exist for sleeping bags; Paddy Pallin sell large storage bags as down should not be compressed when not in use, silk and cotton inner sheets for extra warmth, and sleeping mats.

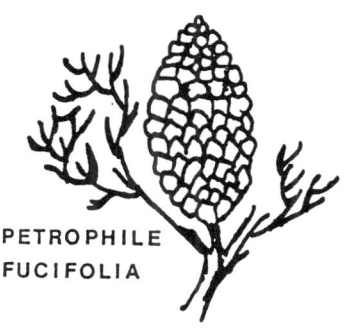

PETROPHILE
FUCIFOLIA

Tent: A simple fly will do perfectly to keep the dew off on clear nights by the coast in summer. However, when venturing into uncertain territory such as the south-west or the Central Plateau, which are notorious for unpredictable appalling weather, a sealed tent is recommended.

Price depends on the material, design, name brand, and size. If cycling in a group, the weight of the tent can be shared. Water-resistance can be improved by the application of a seam-sealant.

Eureka manufacture Australia's most popular tents. A variety of models and sizes are available that range from 1-person bivvy style tents to ones designed for use in snow-expeditions. The Bike and Hike style, featured in the photos in this book, weighs under 2 kilos, has a frame of shock-corded 7000 series aircraft aluminium, and a design that reduces buffeting if pitched with its longitudinal axis aligned with prevailing winds. The cost is approximately $260. It is fast to erect, sleeps two with room for small packs, and comes with a fly that can be zipped open on mild nights. Compactability ensures that it can be taken to the longest cycling and walking expeditions.

Other styles include self-supporting dome tents that need no pegs. These have the advantage of excellent space-to-weight ratios as well as the fact that they can be erected on hard surfaces, and once up, can be picked up and placed anywhere. The only disadvantage with these self-supporting tents is that they can be blown around when no one is lying in them so it's always a good idea to throw in your sleeping gear immediately.

Sleeping mat: Foam closed cell sleeping rolls are unbeatable for their price. Supermarkets sell them for about $15. However, cold conditions as can exist on the Central plateau the ground will drain heat away during the night because the down directly beneath you will be compressed. Proper insulation can be provided with self-inflating foam mattresses that are smaller than their closed-cell counterparts, but about five times the price. They provide a cushion of air that shields the body from the ground. The disadvantage (beside their cost) is that they can puncture. Therma-a-rest models have the strongest reputation and cost approximately $130.

The traditional lilo air mattress is far too heavy and bulky even for extended cycle touring, but of course has the advantage of being far cheaper ($10–$30) and one can explore lakes and rivers and even go surfing with it!

Ground sheet: The common space blanket can

be bought at disposal stores everywhere and are by far the most popular groundsheet.

Uses include: a floor when using a fly so sleeping bags don't get dirty; an extra floor when using a tent to help prevent heat escaping and water leaking in; a picnic blanket for meals where cooking utensils and food can be spread out, and an emergency blanket for victims of hypothermia and heat exhaustion. With the silver side out, the blanket will reflect some 70 per cent of external radiation, keeping the body cool. The dark side is placed outside in the event of hypothermia so all external radiation is absorbed, and internal radiation is reflected back.

Pack Towels: A very useful multi-purpose 68cm x 25cm cloth made from 100 per cent Viscose that can hold up to ten times its weight in water. This water can be 92 per cent wrung out by hand and the remainder quickly air dries. Weighing just 42 grams, it's the ideal towel for the bushwalker and cyclist. Use it to dry yourself, as insulation for hot pots, cleaning the dishes, neckerchief for sweat absorption, compress . . .

Backpack: As mentioned before, when luggage is stored in backpacks as opposed to a pannier, you have the advantage of easier up-hill pushing, easier lifting of the bike, extra storage space, and allowing you to take overnight walks. There are many quality brand names on the market. When choosing, make sure there is plenty of padding on the lower back so that when adopting the crouched cycling position, the harness is not digging into your spine. Although they're becoming out of fashion, some packs still have external compartments for dividing up your gear.

For Tasmanian conditions, your pack should be waterproof, and accommodate enough equipment for at least a four-day walk away from the bike. The combination of a 65–80 litre pack and rear panniers should allow you the greatest flexibility in cycling and walking so that you can explore the furthest corners of Tasmania.

The New Zealand made Tika *Taranaki* has a fully adjustable comfortable harness system and five separate compartments. It weighs under 2 kilos and costs about $300.

General camping equipment

The following is a checklist of equipment that one may need in the bush. It is by no means comprehensive, and individuals may want to add or delete items according to taste. It is wise to draw up a list so you don't forget anything in the last-minute packing rush. What could be worse than realising after a long day's ride that you've forgotten the can-opener?

Cooking	Hygiene	Miscellaneous
Billy	Toothbrush/paste	Lighter/matches
Frying pan	Soap	Candle
Pots	Toilet paper	Maps
Plate	Insect repellent	Water bottle
Cutlery	First aid kit	Small stove
Can-opener	Towel	Metho / gas
Large knife	Tissues	canisters
Scouring pad		Bike tool kit
Cup		Spare tubes
Food		Tent and/or fly
		Sleeping bag
		Compass

Despite the long list, the above shouldn't weigh more than 12-15 kg. Add another 1 kg of food per day and one is looking at about 20 kg of luggage for a week's trip. While this may seem a lot, properly packed panniers, saddle bags, and a backpack can carry up to 50 kg of supplies.

For those owners of racing and conventional touring bikes who are switching to bushbiking, you will most likely have panniers and a rack and these can be easily and costlessly transferred to your new bike. Allocate your luggage in the ratio of 2:3 with the majority of gear at the back for maximum stability.

New panniers on the market have a top section that can be unzipped to reveal backpack straps. Your pannier has just transformed into a day-pack! Other attachments to maximise luggage include handlebar bags that attach to the front forks, rope that can be wrapped around the top tube from the seat post to the neck, water bottles and pumps that can be attached almost anywhere, straps on top of panniers and saddle-bags to put tents, rolls and sleeping bags, and of course panniers across the top of the front wheel as well as alongside it.

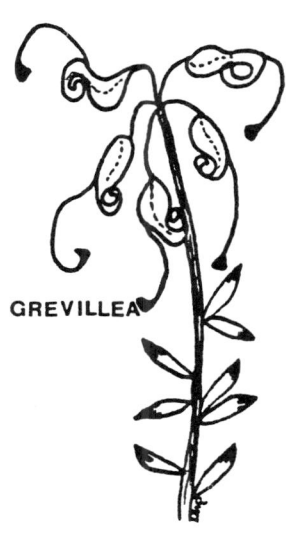

GREVILLEA

FOOD

The following is a list of calorie, carbohydrate, and protein content per 100 g or 100 mL of common food types:

Type	Calories (k)	Carbohydrates (g)	Protein (g)
White rice	103	23	2
Beef steak	396	0	26
Chicken	150	0	30
Baked beans	110	21	6
Mushrooms	165	4	3
Potatoes	77	18	2
Apples	55	13	0.4
Cheese	400	0.5	26
Corn flakes	363	79	8
Eggs (2)	150	1	11
Red wine	95	0.5	0.3

The freeze-dried food from New Zealand that is commonly found in camping stores is popular for long wilderness expeditions. It is extremely expensive, and despite being reasonable quality, is not of adequate quantity. For each meal additional food has to be prepared, which is inconvenient after a long tiring day cycling. Cans and fresh fruit/vegies are recommended but should be consumed as fast as possible to save weight. For lunches and cold snacks, dried fruit and nut mixes give long-lasting nourishment. A quick top-up can be supplied by confectionery.

MAPS

The Department of Environment and Planning has a TASMAP sales shop in the Lands Building (134 Macquarie Street, Hobart). One can also order maps by mail—their postal address is TASMAP GPO Box 44A Hobart 7001. Phone (002) 30-6381. The TASMAP sales office in Launceston is located at Henty House, 1 Civic Square (003) 32-2339. The ones relevant for outdoor use are:

National Parks Maps ($7.95)		Day Walk Maps	
Asbestos Range	(1:25 000)	Ben Lomond	$3.00
Ben Lomond	(1:50 000)	Cradle Mountain	$3.00
Cradle		Hartz Mountains	$2.00
Mountain	(1:100 000)	Mount Roland	$2.00
Frenchmans Cap	(1:50 000)	Mt. Wellington	$3.00
Freycinet	(1:50 000)		
Maria Island	(1:50 000)		
Mount Field	(1:50 000)		
Rocky Cape	(1:30 000)		
Walls of			
Jerusalem	(1:25 000)		

These maps all have detailed information on the reverse side outlining natural and (pre-)European histories, points of interest, regulations, and nomenclature.

TASMAP have agents all over Tasmania where specific maps can be purchased; for example Visitors Centres, Rangers Headquarters, and Information kiosks in the National Parks themselves. In addition, the Hobart Walking Club has released a trekking map of the Eastern Arthur Ranges. At the time of writing, no Forestry Commission maps are publicly available.

About this Guide's Maps

The maps that appear in this book are only to give cyclists an idea where the rides are located. To ensure clarity, there is no topographical information and many of the irrelevant roads, trails, towns, and smaller rivers have been left out.

For the majority of rides in this book, detailed topographical maps are essential. The primary reason why people get lost in Tasmanian national parks is a lack of adequate maps and navigational expertise. A set of 29 x 1:100 000 maps will cover every ride in this book. There are two types of 1:100 000 maps: land tenures ($7.95) and pure topographicals ($6.50). I recommended the land tenures as they are more up to date, and show all state forests, reserves, protected areas, and national parks. In addition they cover the island more efficiently as well as showing 200-metre interval contour lines.

Some of this guide's rides are in extremely remote areas, such as the upper Florentine, Forth, Mersey, Picton, and Weld River Valleys, the Arthur-Pieman area and the Eastern Tiers. For these expeditions and with most of the walks that are detailed in this guide, it is imperative that you have 1:25 000 topographical. Relying on route-notes can lead to frustration especially in forestry areas where new trails are being forged all the time and old ones rehabilitated. Road signs get taken down and tracks get renamed, upgraded, downgraded, closed or re-routed. In these circumstances, 1:25 000 maps will show you the best way to get to where you want to go. As many of them have only just been printed, they're very up to date.

They show the majority of walking tracks and all fire trails that were constructed at the time of field-survey. A scale of 1:25 000 means that 8 cm on the map equals 2 km in reality.

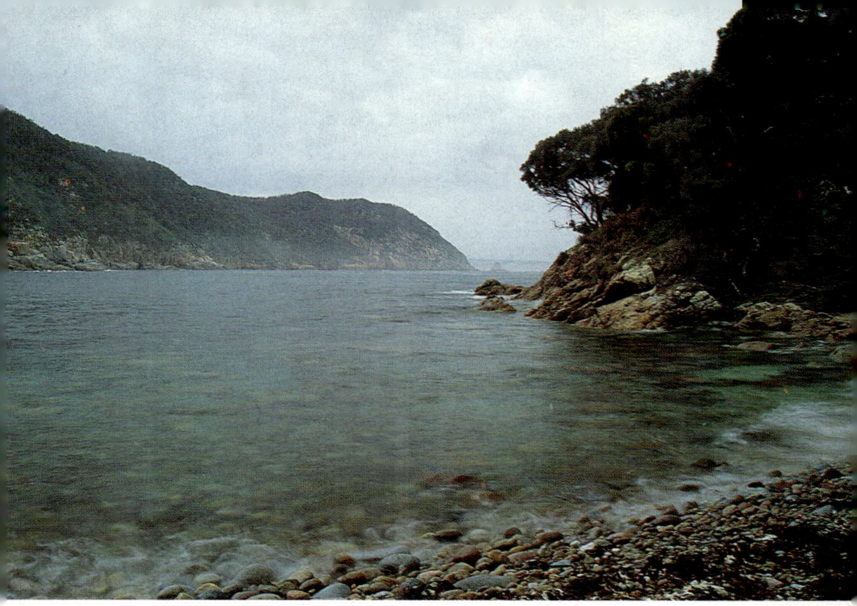

Bluestone Bay, Freycinet National Park (Ride 34)

Apsley River, Douglas-Apsley National Park (Ride 35)

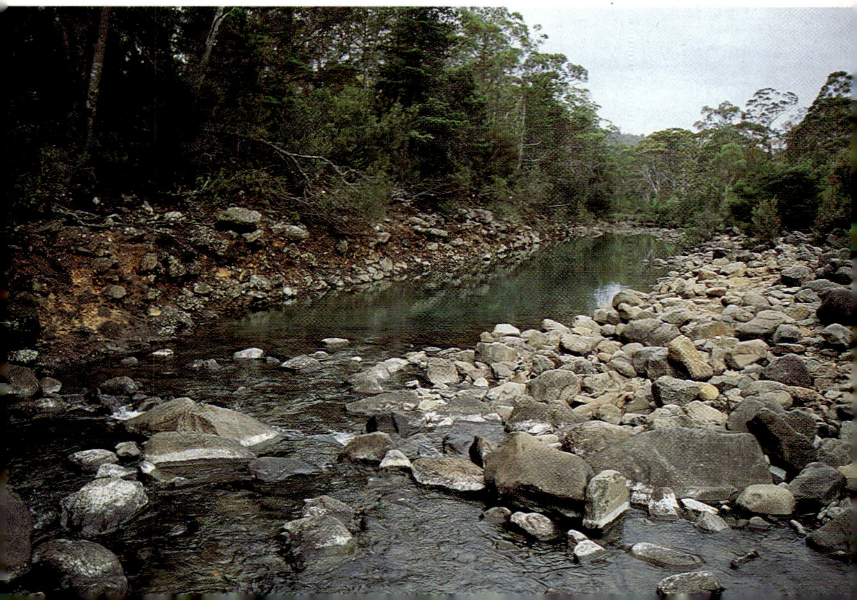

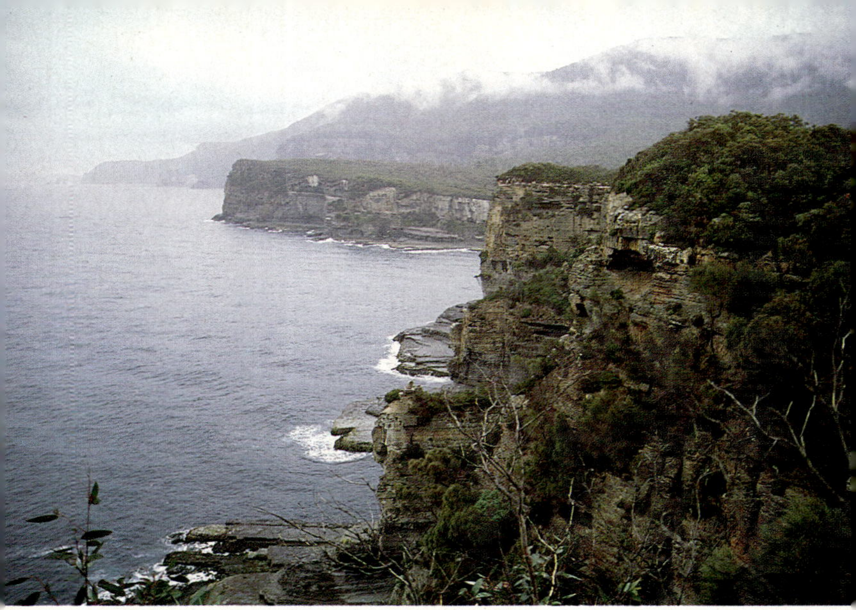

Sea cliffs north of Fortescue Bay, Tasman Peninsula (Ride 38)

The Penitentiary ruins at Port Arthur (Ride 39)

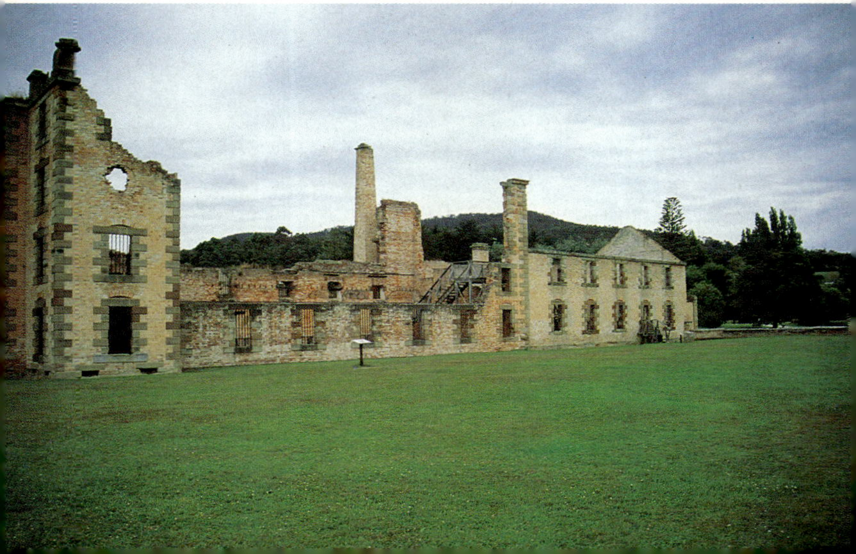

Planning your own rides

The best method for planning a route is to purchase the maps that cover the area you want to cycle and work out a route along the fire-trails (or vehicular tracks as they're represented on the map's legend) that goes the most scenic way to where you are going. The distance of the trail can be measured in centimetres with a piece of string. Simply divide the length of the string by four to obtain the distance of the journey in kilometres. One can also purchase a simple mechanical gadget from Germany that you roll along your intended route and it'll tell you the horizontal distance. They're available at most camping stores. Either way, one would then simply add on 20-30 per cent to account for altitudinal fluctuations and to be conservative.

The average cycling speed on moderately hilly country is about 8–10 km/h, so try not to plan day-trips longer than about 50 km unless you are very fit or the terrain is predominantly downhill, especially if you are laden with panniers. This will leave plenty of time for rest breaks, sightseeing, walking, and unexpected delays. Very rough tracks, great uphills, and navigational errors can reduce a cyclist's average to that of walking or sometimes even slower.

Learn to recognise features on the map using contour lines (lines that join all places of equal height). Orthodox navigation skills involving conversion of bearings and resection are totally unnecessary. One simply has to familiarise oneself with how contour lines represent the landscape. After the first few times in the bush, you should be able to recognise simple and common features on the map: mountains, valleys, ridgelines, saddles, cliffs, etc.

Walking clubs will also teach you the skills necessary for extended wilderness expeditions.

They are located in Hobart and Launceston. Tasmania also has an extensive guide network which will lead small parties through selected tracks. These commercial tour operators include:

Tasmanian Highland Tours
Tasmania Expeditions
Peregrine Adventures
Wilderness Tours
Adventure Tours
Craclair Tours
Taswalks

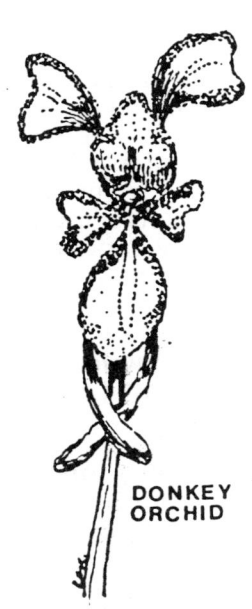

DONKEY
ORCHID

FIRST AID

The most likely cause of injury faced by the cyclist is a fall. A simple medical kit with disinfectant and bandages is adequate for most types of grazing. For minor scrapes, bumps, and small grazes it will be perfectly all right to continue in accordance to the initial plan.

However, for any major loss of blood there will be a loss of stamina, shock, and a risk of infection. At this point the planned route will have to be altered to the easiest and quickest way back to civilisation. Infection can also be caused by serious cases of saddle soreness where the combination of chafing and perspiration causes cracks in the skin where bacteria can enter.

First-aid kits can be obtained from camping stores, the Red Cross, and chemists, or they can be self-made from individual items purchased from a pharmacy or supermarket (this is the cheaper and sometimes better approach). For cycling, the following are recommended:

> Sterilised bandages (about 15 m)
> Aspirin
> Large gauze dressings (non-adhesive)
> Small scissors
> Disinfectant powder
> Cotton wool
> Plaster adhesive tape
> Tea tree oil

Grazing

The aim here is to minimise loss of blood and risk of infection. Clean wound with water. Make sure there aren't any pieces of gravel caught in the open area. Then simply cover with some antiseptic powder or tea tree oil, apply a large gauze dressing and bandage. Treat shock by giving warm liquids and resting the patient. If it is late in the day, and statistics confirm that risk of an accident increases dramatically with time spent on the bike, start looking for a camp site near by so the patient can rest overnight.

Bites

If bitten by a full grown tiger snake in the neck two days' ride from the nearest telephone, there is little one can do. However, the majority of bites are treatable and the current accepted procedure is surprisingly simple to learn (the old days of cutting the wound, sucking out poison, and tourniquets are over):

1. Apply pressure on the wound.
2. At the same time, starting from the top of the limb (shoulder or thigh), bandage tightly and steadily downwards. Several bandages might be needed.
3. Keep the limb *lower* than the heart.
4. Immobilise the limb by splinting it to a straight branch.
5. Treat for shock: tell victim that it wasn't a poisonous snake, or that most of the venom went outside the wound, etc. If one acts calm and collected, chances are the patient's heartbeat will start to fall. This will limit the spread of the venom to the central nervous system.

Treat spider and scorpion bites much the same way. Keeping the bite area cold helps deaden the pain.

All three species of Tasmania's snakes are venomous: the black tiger (*Notechis ater*), copperhead (*Austrelaps superbus*), and to a lesser extent, the whipsnake (*Drysdalia coronoides*), also known as the white-lipped snake. But they are mostly shy, rarely strike, and pose less of a threat to cyclists than to walkers. Their fangs are small so the venom is not injected efficiently into the victim. Since 1925, not more than 20 deaths have occurred from snake bite. The rides on the islands detailed in chapter 10 present the greatest risk from snakes and bandages are essential when touring there.

Heat exhaustion

Symptoms are a loss of blood in the facial area causing it to turn white. The skin will be wet and cold. If there is a salt deficiency, cramps will also be a symptom. Rest in the shade is the best treatment, followed by drinking water with a touch of salt in it. If there is no shade, for example, if you have been travelling on treeless plateau tops, set up a fly or groundsheet over some bushes and ensure there's adequate ventilation.

Hypothermia

Travelling in winter without adequate clothing is perhaps the best way to get hypothermia. The cure is to get out of the wind, replace your wet clothes with dry ones, and put something in between the ground and you, use a space blanket to reflect internal heat and eat plenty of food. Drink *no* alcohol as it only makes you colder. It will be a time to become closer to your companions— literally. Shared body warmth can cure all symptoms of hypothermia, but body reserves will still have to be built up after normal body temperature is reached.

CAMPING

The Parks, Wildlife, and Heritage policy on camping is decentralised. Naturally rules and regulations depend on the area. In designated wilderness areas, one can camp anywhere. In some parks, Cradle Mountain-Lake St. Clair, for example, fees apply. They require bookings for some of their most popular places, especially during school holidays.

In other places, such as in the south-west and Douglas-Apsley, use is limited and one can camp in most places. Some have cabins available complete with pre-cut firewood or coal, while other parks, such as Maria Island, have camping in developed and monitored sites only.

Here in Australia, we cyclists have to be on our best behaviour in order to minimise any future hostilities and zoning of National Parks. Already, the Parks and Wildlife authorities have prevented the use of walking trails as cycling routes due to the fragile nature of the parks. Horseriders have already suffered criticism for their activity in Australia, as have four-wheel-drivers and trail-bikers. In order not to get classified together with motorised transport in any future National Parks management policy, some sort of code of ethics should be adopted by commercial organisations as well as private bikers. Here's what the Department of Conservation and Environment in Victoria has established as a Mountain Bike Code of behaviour:

1. *SELF-SUFFICIENCY:* Carry first-aid kit and tool set.
2. *GROUP-SIZE:* Less than four is considered unsafe, while ten or more will often lead to rapid track degradation and conflict with other users.
3. *CONTROL:* Always ride so you can stop in time for unexpected reasons. Keep your bike well maintained.

4. *UTILITARIAN RIGHTS:* Respect the rights of other users such as walkers and equestrians. Due to the silent nature of the bicycle, both walkers and horses easily get a shock when a cyclist flies past from behind. Always announce your presence. To avoid spooking horses, dismount when passing them and allow them wide berth.

5. *WEED AND DISEASE PREVENTION:* Bicycle tyres have been proved to be a cause of the spread of exotic weeds and plant disease by seeds becoming trapped in the tread and dislodging later. Therefore, cleaning your bike regularly not only makes sense for your bike but also for the environment:

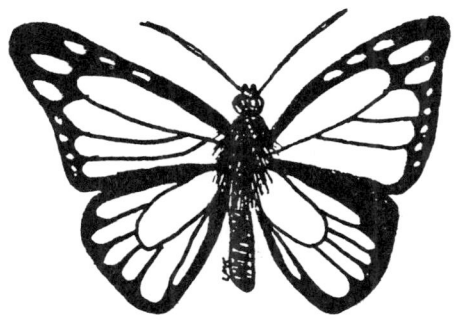

6. *OBEYING SIGNS:* Some tracks, while perfectly possible to cycle on, are closed to all cyclists because they are being rehabilitated. All throughout Australia, gazetted wilderness areas involve the suppression of information on closed trails, revegetation, and the implementation of barriers, penalties and patrols. While the main perpetrators are four-wheel-drivers, mountain biking is not a recreation recognised as being reconcilable with official wilderness areas. Likewise all walking tracks are out of bounds to bicycles due to the rapid damage to the trail and the conflict of use with walkers.

Also be aware of the other regulations in regard to total fire bans, camping permits, fees, fuel stove only areas, and rubbish removal. Leave all gates as found.

7. *SENSIBLE RIDING:* Don't cut corners as this breaks up the soft soil on the road shoulders so that the next rain can easily wash it away, leading to erosion. Likewise skidding is an effective way to accelerate track degradation,* especially if the ground is wet. However, the authorities recommend that you travel *through* mud rather than widen the track by going around large puddles.

---

* Furthermore, the loss of gyroscopic wheel motion as a result from skidding is inherently unstable and often leads to a loss of control.

PHOTOGRAPHY

Cycle touring allows the storage and weight capacity to enable one to carry a good camera outfit. Photographing the Tasmanian bush can be frustrating due to the lack of direct sunlight and the seemingly perpetual drizzle. However, the skilled photographer can use these conditions to his advantage, thus making Tasmania a rewarding place.

Camera: A 35mm camera is recommended that has manual settings so that one can compensate for measuring inaccuracies of the light meter. Fog, high contrast, direct sunlight, position of subject and long shadows can lead to incorrect exposure evaluations. Furthermore, a manual mode gives the photographer more control of his shots with respect to waterfalls and other time exposure shots.

Tripod: In addition to a camera, one needs a tripod. All too often, the cyclist in Tasmania will experience light conditions too dark to shoot freehand (usually 1/15 sec). Rainforest canopies, narrow valleys, flowing rivers and waterfalls all require time exposures of anything up to 30 seconds. A tripod should be lightweight and compact. Numerous models cater directly for the outdoor trekker. Tripods are also an advantage to the solo adventurer to enable self-portraits.

Lenses: Ideally a standard lens, a macro, and a telephoto will give the best results as the number of elements is kept to a minimum. But a cost-benefit analysis dictates that a good zoom lens will do the job of all three and still give more than adequate definition. All the photographs in my guidebooks were taken on a 28–200mm (f3.5-f22) zoom lens.

Filters: For Tasmanian conditions polarising filters are not really necessary, as they reduce the amount of light entering the camera by up to two stops and they become less useful when there is diffused light. Windy, fresh conditions ensure a minimum of haze over landscapes, so most of the time a skylight filter is unnecessary too.

Film: Although the quality gap between negative and slide film is narrowing, transparency (reversal or positive) films still produce the best results in terms of colour saturation and resolution. Tasmania's landscape is a photographer's paradise and the use of a low-ASA-rated film gives it the best justification. A new award-winning high resolution film from Fuji called *Velvia* 50ASA enhances greens superbly in both direct and indirect light as well as giving very fine detail.

The disadvantages with slide films are that they're usually more expensive, more difficult to view, and there's limited scope for corrections in the processing stage. Exposures have to be spot-on, whereas with negative film, error tolerance is greater and the lab can made compensations of up to two stops.

Tips: Good results are the product of three factors:

One-third skill
One-third equipment
One-third environment

* For most types of photography, direct sunlight will give better colour and contrast.

* Early morning and evening are the best times to photograph. This is because the lower angle of the sun's rays through the atmosphere removes blue light giving a warmer shift.

* Prevailing misty conditions are good for mood shots: calm lakes, trunks of beech trees, dew droplets on webs, moss, etc.

* Avoid using flash as this washes out colour. Cave formations are best captured using a tripod and a long exposure.

* For landscapes, where possible, include a foreground.

* Avoid having the horizon passing through the middle of the frame. In most cases, make a habit of angling the camera slightly down.

* When using a polarising filter, photograph as much 'with' the sun as possible, although good polarising effects also occur when shooting at 90 degrees to the sun.

* For shots of cyclists fording water crossings, choose a fast exposure and follow the cyclist into the water while taking the shot. This will blur the background thereby enhancing the sensation of speed.

* For shots of cyclists or walkers at lookouts, choose a smaller aperture so that there is more depth of field, i.e. both the foreground and background will be in focus.

* Rivers, seascapes, and waterfalls can have the classic softened effect by slowing the exposure to as much as 10 seconds. However, too long an exposure will start to produce a blue-shift without the suitable correction filter.

Not all that looks good to the eye will look good on film. Only experience will improve your judgement of what will make a good photograph. Comparing results to records of exposure settings will also improve the accuracy of your compensation adjustments so that a smaller percentage of photographs is wasted.

International fame and fortune awaits the photographer who can capture the legendary Tasmanian tiger (*Thylacine cynocephalus*). Although the probability is declining each year, there is the remotest possibility that it still exists. The last ones were found in the Florentine Valley (Ride 83) in 1933 by Elias Churchill and near Mawbanna in 1930. Sceptics claim that the lack of unconfirmed sightings, remains and droppings is evidence enough of its extinction. Still, many believe in its existence, and scientific expeditions are still frequent. A number of generous bounties exist for people who can obtain verifiable evidence of its existence. Another potential bonanza, although even less chance, is the Tasmanian emu, believed extinct since 1865. So it's wise to always keep a film in your camera.

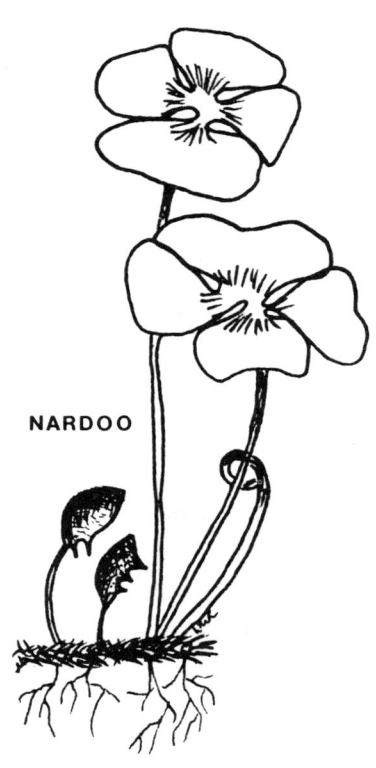

NARDOO

3

THE STATE

An Introduction

Tasmania contains some of the most aesthetic wilderness areas in the world. The south-west region of the island, together with Fiordland in New Zealand, and western Patagonia and Tierra del Fuego in South America, are the four major temperate wildernesses in the Southern Hemisphere. Standing on a peak on the Sentinel Range dividing Lake Gordon from Lake Pedder, the adventurer can see nothing but a panoramic vista of rugged quartzite mountain ranges all around.

For mainlanders and international visitors, 12,000 years of isolation from the world has seen the Tasmanian plant and wild adopt unique characteristics.

Being a small state (about the size of Ireland, with 455,000 people), road quality is generally of a high standard throughout Tasmania as is the level of signposting. All major roads are labelled with a letter prefix signifying economic importance. This will, in most cases, be correlated with grading. An 'A' with one number represents the sealed highways, a 'B' road with two numbers connects the secondary townships, while 'C' roads with three numbers are unsealed with less traffic and more often than not lead to more scenic places. On all three types, conventional touring bikes can be used, although a run of bad weather can turn 'C' roads into a quagmire. For management trails, highland vehicular tracks, coastal four-wheel-drive trails, and old logging roads, a mountain bike is essential.

The map that shows all major roads and the prefix codes is the RACT 1:600 000 Touring Map of Tasmania. Cycle touring is very popular for overseas visitors who do a circumference of the island: Hobart-Strahan-Burnie-Launceston-Bicheno-Hobart. Such a tour is about 1100 km and takes a couple of weeks. The relevant guide to obtain for these road tours is the 76-page booklet *Bicycling Tasmania* by Ian Terry. It contains 20-odd rides on roads connecting the major cities and tourist points of interest and is written for those with conventional touring bikes and little knowledge of Tasmania.

While the traditional 'circumference' tour gives the cyclist a good overview in a relatively short period of time, it omits the true interaction between man, machine and nature that can only be achieved on a mountain bike in the several hundred thousand hectares of forests covering the island. With the furthest point being less than 400 km from any other, a racer or touring bike is not a necessity.

One point of law to note is that while in other states cyclists are allowed to ride two abreast if they're less than 2.5 m from the left hand side of the road, the Tasmanian Traffic Code states that only single file riding is permitted.

Despite its isolation, Tasmania has a rich history and the evidence of this is proudly promoted by local tourism. Indeed it seems that anything older than a few decades is automatically labelled with a Historical Site sign and photographed in postcards for sale at the local milkbar.

The cyclist prepared to travel on the rough rainforest trails on the west coast will be rewarded with a unique mix of old colonial-period mining ruins set amid spectacular landscape scenery. This is what sets Tasmania apart, making it a perfect venue for mountain biking.

TRANSPORT

To Tasmania

Getting your bike to Tasmania is relatively cheap. While you might be paying $200 for a Sydney-Hobart airfare, you can fly with your bike as excess luggage, paying just $24, or $20 from Melbourne. You will have to make the bike as thin as possible such as by turning the handle-bars parallel with the frame and unscrewing the pedals. All domestic carriers plus several smaller regional operators provide regular services across Bass Strait.

For cyclists using the ferries, there are two options. The fastest is the wave-piercing *Seacat Tasmania*. With its four 3.8 million watt engines it takes under five hours from Port Welshpool in Victoria to George Town in Tasmania. The problem for cyclists is that it departs 200 km from Melbourne. The destination, George Town, is about 50 km from Launceston. The one-way cost is $15 for a bike (regardless of season) and $109 for a passenger.

This makes the second alternative, the *Abel Tasman*, a more convenient vessel as it leaves Melbourne directly and arrives at Devonport (90 km from Launceston). Prices vary considerably because of the necessity of accommodation. With its service speed at only 18 knots and consequent trip time at 15 hours, a room must be rented and the cheapest hostel accommodation in summer costs just over $100 one way. Bicycles vary between $10 and $20 depending on season. Students receive a discount. A connecting bus service then can take you to Launceston or Hobart. Both vessels have very regular services departing several times a week, but in summer bookings are necessary well in advance and can be performed at any travel agent.

Medication is advisable for those prone to motion

sickness. To minimise sway, sit on the central longitudinal axis. Bass Strait is one of the roughest stretches of ocean in the world and both vessels rock considerably.

Within Tasmania

Although there are 1000 km of railway tracks on the island, there are no longer any passenger services (apart from a tourist steam-train at Devonport). Therefore the Wilderness Transport Network in Tasmania is ideally suited for domestic and international visitors with no automobile transport. It provides transport to and from the major cities such as Devonport, Launceston, and Hobart to the most popular national parks and many of the staging areas listed in this guide:

Staging Point	Area Accessed
Mt. Field National Park	National Park and Florentine Concession state forests. Reserves in the Tyenna River valley.
Scotts Peak Dam	Lake Pedder, Strathgordon, Gordon Dam, Scotts Peak Dam, Mount Anne, The Sentinels.
Dover-Lune River	Hartz Mountains National Park, Thermal Pool, D'Entrecasteaux Historic Site, the southern state forests, Hastings Caves State Reserve, Esperance River Forest Reserve.

Lake St. Clair	Central Plateau Conservation Area, Franklin River, Lake King William, walking to south part of Overland Track.
Strahan	West coast: Ocean Beach, Henty Dunes, Queenstown, Huon Pine rainforest, Gordon River cruises, scenic flights, Zeehan
Cradle Mountain	Cradle Valley, Waldheim, Lake Dove, Mount Roland Protected Area, King Solomon's Cave State Reserve.
Walls of Jerusalem	Mersey River, Forth River, Fish River, Lake McKenzie, Lake Parangana, Lake Rowallan, Central Plateau, Cradle Mountain National Park eastern perimeter state forests.
Burnie	North-west state forests and forest reserves, Arthur River, Arthur-Pieman Protected Area, The Nut, Rocky Cape National Park.

Ben Lomond	Only in winter (1 July onwards). North-east state forests and forest reserves, Hollybank, Mt. William National Park, Ansons River, Mt. Barrow State Reserve, Douglas-Apsley National Park.
Hobart	Bruny Island, Seven Mile Beach, Tasman Peninsula (Port Arthur), Fortescue Forest Reserve, Maria Island, Freycinet Peninsula.
Launceston	Asbestos Range National Park and surrounding state forests, Mt. Barrow State Reserve, Bell Bay, northern beaches, Cataract Gorge.

The buses depart about 6-8 times a day. Fares range from about $65 to $170 return. Single fares are half these prices, and mountain bikes are an additional $10. You have to let the network know in advance of your intention to take bikes so they can hook up a cage trailer to the bus.

Bookings, timetable, and price information can be obtained by ringing 008-030-505. For the hard-core mountain cyclist with little time to travel from the ferry/airport to the wilderness, this is the ideal service. One can also be picked up after completing a ride and driven pack to the city. A good idea is the Wilderness and Highway Pass, giving unlimited travel. One week costs $120 while two cost $159.

Other bus services include:

* TASMANIAN REDLINE COACHES:
    (Bikes are standard rate of $8.00.
    No requirements for removal of
    handle-bars, pedals, etc.)

    112 George St., Launceston (003) 31-9177
    199 Collins St., Hobart (002) 34-4577

MIDLAND—NORTH WEST COAST ROUTE
Hobart-Launceston-Devonport-Burnie-Wynyard-Smithton
Runs 7 times a day weekdays, and 3 times a day
weekends in addition to return service.

EAST COAST
Hobart-Bicheno-Swansea-St. Helens-St. Marys-Derby-Launceston
Runs several times a day weekdays, once only night
service at weekends
Return service also available

WEST COAST
Hobart-Derwent Bridge-Queenstown-Burnie
1 service daily Tue-Sat
Return service same schedule
No service Sun and Mon

* HOBART COACHES:
    (Bikes are a standard rate of $8.00.
    No requirements for removal of pedals.)

83 Cimitiere St., Launceston (003) 34-3600
60 Collins St., Hobart (002) 34-4077
                        (008) 03-0620

MIDLAND—NORTH WEST ROUTE
Hobart-Launceston-Devonport-Burnie
Runs 4 times a day weekdays and twice a day
weekends in addition to return service

EAST COAST
Hobart-Triabunna-Swansea-Bicheno-St. Helens
Twice a day in addition to return service
Doesn't run Saturday

PENINSULA
Hobart-Port Arthur: each late afternoon weekdays
Port Arthur-Hobart: each early morning weekdays

* HALEY'S COACHES
  St. Marys-St. Helens-Derby-St. Helens
  Once a day weekdays only

* PEAKES COACHES
  St. Marys-Bicheno-Swansea-Bicheno-St. Marys
  Once a day weekdays only

* BICHENO COACH SERVICES
  Bicheno-Coles Bay-Bicheno
  Once a day Mon-Sat

* PENINSULA COACH SERVICE
  Hobart-Port Arthur-Hobart: once a day weekdays

* MAXWELL'S COACH AND TAXI SERVICE
  (004) 92-1431
  Devonport, Launceston, Hobart to Mersey
Valley, Walls of Jerusalem, Arm River, Forth River,
Frenchman's Cap, Lake St. Clair, Franklin River,
Strahan, Cradle Valley, Derwent Bridge, Bronte.
By appointment only.

ACCOMMODATION

Perhaps the most popular form of accommodation in Tasmania is the youth hostels, which are located in convenient and scenic locations close to the parks. Lune River Youth Hostel, for example, is a short ride from Hastings Cave State Reserve and the Thermal Pool in the very south of Tasmania.

Membership is essential, but tariffs are low. Note that several hostels do not have permanent caretakers and a key is needed from head office in Hobart located at 28 Criterion St, telephone (002) 34-9617. The publication *For Backpackers by Backpackers* gives accommodation and travelling information for domestic and international visitors and is available from the YHA.

All hostels will mind your bike while you're walking if you prefer not to hide it in the bush. Many hostels also hire out hybrid ATB bikes.

The following is a list of the hostel locations:

Location	Phone	Area serviced
Stanley	(004) 58-1266	North-west coast
Wynyard	(004) 42-2013	North-west coast
Devonport	(002) 50-2311	Central north coast including Asbestos Range National Park
Deloraine	(003) 62-2996	Central north
Launceston	(003) 44-9779	Central north-east
Winnaleah	(003) 54-2152	Mt. William National Park
St. Helens	(003) 76-1661	North-east coast
Scamandar		East coast
St. Marys	(003) 72-2341	Douglas-Apsley National Park

Location	Phone	Area serviced
Bicheno	(003) 75-1293	East coast including Douglas-Apsley National Park
Coles Bay		Freycinet Peninsula
Swansea	(002) 57-8367	East coast
Triabunna	(002) 57-3439	East coast
Oatlands	(002) 54-1320	East-inland
Bellerive	(002) 44-2552	Hobart (east)
Port Arthur	(002) 50-2311	Tasman peninsula
Hobart	(002) 28-4829	Derwent River valley
Cygnet	(002) 95-1551	Snug and Huon River valley

Location	Phone	Area serviced
Lune River	(002) 98-3163	Southern state forests and Ida Bay
New Norfolk		Upper Derwent River
Mt. Field	(002) 88-1369	Mt. Field National Park (Gateway to south-west)

Associated hostels are located at:

Location	Phone	Area serviced
Bronte Park	(002) 89-1126	Central Tasmania including Central Plateau, Lake St Clair, and also closest hostel to Strahan area.
Lumeah	(002) 93-1265	Bruny Island

There are also numerous caravan parks and official camping grounds. For example the Cradle Mountain Camping Ground is run by P&O who lease the site from the Department of Parks, Wildlife, and Heritage. Naturally, fees apply.

However, there is unlimited accommodation at no charge in the many natural campsites and huts in the national parks and state forests. Usual facilities provided are picnic tables and fireplaces. More popular camping grounds have pit toilets, rubbish pits, shelters, fresh water, and firewood or electric/gas BBQs.

GUIDED TOURS

If you are a novice mountain biker, new cycling clubs, societies and other more commercial touring organisations are popping up everywhere.

Some of the more commercially orientated tours will provide support vehicles that carry all food and supplies, and provide transport for large uphills, etc. Group sizes are usually limited to between 10 and 15 and *you do not need to own a bike!* Renting one costs a few dollars extra. This is really an excellent way to discover whether you like the sport BEFORE spending $1000+ on equipment.

One tour operator, Peregrine Adventures, has a range of cycling, caving, sailing and walking tours. The mountain bike tour centres on the north-east around the St. Helens coast and associated hinterland. One such tour was featured on the national televsion program *Getaway*, in fact the very first segment screened. A 4WD support carries all your gear over the 2–3 day tour.

Other tours offered over summer and autumn take one along the north-east coast exploring Mt. William National Park and its hinterland. For $390, you get four days entertainment including meals and camping gear. Bikes are supplied, and they also hire them out. Phone (002) 310-977 for details.

Bicycle Tasmania

Bicycle Tasmania represents cyclists' needs by lobbying state and local governments on a variety of issues, mainly related to traffic. Bicycle User Groups (BUGs) have been established in the three major cities of Hobart, Launceston, and Devonport, and have regular meetings discussing local events of concern to cyclists and organising social and competitive rides. People interested should contact

Bicycle Tasmania at 102 Bathurst St, Hobart 7000 or phone (002) 44-1864.

Sightseeing

Besides cycling, there are numerous other ways to experience what the island has to offer. Tour operators can take you fly-fishing on the central plateau, or four-wheel-driving at Mt. McCall, or cruising up the beautiful Gordon River, caving the longest cave in Australia, rafting, and even scenic flights over the World Heritage Areas: south-west (based from Hobart), Franklin River and Frenchman's Cap (Strahan), and Cradle Mountain (Cradle Valley).

The most popular non-natural tourist destinations are the Cadbury Chocolate Factory at Claremont, the Port Arthur convict settlement ruins, and the Cascade Brewery at the base of Mt. Wellington. The most visited natural features are Cataract Gorge at Launceston, the Tasman Peninsula coast, Russell Falls in Mt. Field National Park, and Cradle Mountain.

Walking

As previously mentioned, many of the most spectacular places are located within prime wilderness tens of kilometres from the nearest road. A cycling tour of Tasmania is never complete without at least a few one day walks, and often an overnight one will exercise different muscles as well as offering some variety.

The definitive walking guide to Tasmania is Tyrone Thomas's *100 Walks in Tasmania* containing detailed topographical maps covering a range of walks from strolls through the cities to week-long expeditions into the south-west.

Other guides exist as well, dealing exclusively with specific areas such as Cradle Mountain-Lake St. Clair and Federation Peak.

Like cycling, there is a code of behaviour for walking/camping. Much of it is common sense. The Tasmanian Department of Parks, Wildlife and Heritage recommend:

* Washing your dishes and your body should be done at least 50 m from streams as soap, detergents, and food scraps are all harmful to aquatic life.
* Human waste should be buried at least 100 m from streams. This reduces the incidence of gastroenteritis (diarrhoea and vomiting) caused by exposed faecal matter.
* Camp at low impact sites at least 30 m away from watercourses. Sand and hard surfaces are better than wet, soft, boggy, vegetated areas. Choose existing campsites rather than making your own. This can be achieved by proper planning.
* The use of modern tents is encouraged. Pitched properly they are mostly waterproof and don't require the digging of perimeter trenches. They come with fibreglass or aluminium frames so saplings do not need to be cut down for poles, and foam/inflatable mats make obsolete the traditional practice of cutting fern fronds for bedding.
* Carry rubbish out with you. Buried rubbish can be dug up by animals.
* Where fires are allowed, use existing fireplaces, do not encircle them with rocks, use only fallen dead wood, keep it small, don't use it as a rubbish tip, and extinguish it completely when leaving. For remote places such as in the Arthur Ranges, leave some kindling for the next party.
* Keep group sizes to a minimum (4–8).
* Spread out in open untracked country so the impact on vegetation is minimised. Keep on rocks where possible.
* Wear lightweight walking boots and soft sandshoes rather than heavy duty GPs.

Presently there's a trend towards the introduction of walking fees for Tasmania's more popular overnight walks. This is due to the expensive operation of duckboarding long sections of trails that are susceptible to erosion. Examples of overuse leading to deterioration include the South Coast track in South-West National Park and Lake Osbourne walk track in the Hartz Mountains. Walkers on the Overland Track must pay $20.00 for the privilege of traversing the national park. In addition to track, hut, and signpost maintenance, this fee also pays for coal supplied for heating purposes in the numerous huts.

Bird Watching

This is a popular pastime in the island state and both cyclists and walkers looking for native species will see at least a few of most common Tasmanian birds listed below. They are classified according to their habitat.

BIRDS OF WET FORESTS

Brown Goshawk
Wedge-tailed Eagle
Yellow-tailed black
  Cockatoo
Green Rosella
Grey Shrike-thrush
Fantailed Cuckoo
Golden Whistler
Yellow Wattlebird
Grey Fantail
Black-headed
  Honeyeater
Strong-billed
  Honeyeater
Crescent Honeyeater
Striated Pardalote

BIRDS OF DRY FORESTS

Brown Falcon
Superb Fairy Wren
Pallid Cuckoo
Dusky Robin
Laughing Kookaburra
Scarlet Robin
Black-headed Cuckoo-
  shrike
Flame Robin
New Holland
  Honeyeater
Eastern Spinebill
Brown Thornbill
Yellow-throated
  Honeyeater
Silvereye

Beautiful Fireta   Spotted Pardalote
Forest Raven   Sulphur-crested
                                Cockatoo

Climate

In short Tasmania is cold, wet and windy!

It is plain to see by the tables presented on the following pages that the first three months of the year are the warmest and driest, but warm, waterproof clothing is still essential. The south-west is the second wettest place in Australia after the Queensland tropics, and especially susceptible to spectacular weather transformations. Any extended walking trips should be carried out during February and March when the sky is most stable. During winter, low pressure systems cross Tasmania and mix with moist airstreams to produce clouds. In fact so much cloud that the Lake Gordon area only receives two days' worth of sunshine per month. The east coast is driest at all times and the north-east is the only area which can be comfortably toured all year round. Wind is less of a problem due to the mountainous nature of the island, but cyclists traversing the Arthur-Pieman Protected Area and the west coast will be guaranteed a constant strong crosswind that will make coastal riding and camping somewhat unpleasant.

As a rule, cyclists/walkers/campers should bring plenty of warm clothing and a waterproof jacket, no matter what time of year one travels. Be prepared that firewood can be damp and therefore difficult to light. At the same time one must watch out for fire-danger periods when dry windy conditions can whip up flames into an inferno. The locals have seen this all too often in the past.

A big advantage with Tasmania's southerly latitude is that daylight hours are much longer. During the period around the summer solstice, up to 16 hours are available to the cyclist.

The following is a summary of precipitation, rain days, and temperatures for three areas in the major parks:

MEAN PRECIPITATION (mm)

	Cradle Valley	Lake St. Clair	Strathgordon
Jan	150	81	159
Mar	157	85	140
May	284	138	234
Jul	328	164	267
Sep	280	159	273
Nov	212	124	179

RAIN DAYS PER MONTH

	Cradle Valley	Lake St. Clair	Strathgordon
Jan	16	14	18
Mar	18	15	17
May	21	21	22
Jul	24	22	24
Sep	22	21	24
Nov	19	19	20

MEAN DAILY MAXIMUM TEMPERATURES

	Cradle Valley	Lake St. Clair	Strathgordon
Jan	17	19	19
Mar	14	16	17
May	8	10	12
Jul	5	7	9
Sep	8	10	11
Nov	13	14	16

FUEL STOVE ONLY AREAS

These are declared environmentally sensitive regions within National Parks and Conservation Areas where campfires have been banned. This is due to the past effects of bushfires (often started by out-of-control campfires) on Tasmania's high altitude and high precipitation vegetation. Since 1960, 16 per cent of alpine flora and 8 per cent of rainforest has been burnt. Several of the species that grow in these communities such as Huon Pine, King Billy Pine, pencil pine, and deciduous beech do not regenerate. One such fire started at a campsite in December 1980 on the northern shore of Lake Vera and burnt out 6450 ha of the Franklin-Lower Gordon Wild Rivers National Park. The hut located there, as with the many huts along the Overland Track, now have coal supplied for heating.

Banning campfires with a $5000 penalty also reduces the likelihood of native trees being cut down for wood which expands small clearings into larger ones leaving visual scarring. Furthermore many people use fires as a rubbish-place. Since extremely hot large fires are needed to disintegrate tins, cans, and bottles, park rangers have found more often than not, campsites are left with a lot of half-burnt rubbish.

The Tasmanian bush, with high winter rainfall and drying summer winds, is especially susceptible to ignition. The people of Hobart discovered this in 1967 when a wall of fire swept around Mt. Wellington and destroyed homes, businesses, and 51 lives. Over the last two decades there have been numerous cases of campfire escapes, lightning, management fires becoming out of control, and arson. These fires often have the heat intensity to enter rainforest and wetland areas.

Peat soils are especially susceptible to fire. Being

the very early stages of coal beds, peat covers extensive areas of western Tasmania. It's made up of decomposed, compressed organic matter, is dark, greasy, and feels springy if walked on. Fires can burn down into the soil and smoulder for months thus serving as potential ignition sources during future hot, dry weather. There is a fine of up to $1000 where a fire is lit on peat soil, whether it be in or outside a Fuel Stove Area.

The only exceptions that the Department of Lands, Parks, and Wildlife allow are in the case of genuine emergencies. Only use dead, fallen wood and keep the fire small.

The Fuel Stove Only Areas are:

Franklin-Lower Gordon Wild Rivers,
National Park
Cradle Mountain-Lake St. Clair National Park
Walls of Jerusalem National Park
Southwest National Park

4

THE CITIES' SURROUNDS

RIDES AROUND HOBART

The second oldest capital in Australia (settled on 7 September, 1803), Hobart is the tourist and political capital of Tasmania. Located in the south of the island on the mouth of the Derwent River, it is protected from the roaring forties by big Mt. Wellington. The massive dolerite mountain (dubbed by locals as simply 'the mountain') stands at 1271 m and is covered in snow in winter. From the summit, a popular lookout commands views of all of Hobart and surrounds. The local hostel provides a service for member cyclists where a bus drives up the 20 km to the summit and one can ride back down. Hobart, which became the capital in 1856, has a population of approximately 175,000, one-third of the state. This is very atypical of distribution in Australia where capital cities usually contain two-thirds of their state's population. Due to its colonial heritage many buildings within the CBD and surrounds are of historical interest, being of predominantly Georgian architecture. Places of interest in and around the city include the Saturday morning Salamanca Markets, the Cadbury Chocolate Factory, the Cascade Brewery, Bellerive Oval, Wrest Point Casino, the Royal Botanical Gardens, the colonial buildings of Battery Point.

To the east is the airport and aerodromes where scenic flights provided by TASAIR and PAR AVION take you over the World Heritage Area to Federation Peak (1224 m) via Precipitous Bluff (1120 m), Cox Bight, Bathurst Harbour, and Mt. Anne. You can also charter the plane to see any other part of the south: Freycinet National Park, Maria

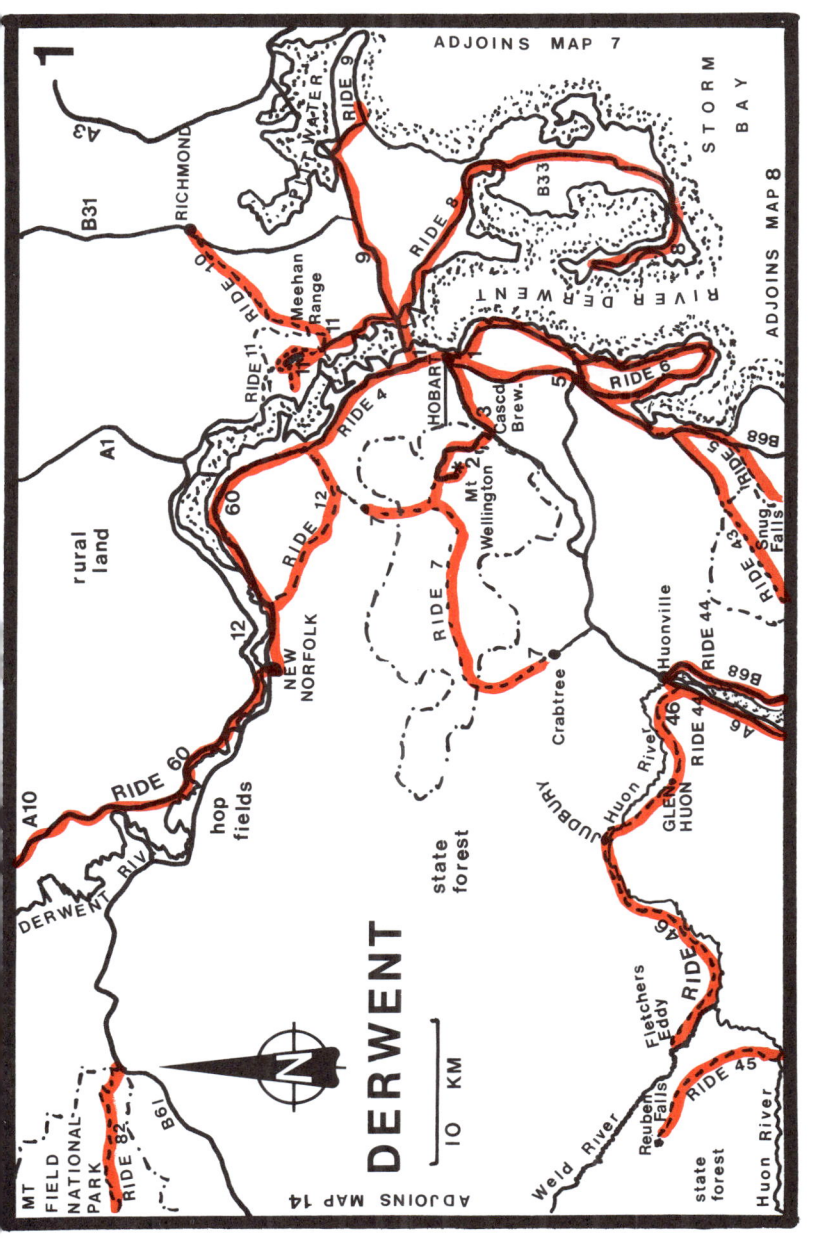

Island, or the Tasman Peninsula. The going rate is about $250 an hour.

Accommodation for cyclists preparing their adventures is plentiful: there are hostels, cabins, caravan parks, motels, hotels, and resorts. One in the city centre is the Tasmanian Backpackers at 87 Bathurst St. Rates are cheap, there are links with Redline Coaches to and from the airport, as well as bicycle hire. Phone (002) 34-4516 for details.

Cycling shops are located at:

McBain Sloane Cycles
132 Bathurst St, Hobart
Ray Appleby Cycles   also at
125 Elizabeth St, Hobart   112 Charles St, Moonah
Ken Self Cycles
124 Elizabeth St, Hobart
Eastern Shore Mowers & Cycles
44 Lincoln St, Lindisfarne
Treadlies
Channel Court Shopping Centre, Kingston

Mountain bikes can be hired from:

Peregrine Adventures
28 Criterion St, Hobart

If you're a YHA member, bike hire is available from the hostel at Adelphi Court, 17 Stoke St, New Town.

From the Transit Centre in Collins St, coaches leave for Launceston, Devonport, Burnie, St. Helens, Bicheno, Derby, St. Marys, Queenstown, Swansea. Timetables are available from the government tourist information centre just north of the mall in Elizabeth Street.

Information and maps on national parks can be obtained from the Department of Lands, Parks, and

Wildlife at 134 Macquarie St and state forest information from the Tasmanian Forestry Commission at 199 Macquarie St.

Your slide and negative films can be processed in 30 minutes at Cameraworld on the corner of Murray St and Collins St.

RIDE 1: HOBART

FROM: Hobart Youth Hostel, Adelphi Court, Stoke St, New Town
TO: Domain, Battery Point, Wrest Point Casino [RETURN]
LENGTH: 33 km
TIME: 1 easy day
RIDE/TRACK GRADE: 2/1
HEIGHT VARIATION: 20 m
FACILITIES: Everything
SPECIAL GEAR: Money
MAPS: RACT Touring Map of Tasmania (free from any tourist info centre). (See Map 1: *DERWENT*)

This ride offers the beautiful Royal Botanical Gardens, some of the cultural heritage of the colonial nineteenth century, and a chance to blow all your money at the Casino. The ride starts at the youth hostel because that's where many tourist cyclists reside. Furthermore, there is bike hiring available here. But no matter where you're residing, make your way to the Queen's Domain on the Derwent River Harbour. This is a beautifully maintained parkland with views from the centre over the New Town cemetery and up the Derwent valley. Continue to the Royal Tasmanian Botanical Gardens, which are internationally renowned for their exotic trees, fuchsia and cacti houses, and the exquisite Japanese garden.

Exit through Lower Domain Road. Head right along the Tasman Highway and keep left at the giant round-about. Follow Brooker Avenue around where it becomes Macquarie Street. At Dunn Street head left and then immediately right onto Davey, thus avoiding most of the heavy traffic on Macquarie Street. Franklin Square with its old fountain and statues is on the right opposite the Hydro-Electric Commission (HEC) headquarters where, in the 1970s and early '80s, countless conservationists marched to protest against the Lake Pedder and Franklin Dam schemes. When you reach Murray Street, turn left and cycle around Battery Point keeping the parks on the right. This was the second place to be settled in Australia, and is named after the Mulgrave Battery that defended the original establishment in the early 1800s. In the 1850s, it became a mariners' village.

Salamanca Place's warehouses and wharves have become famous as the old colonial Georgian-style buildings still remain largely intact. Each Saturday morning the markets here draw huge crowds. But the place really comes alive at the very end of each year with the conclusion of the classic Sydney-to-Hobart yacht race. There are about 20 heritage sites of interest including cottages dating from the whaling days of the 1830s. Follow the road around where it becomes Castray Esplanade and turn left at Dewitt, and left at Cromwell past St. George's Anglican Church built in 1836. Follow Cromwell to the end and turn right. Napoleon Street will take you all the way to Sandy Bay Road and then it's just a short cycle south to Wrest Point Casino. Strict dress rules only apply in the evening and you should be able to get in if you don't look too scruffy. The entrance is on the very right of the convention centre. When you've lost all your money, return to where you're staying, return to New Town via Nelson Road and Regent Street to avoid the heavy traffic on Sandy Bay Road.

RIDE 2: MT. WELLINGTON

FROM: Mt. Wellington summit (1271 m)
TO: Hobart
VIA: Mt. Nelson
LENGTH: 26 km
TIME: 1 easy day
RIDE/TRACK GRADE: 3/1
WALKING: Optional walking in the Mt. Wellington Protected Area
HEIGHT VARIATION: 1260 m
TRANSPORT: Youth hostel bus service to summit
FACILITIES: Shops in most suburbs
SPECIAL GEAR: Wind-proof parka
MAPS: BP Touring Map of Tasmania. (See Map 1: *DERWENT*)

Only members of the youth hostel will be able to benefit from the bus service carrying cyclist and bicycle to the summit of this dolerite peak. Non-members will either have to push up the 1270 m hill or turn the page. A fine day is preferable as the summit can often be obscured in mist. But even if there is a whiteout, the hair-raising ride down from out of the clouds is still worth it.

The summit is composed of extruded columnar or fluted dolerite 350 m thick sitting on a sandstone base. In winter snow covers the mountain to as far down as 400 m and the roads have to be closed. After enjoying the views and walking around, check brakes and head straight down along the winding road. Watch out for coaches that can cramp you for room on the treacherous blind corners.

When you're at the bottom a few minutes later, head left along the Huon Highway and then right down Ridgeway Road, past the reservoir. At the end cross under the Southern Outlet and backtrack along Proctors Road and then left up over Mt.

Nelson (340 m) for more good views over the Derwent Estuary at the Signal Station Reserve. The station was built in 1811 and was used to announce the presence of ships bound for Hobart. The Signalman's residence (1897) is now a tea house. Backtrack along Mt. Nelson Road, then continue north down the other side through a residential area along a road with numerous hairpins, which will get you to Sandy Bay and Wrest Point.

One can then do Ride 1 in reverse from the casino through Battery Point, the CBD, domain, and back to the hostel.

Consult Ride 7 for route descriptions over the Mt. Wellington Range.

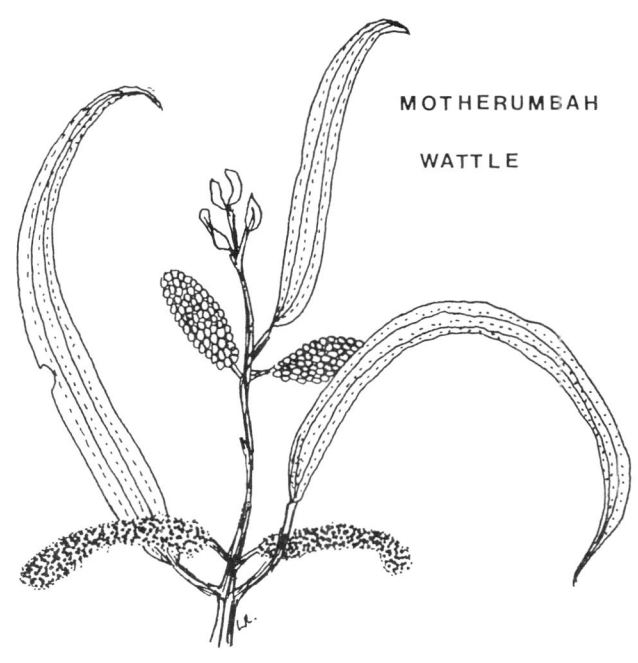

MOTHERUMBAH

WATTLE

RIDE 3: THE CASCADE BREWERY
(INCLUDING WELLINGTON FALLS)

FROM: Hobart CBD
TO: Cascade Brewery [RETURN]
VIA: Neika, Wellington Falls
LENGTH: 30 km
TIME: 1 day
RIDE/TRACK GRADE: 6/5 (2/1 if just travelling to brewery)
WALKING: 2 km steep walk to access falls
HEIGHT VARIATION: 750 m (70 m if just doing Brewery Tour)
TRANSPORT: None
SPECIAL GEAR: None
MAPS: BP Touring Map of Tasmania. (See Map 1: *DERWENT*: If going to falls, Mt. Wellington 1:15 000 Day Walk Map)

This ride is really in two separable stages. One can do just the brewery tour and cycle back to Hobart. Or one can do just the ride to Mt. Wellington Falls, or both. This description is written for those who've booked the morning tour and therefore have time to see the falls. One would have to get up very early to see the falls first and still be in time for the lunch tour.

Not only is it Australia's oldest brewery, but it's also the country's oldest existing manufacturing enterprise. On this tour you can witness how Australia's finest premium lager is made as well as learning the distinguishing characteristics and ingredient ratios between different blends of beer: bitter, ale, stout, draught, etc. The tour costs $9.00 for adults with a student concession rate of $4.50 available. It is wise to book in advance. There are two tours in the day: one at 9am, the other at 1pm and they last for about 90 minutes.

The history of the brewery is interlinked with Hobart's origins. In 1824, Governor Sorell granted an English migrant named Peter Degraves (b.1778) 2500 acres at the base of Mt. Wellington. On the bank of the Guy Fawkes Rivulet, he built a sawmill and watermill to power it, providing timber to a growing Hobart. These were the days before the gold rush on the mainland, when the convict settlements in Tasmania were still of relative importance.

Ten years later he built the brewery building in the freestone Georgian style, as well as other prominent buildings in Hobart city such as the Theatre Royal.

Conditions were ideal for brewing. The maritime temperate climate and fertile soils around the New Norfolk area supported a high quality yield of hops and barley. Today the Cascade Brewery Co and its subsidiary Boag inject a lot of money into the Tasmanian economy by tax revenue created by exporting the Premium Lager to Europe and the Australian mainland, through employment, and by sponsorship of sports.

On the tour you will see how the barley is delivered, sieved, and germinated to create malt. This brewery is one of the few that still malt their own beer and so have greater control of their ingredients. The other inputs, pure water, yeast, and hops are added, before the beer is matured and carbonated. You then enjoy a beer or three at the workers' bar before viewing the assembly bottling, labelling, and packaging process. The tour concludes with another beer of your choice to take away.

Commence the ride to the brewery from the CBD following Macquarie Street west. This narrows into Cascades Road and the old tall Brewery building is soon evident on the right. On the opposite side is the old managing director's residence with some superb gardens including the oldest holly tree in Australia. It has been converted into a convention centre.

Those completing the early tour have the option of riding several kilometres south to follow a management trail that contours around Mt. Wellington to some lovely falls. Follow Strickland Avenue around all the way to the Huon Highway. Go up the Highway and past the Mt. Wellington turnoff at Fern Tree. This township was almost destroyed in the disastrous 1967 bushfires. Another few kilometres will bring you to the old Neika schoolhouse. A barrier blocks public vehicles from proceeding up the Pipeline Track which is maintained by the Hobart City Council for water supply purposes. After an initial climb, the 15 km return distance is level and easy going, although windy. Watch out for management vehicles around blind corners. At the end, hide the bikes and cross the North West Bay River via a bridge and a short distance later again via a weir. A steep track over rocks will lead to the 40 m falls, almost always flowing well. There are views over the Derwent Estuary too.

Return to the bikes and cycle back to Hobart via Ridgeway Road (right just after the Mt. Wellington turn-off). This avoids the traffic on the Huon Highway.

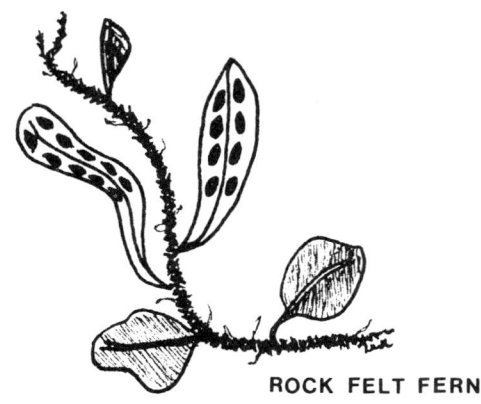

ROCK FELT FERN

RIDE 4: CADBURY CHOCOLATE

FROM: Hobart Youth Hostel, Stoke St, New Town
TO: Claremont [RETURN]
VIA: Collins Cap
LENGTH: 24 km
TIME: 1 day
RIDE/TRACK GRADE: 5/2
WALKING: Optional walking on the Mt. Wellington Range
HEIGHT VARIATION: 600 m
MAPS: BP Touring Map of Tasmania and Collinsvale 1:25 000 topographical. (See Map 1: *DERWENT*)

Bookings are essential for this tour. Contact the Government Tourist Information Centre on Elizabeth St. Times are in the morning so an early rise is required.

From the youth hostel or wherever you are staying make your way along New Town Road through the retail sector of Glenorchy and to the address written on every Cadbury chocolate wrapper in Australia—Cadbury Road, Claremont. The site occupies about 100 ha of land along the Derwent, making it the largest confectionary plant in Australia.

The tour guide is no Willy Wonka, but the process of mass-producing Australia's favourite chocolate is quite fascinating. There are plenty of samples, and it will give cyclists who are undertaking some of the more challenging wilderness rides in the book the chance to stock up on carbohydrates.

RIDE 5: SNUG FALLS

FROM: Hobart
TO: Snug [RETURN]
VIA: Kingston (Antarctic Administration Head-quarters Museum)
LENGTH: 92 km
TIME: 2 days
RIDE/TRACK GRADE: 3/2
WALKING: 2.5 km return walk to Snug Falls
HEIGHT VARIATION: 120 m
FACILITIES: Caravan Park at Snug
MAPS: BP Touring Map of Tasmania. (See Map 1: *DERWENT*)

Snug Falls are perhaps the most popular in the vicinity of Hobart and the walk is very easy. Subsequently this is a relatively simple overnight ride staying at the caravan park at Snug (rates are $8 for a tent). One can choose one of two ways of cycling from Hobart to Snug: (1) the Southern Outlet through Kingston and Margate or (2) the Sandy Bay Road past the historic Taroona Shot Tower, Kingston, and then Margate. The second option, being along the coast, is the most scenic but is windy; the first is fastest but the cyclist must endure heavy traffic. If choosing the first option, stop at the shot tower (48 m). It was solely designed and built in 1870 by Joseph Moir and is supposedly the tallest freestone tower in the world. Those climbing its 100-odd steps will be rewarded with good views over the Derwent Estuary. There is also a museum outlining its purpose. At Kingston, stop in at the Antarctic Division headquarters and discover the history and administration of a little known but gigantic Australian territory. The staff are responsible for all Australian activity in Antarctica, including annual expeditions and the maintenance of science programs at the four permanent stations and summer bases.

From the Snug School, take the Snug Tiers Road and then Snug Falls Road 1 km later to the carpark 3.6 km from the township. All turnoffs are well signposted and no topographical maps are needed. The easy walk is wide enough to cycle along, but unfortunately this is not permitted. Leave the bikes at the carpark and walk the 1.25 km down to Snug River amongst swamp gums. Return time is about 30 minutes. If you've just set a record time cycling from Hobart then you might like a dip in the pool at the 20 m fall's base. Otherwise a warm shower at the caravan park adjoining the Derwent might be welcome. Camping at the Fall's carpark or by the river is not permitted.

Just 8 km south of Snug is Kettering where the ferry to Bruny Island leaves. See Rides 90-94.

RIDE 6: TINDERBOX PENINSULA

FROM: Hobart
TO: Tinderbox [RETURN]
VIA: Kingston Beach
LENGTH: 62 km
TIME: 1 full day
RIDE/TRACK GRADE: 4/3
HEIGHT VARIATION: 65 m
FACILITIES: Shops at Kingston and Kingston Beach
MAPS: BP Touring Map of Tasmania. (See Map 1: *DERWENT*)

Attractions on this tour include Wrest Point Casino, the historic Shot Tower, Kingston Beach, views of Bruny Island, and the museum at the Antarctic Division Headquarters.

One can choose one of two ways of cycling from Hobart to Kingston Beach: (1) the Sandy Bay Road past the historic Taroona Shot Tower and then down to Kingston Beach or (2) the Southern Outlet through Kingston. The first option, being along the coast, is the most scenic and the one I've chosen for this ride. The second option is the fastest but freeway conditions make it uninteresting. I suggest to do a loop using both these routes so as to avoid backtracking.

Start at the CBD and head down Sandy Bay Road from Davey Street. If you like gambling, then the Wrest Point Casino will be happy to take your money. Further south is the Taroona Shot Tower (48 m) which the cyclist can inspect. It was solely designed and built in 1870 by Joseph Moir and is supposedly the tallest freestone tower in the world. Those climbing its 100-odd steps will be rewarded with good views over the Derwent Estuary. There is also a museum outlining its purpose. When freewheeling down to Kingston Beach, avoid the traffic on the narrow windy descent by taking Tyndall Road left and then Osbourne Esplanade along the very wide Derwent River. The surf here usually resembles the Nullarbor Plain.

Continue south through residential areas to Blackmans Bay and then the C623 to Tinderbox. This is officially the end of the Derwent River, which began 160 km upstream at Lake St. Clair (737 m). There are good views from Passage Point over the D'Entrecasteaux Channel and Bruny Island (see Rides 90–94). Located here are navigation lights guiding ships into Hobart. The water immediately lining Tinderbox is a marine reserve.

The road becomes unsealed but is still of good quality before Howden is reached on Stinkpot Bay. Head north-west to the Channel Highway and to Kingston. Stop in at the Antarctic Division Headquarters 2 km before Kingston and discover the history and administration of a little known but gigantic Australian territory. The staff are responsible for all Australian activity in Antarctica, including annual expeditions and the maintenance of science programs at the four permanent stations and summer bases. From Kingston, the Southern Outlet takes you on a no-frills 13 km direct line to Hobart.

RIDE 7: MOUNT WELLINGTON RANGE

FROM: Collinsvale
TO: Grove
VIA: Collins Bonnet
LENGTH: 42 km
TIME: 1 long day
RIDE/TRACK GRADE: 9/7
HEIGHT VARIATION: 1200 m
WALKING: To summit of Collins Bonnet (1260 m)
TRANSPORT: Car shuttle between Collinsvale and Grove
FACILITIES: None
SPECIAL GEAR: Warm, windproof and waterproof gear, thorn proof tubing and kevlar belted tyres recommended
MAPS: Collinsvale and Longley 1: 25 000 topographical maps. (See Map 1: *DERWENT*)

The range that extends behind Mt. Wellington offers spectacular mountain biking country very close to Hobart. Although proposals to declare this an official wilderness zone are in preparation, the trails are still open to bikes and experienced cyclists should hurry before the area becomes the sole domain of walkers. WARNING: because of the restrictions in regard to camping on the plateau, this ride must be performed in one day. You should make an early start and be dropped off at Collinsvale and picked up at Crabtree (named after James Crabtree, a free settler who managed the Hollybank Mill in 1854). Cyclists must be fit and carry a minimum amount of gear.

Drive north from Hobart to Berriedale (21 km) and thence to Collinsvale (10 km) at 300 m altitude. Head south along Collinsvale Road past the sports oval and Church Road on the left. Take the Mount Hull Road left. Two kilometres further you will see a gate on the left preventing vehicular entrance onto the plateau. This is the drop-off point on the boundary of the Mt. Wellington Protected Area (15 000 ha). This reserve is also the catchment for the Glenorchy Water Reserve, the Hobart Water Supply, and the Lachlan Water Supply. The trail climbs very steeply up to 1100 m, quickly becoming 4WD standard and pushing is all one can do. Head right 2 km further at 690 m altitude. Keep right at a junction 1 km further with some fantastic views over south-eastern Tasmania. You are now heading west. At 750 m, urn gums are the dominant tree.

Once the 900 m contour line is reached, the orange dolerite starts to take over from the sandstone as the main geological feature. In another kilometre there'll be another junction with a track heading right off the plateau. Keep left rising 5 km later to the maximum altitude of the ride—over a spur jutting north from Collins Bonnet. At this altitude (1100 m) the picturesque gnarled snow gum takes over from the urn gum. A 1 km walking track leads from just before the spur to the very summit for extensive views west over the World Heritage Area. Head back to the bikes on the spur. This is where the descending begins and the fun starts. Head west along the ridge top through pine-apple grass and sphagnum moss. In the next 5 km ignore turnoffs to the right, left, and right. Pass Mount Marion (1130 m) on your right and keep cycling along the trail as it leads between Mt. Patrick and Mt. Charles. 11 km from Collins Bonnet you'll encounter another gate then 250 m later turn left. Prepare to lose 800 m of altitude in a real hurry. The state forest that replaces the Protected Area is a blur of white and blue gums, black she-oaks, white peppermints, and native cherry. Cycle through the small village of Crabtree before rejoining the Huon Highway at Grove. Hobart is 31 km away to the north, if you are not being picked up.

A much less challenging alternative to this ride is to be dropped off at the summit of Mt. Wellington (1270 m) by your transport or utilising the YHA service. Head back down Pinnacle Road for 3 km before coming to a sweeping right-handed bend near Mt. Arthur (1100 m). A trail past a barrier leads to Collins Bonnet, dropping to 730 m and then back up to 1100 m. The Mt. Wellington Day Walk map is necessary.

RIDE 8: CAPE DIRECTION

FROM: Hobart
TO: Cape Direction [RETURN]
VIA: Lauderdale
LENGTH: 88 km
TIME: 2 days
RIDE/TRACK GRADE: 3/3
HEIGHT VARIATION: 45 m
MAPS: Taroona, Cremorne, Blackmans Bay, and Communication 1:25 000 topographicals. (See Map 1: *DERWENT*)

This ride takes you to the meeting place of the Derwent River and the sea, opposite Tinderbox (Ride 6). The cyclist can explore a small peninsula that is attached to Tasmania by a narrow neck dividing three bays: Frederick Henry, Ralph, and Storm.

Cross the Tasman Bridge and proceed right to Bellerive. Cambridge Road and Clarence Streets will take you to Lauderdale. Follow the main road to Opossum Bay via Hope Beach.

RIDE 9: SEVEN MILE BEACH

FROM: Hobart
TO: Sandy Point [RETURN]
VIA: Hobart Airport
LENGTH: 51 km
TIME: 1-2 days
RIDE/TRACK GRADE: 3/2
HEIGHT VARIATION: 60 m
FACILITIES: Picnic tables, barbecues, toilets.
MAPS: BP Touring Map of Tasmania and Carlton
1:25 000 topographical. (See Map 1: *DERWENT*)

The Seven Mile Beach Protected Area offers an enjoyable venue for a moderate day's cycle from Hobart. Head out to the airport. Just after the turn-off, head right and onto the Seven Mile Beach peninsula with its sand dunes protecting Pitt Water from the ocean. This area is one of the few where mountain cycling is officially accepted by the Parks and Wildlife authorities.

RIDE 10: RICHMOND

FROM: Hobart
TO: Richmond [RETURN]
VIA: Cambridge
LENGTH: 62 km
TIME: 1 day
RIDE/TRACK GRADE: 3/2
WALKING: None
HEIGHT VARIATION: 240 m
MAPS: BP Touring Map of Tasmania. (See Map 1: *DERWENT*)

Richmond has many attractions worth seeing. Not only is there the oldest bridge in Australia, but essentially the whole main street of the township is a museum of old Georgian buildings. Cross the Derwent on the Tasman Bridge and head left to Lindisfarne and then right up to Risdon Vale. It's 3 km up hill to Grass Tree at 240 m and then a very flat 12 km to Richmond.

There's the Colonial Hotel with its traditional balcony, St. Luke's church with a disproportionately large clock/bell tower, and the oldest post office in Australia. Richmond Gaol was built in 1835 by Lee Archer and predates Port Arthur as a convict prison. It is considered to be the oldest surviving convict jail in Australia. Then there is the six-arch stone bridge over the Coal River, built by convicts in 1823–26 and today popularly photographed when the sun is low to capture the brilliant golden shades in the sandstone. It is 11 years older than any on the mainland and was used as a thoroughfare for traffic between Hobart and the eastern coast.

There's also the ever-present tea rooms, art galleries, and craft shops. Return to Hobart the same way.

RIDE 11: MEEHAN RANGE

FROM: Hobart
TO: Meehan Range State Recreation Area [RETURN]
VIA: Mt. Direction (448 m)
LENGTH: 52 km (longer for alternatives mentioned)
TIME: 1 long day
RIDE/TRACK GRADE: 7/6
HEIGHT VARIATION: 450 m
FACILITIES: Picnic grounds, shops at Risdon Vale
MAPS: Richmond 1:25 000 topographical and BP Touring Map of Tasmania. (See Map 1: *DERWENT*)

Named after James Meehan, surveyor of the Hobart-Launceston road in 1812, the range (beginning at Jens Hill in the north) is one of the few remaining locations in Tasmania where mountain biking is encouraged by the National Parks and Wildlife Service.

Head across the Tasman Bridge and right to Bellerive. Continue along the Tasman Highway and left onto East Risdon Road leading down to Kangaroo Bay Rivulet. Up the other side, turn right to Flagstaff Gully Road and over Flag Staff Hill to cross under the power lines heading left and join up with Sugarloaf Road near Risdon Vale. Continue down to the Risdon Brook Reservoir turn-off marked by gates just north of the East Derwent Highway turnoff. Where motorists have to leave their cars behind at the picnic area 500 m from the road, the cyclist can continue into the Meehan Range State Recreation Area to Mt. Direction taking the trails along the left or right of the lake's shore (60 m). This is the water supply for Lindisfarne and swimming is not permitted. Take the tracks following the western shore. Near the northern end a track climbs steeply through dry sclerophyll forest for 2 km to Mt. Direction at 448 m giving

118

fine views across the Derwent River valley to Mt. Wellington.

The return trip to Hobart can be extended by more mountain biking trails. Head back down to the intersection and turn left following the trail down to Risdon Brook and then left rising up to 310 m to Split Rock Saddle 4 km away. Follow Catchpole Gully and down to the reservoir again where it's 4 km back to the carpark and another 20 km to Hobart via Lindisfarne. Please note the Richmond 1:25 000 topographical is essential to negotiate the network of management and abandoned trails throughout here.

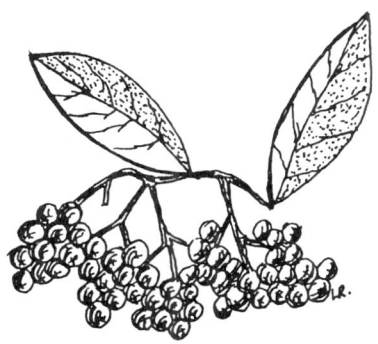

COMMON BUSH BERRIES

Another alternative is to return to the East Derwent highway via a prominent rocky outcrop known as Gunners Quoin. From the brook on the northern side of the reservoir, head left then left again to Quoin Gully. Ford the creek and rise up to 300 m passing the landmark on its left. There's a terrific downhill then to Baskerville Road, only 1.1 km from the highway. Claremont with the Cadbury-Schweppes factory is on the other side.

RIDE 12: NEW NORFOLK
(GARDEN OF THE ANTIPODES)

FROM: Hobart
TO: New Norfolk [RETURN]
VIA: Malbina
LENGTH: 74 km
TIME: 1-2 days
RIDE/TRACK GRADE: 4/2
HEIGHT VARIATION: 380 m
MAPS: BP or RACT Touring Map of Tasmania. (See Map 1: *DERWENT*)

The Derwent Valley is an example of a river drowned when an Ice Age 30 000 years ago lowered the level of the water, forcing the river to cut down to a 100 m lower level. When the sea rose again about 6000 years ago, the enlarged valley became flooded. The Tamar in the north is also an example of this.

Most of Australia's hops requirements are grown in New Norfolk in well ordered fields of vertical crops and cyclists can visit the National Trust classified historic circular hops kiln constructed in the 1860s and associated museums that describe the way of life in nineteenth century pastoral Van Diemen's Land.

From Hobart head north along Main Road through Glenorchy and onto the Lyell Highway (A10). Shortly after at Berriedale turn left and take the C615 up to Molesworth. Some steep climbs are located on this 14 km short-cut to New Norfolk, peaking at 380 m. Past Malbina, with views of the Derwent, turn left again back on the A10. The hop museum, called Oast House, is located 2 km before New Norfolk and 800 m to the right off the A10. There are tea rooms, a craft gallery, and the usual antiques.

At New Norfolk the colonial attractions include

120

the Old Colony Inn with an antique museum (located in Montagu St), the old Peg Factory, one of the largest antique dealers in Australia. Across the only bridge and right to Boyer is the Australian Newsprint Mills which give relatively informal tours by prior arrangement. They were established in 1941, being supplied by the Florentine Valley grants. Phone (002) 61-0433 for details.

Follow the Derwent back on either bank to reach Hobart again. Otherwise there is a youth hostel at New Norfolk located in an old Toll House beside the Derwent.

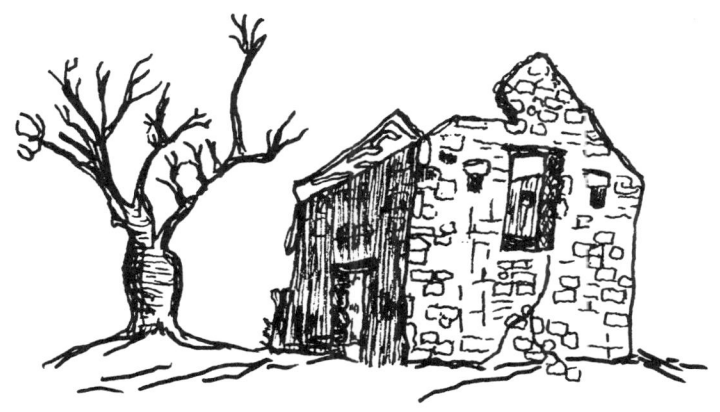

RIDES AROUND LAUNCESTON

The third oldest city in Australia, Launceston was settled in 1806. It is situated at the confluence of the North and South Esk Rivers, which form the Tamar. Despite its age, Launceston's population is just 80 000. Like Hobart it has kept intact a lot of its colonial heritage. But unlike the capital, Launceston does not have a big mountain as its main tourist attraction. Instead it has the Cataract Gorge, one of Tasmania's most visited places and very close to the city centre. For those wishing to unload some burdensome cash, there is also a casino. Other attractions include the woollen mills that produce high quality fine wool, a paddlesteamer journey on the Tamar, a rare Australian planetarium, and countless tea gardens, art galleries, craft exhibitions, antique stores, old cottages and homesteads, and dozens of other historical sites. The first ever interstate cricket match was played here between Victoria and Tasmania in 1850.

Building architectural styles can be classed as follows:

Georgian:	–1860
Gothic Revival:	1860–1890
Queen Anne:	1890–1920
Bungalow:	1920–1940
Contemporary:	1940–

Two of the best examples of colonial homesteads are Franklin House (1838) by Britton Jones and Entally House (1820) built by Thomas Reibey Jnr. You can learn the charming story of Mary Haydock (15 years old), convicted and transported after taking a joyride on a squire's horse, and Sub-Lieutenant Thomas Reibey, the patient guardian who eventually married her and together built a corporate conglomerate.

A richer, less restricted hinterland has created the most wealthy agricultural region in Tasmania and Launceston provides many of the social, commercial, and cultural services that the mid-north requires.

Cycling shops are located at:

Kinnane Cycle Co
187 Wellington St, Launceston
Geard's Cycles
335 Wellington St, Launceston
McBains Cycles
10 Paterson St, Launceston

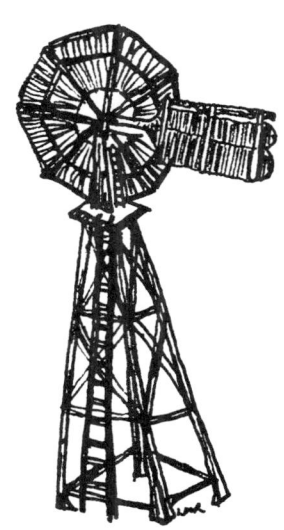

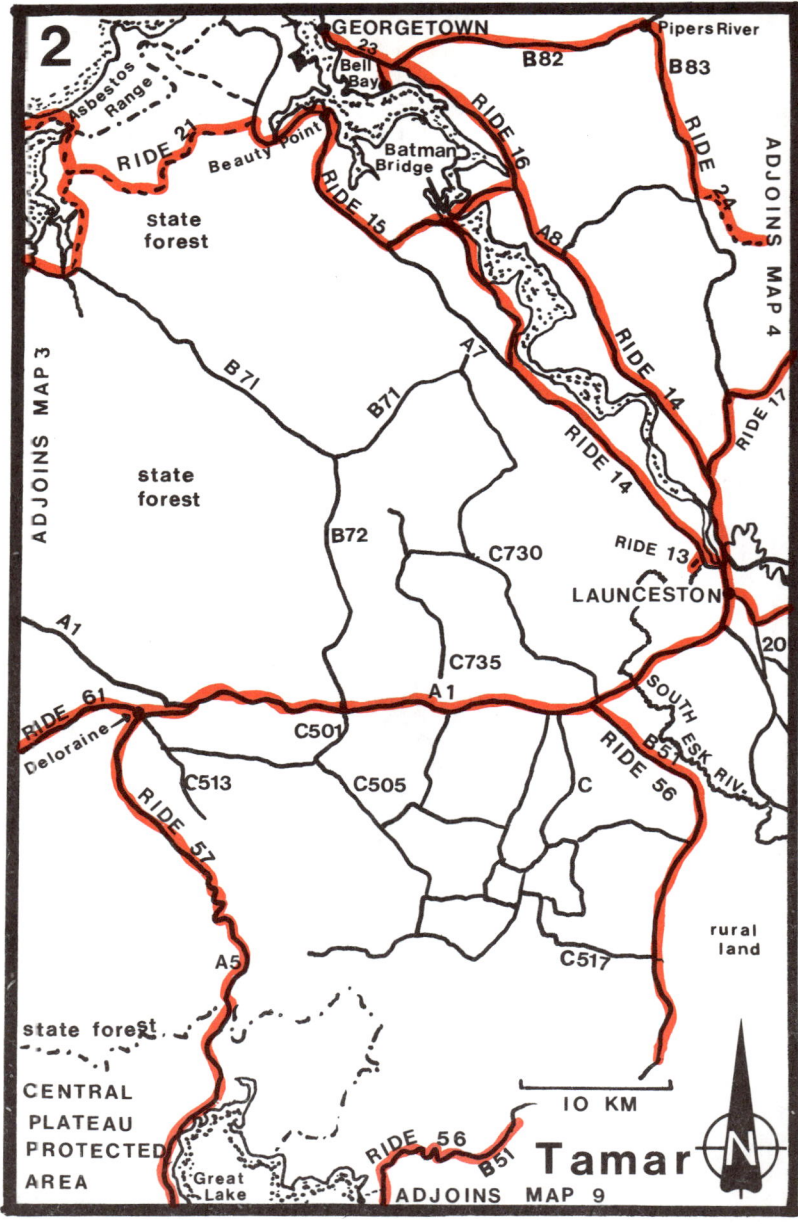

2

GEORGETOWN

Pipers River

Asbestos Range

23

Bell Bay

B82

B83

RIDE 21

Beauty Point

Batman Bridge

RIDE 16

RIDE 24

ADJOINS MAP 4

state forest

RIDE 15

A8

ADJOINS MAP 3

B71

A7

RIDE 14

RIDE 17

state forest

B71

RIDE 14

B72

C730

RIDE 13

LAUNCESTON

A1

C735

20

RIDE 61

A1

Deloraine

C501

SOUTH ESK RIV.

RIDE 56

B51

C513

C505

C

RIDE 57

A5

C517

rural land

state forest

CENTRAL

PLATEAU

PROTECTED

10 KM

AREA

RIDE 56

Tamar

Great Lake

B51

ADJOINS MAP 9

N

RIDE 13: LAUNCESTON TOUR

FROM: Launceston Youth Hostel, Thistle St, West Launceston
TO: Cataract Gorge
LENGTH: 36 km
TIME: 1 easy day
RIDE/TRACK GRADE: 3/2
WALKING: Along Cataract cliff tops
HEIGHT VARIATION: 200 m
FACILITIES: Souvenir kiosks
MAPS: RACT Touring Map of Tasmania (reverse side) or Launceston and Prospect 1:25 000 topographical. (See Map 2: *TAMAR*)

> *Upon opening the entrance I observed a large fall of water over rocks, nearly a quarter of a mile up a straight gully between perpendicular rocks about 150 ft high. The beauty of this scene is probably not surpassed in the world*
>
> —William Collins, the first European to visit the area in 1804, describing Cataract Gorge

Head down Thistle Street and follow Neika, Brougham, Hillside, Garnet, York, and Margaret streets to Paterson Street. Turn left along the Tamar past Ritchies Flour Mill, under the West Tamar highway and across Paterson Bridge. There are good views here straight up the dolerite-cliffed Cataract Gorge. It is a hilly 3 km from here to the Cliff Grounds Reserve via Trevallyn and Gorge Roads.

Spend some time exploring this natural phenomenon. This side of the gorge with its dolerite cliffs has been anglo-saxonised while the other remains in its natural state. The chairlift over the First Basin, constructed in 1972, supposedly contains the longest unbroken span in the world: 308 m. Note that this is a chairlift record—cablecars in the Swiss alps are suspended many kilometres between supports. Despite looks, statistics apparently prove that chairlifts are the safest form of transport.

On the other side one can also do some walking both down and upstream.

Another undulating short cycle through Trevallyn via Gorge Road and Bald Hill Road will take you to a lookout surveying the distance you've ridden plus views along the Tamar as it makes its way north. Head back down to Veulalee and turn right and then left onto Reatta peaking at 205 m 6 km from the Cliff Grounds. On the left is Trevallyn State Recreation Area (450 ha). Two kilometres further is a lookout over Deadman's Hollow on the South Esk. The old turbine-powered Duck Reach Power Station here was completed in 1895 to service Launceston, the first city in the southern hemisphere powered by hydro-electricity. It ceased operating in 1955. Return via same route.

Other venues for cycling around Launceston are to City Park (1827) containing an old Napoleon pear tree, the Maritime Museum, and the Waverley Woollen Mills (1874). The latter has an international reputation for manufacturing very high quality woollen products due to purer production methods. Next door is the National Automobile Museum. In the CBD are the information and map sales centres, and National Parks headquarters, where details in preparing the other more challenging rides outlined in this guide can be obtained. The Country Club Casino is located on the south-western outskirts of the city.

RIDE 14: TAMAR VALLEY TOUR

FROM: Launceston
TO: Batman Bridge
VIA: Exeter
LENGTH: 78 km
TIME: 1 long day
RIDE/TRACK GRADE: 4/2
HEIGHT VARIATION: 75 m
FACILITIES: Speciality stores
MAPS: BP Touring Map of Tasmania. (See Map 2: *TAMAR*)

This popular ride is one for cyclists who've just arrived in Tasmania. It gives them an introduction to the idyllic rich apple and pear growing regions of the mid-Tamar as well as throwing in the odd lavender farm and a few dozen tea gardens set in colonial cottages.

The Tamar Valley is an example of a river drowned when an Ice Age 30 000 years ago lowered the level of the water so the coast was about 30–40 km further out, forcing the river to cut down to a 100 m lower level. When the sea rose again about 6000 years ago, the enlarged valley became flooded. The Derwent in the south is also an example of this.

The route descriptions are simple. From Launceston take either the West or East Tamar Highway north for 34 km and cross the Batman Bridge at Whirlpool Reach. It was opened in 1968 at a cost of $3.5 million, set at a site where erosion-resistant dolerite restricts the Tamar River to one of its narrower sections. The 100 m A-frame tower supporting the 206 m span has its foundations in the bedrock on the west bank and is inclined at 20 degrees to the vertical directing any lateral thrust away from the softer clays of the east bank. It's quite a spectacle approaching the bridge and makes for an interesting photographic opportunity. It was named after John Batman, one of the founders of Melbourne, who moved there from northern Tasmania.

Return to Launceston via the other bank.

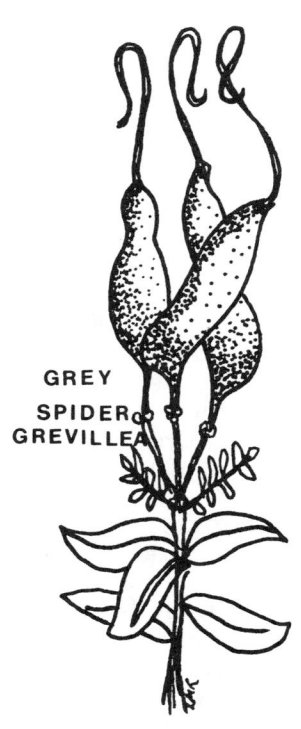

GREY
SPIDER
GREVILLEA

RIDE 15: TAMAR VALLEY WEST

FROM: Launceston
TO: Beauty Point [RETURN]
VIA: Exeter
LENGTH: 90 km
TIME: 2 days
RIDE/TRACK GRADE: 3/2
HEIGHT VARIATION: 50 m
FACILITIES: Caravan park at Beauty Point if 2 day trip
MAPS: BP Touring Map of Tasmania. (See Map 2: *TAMAR*)

Beauty Point is a picturesque deepwater port near the end of the Tamar's flow. Along the way is pleasant rural scenery, the big Batman Bridge, and the largest teddy bear in the world. Follow the western bank of the Tamar ('Penrabbel' in the native tongue) for 45 km to Beauty Point via Exeter and Beaconsfield.

Attractions along the way are:

Grindelwald Swiss Village
St. Matthias Winery
Waterbird Haven Trust
Rosevears Hotel and Brewery
Rebecca Monument
Brady's Lookout
Paper Beach
Supply River Flour Mill Ruins
Marions Vineyard
Beaconsfield Grubb-Shaft Museum and Mine Ruins (1905)
Redbill Point State Recreation Area

RIDE 16: TAMAR VALLEY EAST

FROM: Launceston
TO: Georgetown [RETURN]
VIA: Mt. Dismal
LENGTH: 111 km
TIME: 2 days
RIDE/TRACK GRADE: 3/2
WALKING: None
HEIGHT VARIATION: 80 m
FACILITIES: Caravan park at Georgetown if 2 day trip
MAPS: BP Touring Map of Tasmania and Lilydale 1:25 000 topographical. (See Map 2: *TAMAR*)

The destination of this ride is George Town, the OLDEST town in Australia. Yes, since Sydney, Hobart, and Launceston have been elevated to 'city' status, that makes George Town technically the oldest, a cunning device of publicity employed by the local tourist authorities. Anyway, at George Town one can see the hi-tech Sea Cat, a few small lighthouses along the road to Low Head, and the colossal Comalco aluminium smelter and thermal station and Bell Bay (see Ride 23 for details).

Take the East Tamar Highway (A8) 53 km north. On the way is Hillwood Strawberry Farm and Mt. George Lookout. Past George Town is Low Head where a series of old semaphore signal stations relayed messages in a 215-bit code to Launceston about boating activities in the Tamar. These were relayed at Mt. Direction.

RIDE 17: HOLLYBANK
(TASMANIA'S COUNTRY GARDEN)

FROM: Launceston
TO: Hollybank Forest Reserve [Return]
VIA: B81 road to Lilydale
LENGTH: 48 km
TIME: 1 day
RIDE/TRACK GRADE: 3/3
WALKING: Numerous short strolls
HEIGHT VARIATION: 340 m
FACILITIES: Picnic (BBQ) facilities, toilets
MAPS: RACT Map. (See Map 2: *TAMAR* & Map 4: *BEN LOMOND*)

Hollybank Forest Reserve (140 ha) is one of the most accessible and developed of the 40-odd forest reserves managed by the Tasmanian Forestry Commission. About 100 000 visitors a year come to see the variety of imported species—everything from conifers to deciduous trees as well as native species.
HISTORY: William Crabtree was the first to settle there. He managed a mill there and planted some of the larger exotic trees in the 1850s. It was sold for £20 in 1886 to William Orr, who built a cricket pitch there but sold it to the Ash Plantation Co. who used the timber to manufacture high quality cricket bats and tennis rackets. It planted 100 000 ash trees as well as douglas fir, larch, western hemlock, and the largest species of tree in the world, the majestic californian redwood (sequoia). No sporting equipment was ever made as growth rates were too slow. It became a reserve in 1977, one of the first in Tasmania.
TODAY: Some evidence of early commercial development still remains but most has been demolished. A leisurely cycle around the circuit will take you amongst the following trees: silver

birch, red oaks, white gum, beech, pin oak, holly, Japanese cedar, redwood, douglas fir, plum, silver wattle, elm, cypress, Tasmanian blackwood, radiata pine, laurel, Corsican pine, lime, and Caucasian fir. They are arranged in plantations, lining the road, and in an arboretum. Extensive picnic grounds are provided. No camping is permitted.

ROUTE: Simply take the B81 from Launceston following street signs to Lilydale. The turnoff is well signposted on the right 21 km from Launceston and 8 km before Lilydale. Hollybank Forest Reserve is 2 km from the Lilydale Road heading north from Excalibur.

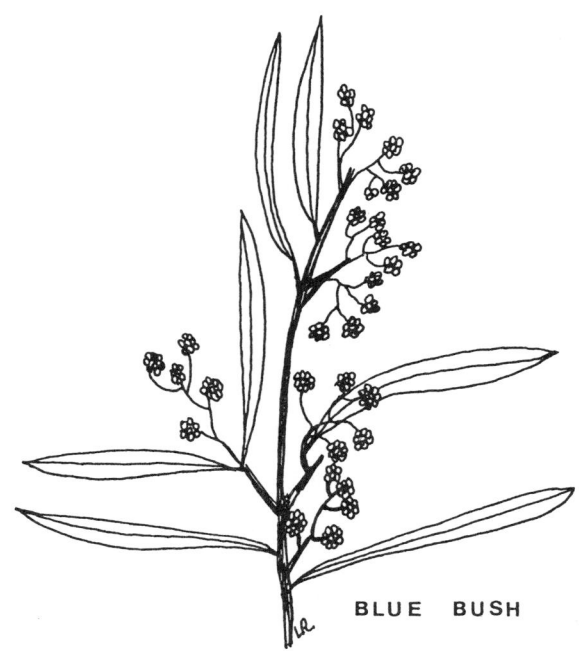

BLUE BUSH

RIDE 18: MOUNT ARTHUR

FROM: Launceston
TO: Mt. Arthur (1188 m) [RETURN]
VIA: Underwood
LENGTH: 82 km (41 km each day)
TIME: 2 days
RIDE/TRACK GRADE: 6/5 (most is sealed road)
WALKING: To summit of Mt. Arthur (2 hours)
HEIGHT VARIATION: 1184 m (including walk)
FACILITIES: Supplies at Lilydale
MAPS: Lilydale 1:25 000 topo. (See Map 4: *BEN LOMOND*)

The Mount Arthur summit offers fantastic panoramic views south to Mt. Barrow and Ben Lomond, west to Launceston and the Tamar valley, and north to George Town and Anderson Bay. The walk ascends through silver wattle, forests of gum-trees, and montane rainforest (montane meaning 'high altitude').

Take the Lilydale Road (B81) to Lilydale (29 km) at 170 m altitude. On the way you pass Hollybank Forest Reserve—worth seeing (see Ride 17 for details). At Lilydale you should stock up on supplies as there are no facilities in the state forest. Head 3 km south to Mountain Road (225 m). From here it is a steady uphill climb to the Grammar School Hut where the track deteriorates. The bikes have to be left behind 500 m later as the trail turns into a walking track. It is moderately graded but still steep, comparable to Mt. Roland. Note the vegetation changes as altitude is increased. From the bare treeless summit at 1188 m with its firetower there are fine vistas over mid north-east Tasmania. One can camp anywhere down the bottom in the Mount Arthur state forest.

RIDE 19: MOUNT BARROW

FROM: Launceston
TO: Mt. Barrow State Reserve
VIA: North Esk River Valley
LENGTH:
   Day 1: 52–66 km depending on camping preferences
   Day 2: 58–72 km depending on Day 1's campsite
   65 km if travelling back to Launceston
Day 3: Ben Lomond National Park to Launceston
90 km
Total distance is 199 km
TIME: 3-4 days
RIDE/TRACK GRADE: 9/5
HEIGHT VARIATION: 1413 m
FACILITIES: Picnic tables, shelters
SPECIAL GEAR: Cold weather gear and plenty of water
MAPS: Nunamara, Ben Nevis, Blessington, Giblin 1:25 000 topographical and Ben Lomond National Park 1:50 000 map (See Map 2: *TAMAR* & Map 4: *BEN LOMOND*)

Suitable only for fit and experienced riders, this journey takes you to an isolated summit-lookout with panoramic views of the north-east. Take the Scottsdale Road (A3) for 35 km to the C401 turn-off. The Mt. Barrow lookout is signposted. Unlike Mount Arthur, the cyclist can take his bike to the very summit. You'll have to push your bike up and up and up and up to 1413 m! It'll get colder but you'll be too hot and exhausted to put on any windbreakers or jumpers until you reach the top.
   Examples of frost shattered rocks dominate the slopes of Mt. Barrow, moved by solifluction. These deposits are known as block streams and account for acceleration of slope retreat. During winter the summit is clad in snow. When it's not in the clouds,

there are excellent views south to the Ben Lomond plateau as well as the rest of mid north-eastern Tasmania. Once at the top you'll feel colder especially from the wind. If there is no sign of a cold front, you can camp at the picnic area with shelters and barbecues so long as you make as little disturbance to the location as possible. Sunset and sunrises can potentially be awe inspiring from such a prominent vantage point. The track also continues to South Barrow but the views are much the same, although better photographs of the North Esk River catchment can be obtained here. Otherwise head back down, taking great care on the sharp hairpin corners. Return to the first turn-off and head right to the non-existent township marked on the map as Tayene. Head right along the C405 into state forest along the tributaries of the North Esk River. A makeshift campsite can also be found here. The day's distance will have been about 66 km.

The next morning one can head back to Launceston via the well graded Blessington Road (C401). Or one can camp in the foothills of the mighty Ben Lomond plateau. The relevant topographicals are needed to find your way through the maze of old forestry roads to the Nile River on the western flank. Once the road from Mt. Barrow comes out at Blessington Road crossing the North Esk River (400 m), turn left and then right where the signposts direct winter skiers to the alpine village. Take the Ben Lomond Road for 11 km up to 760 m where a fire trail heads right. It contours around the base at the same height before meeting with O' Plain Creek and climbing dramatically to 1100 m through a saddle between Ragged Jack mountain and the plateau. Keep following the trail as it flanks the plateau. Some good rocky downhills that'll challenge your mountain biking skills and brakes lead to the beautiful Nile River at the entrance to the National

Park 26 km from the turn-off. The water is completely drinkable. The day's distance will have been 55 km.

The final leg to Launceston is 90 km from the Nile River. This is too far to complete in one day as there is the 26 km fire trail to negotiate and overnight camping provisions attached to carry as well. This can be broken into two easier days by backtracking to the North Esk River. One can also exit the campsite by following the Nile River downstream.

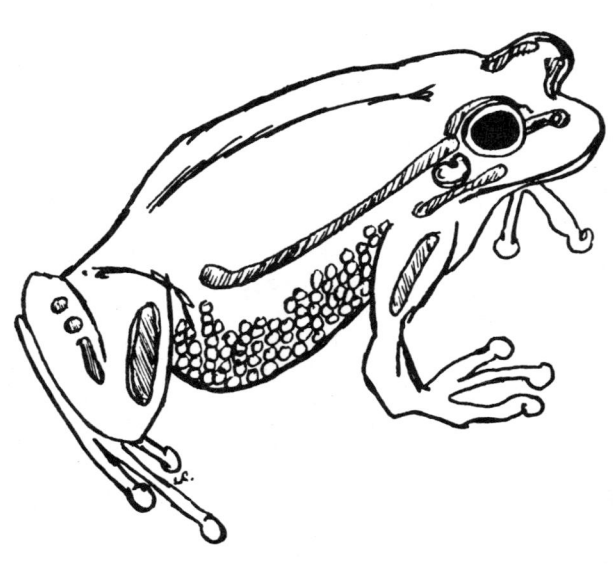

RIDE 20: BEN LOMOND

FROM: Ben Lomond National Park
TO: Launceston
VIA: Deddington and Evandale
LENGTH: 62 km
TIME: 1 day
RIDE/TRACK GRADE: 5/5
WALKING: Short snow-walk to Legges Tor
HEIGHT VARIATION: 1550 m
TRANSPORT: Wilderness Transport Network bus to alpine village. Only in winter.
FACILITIES: Small kiosk
SPECIAL GEAR: Cold weather gear, UV glasses
MAPS: Ben Lomond National Park 1:50 000 map and BP Touring Map of Tasmania. (See Map 2: *TAMAR* and Map 4: *BEN LOMOND*)

Named after its Scottish counterpart by Colonel William Paterson in 1804, the Ben Lomond plateau remained untouched for 100 years until Legge explored the plateau over successive excursions. The nomenclature is largely attributable to him, especially those related to the River Nile. In tribute to him is Legges Tor, the highest point on the plateau marked by a cairn of dolerite rubble. It's also the second highest peak in the state and the highest most cyclists will attain, as Mt. Ossa (1617 m) in Cradle Mountain-Lake St. Clair National Park is strictly an overnight walk.

The plateau was formed by the forces of glaciation in the ice ages of 20 000 years ago. Dolerite was formed by the cooling of magma extruded vertically through sedimentary rock. It contains less silica than columnar basalt and is 100 million years older.

The Wilderness Transport Network runs a service to the alpine village in winter. Take a short walk through snow over boulder-fields to Legges

Tor. One can then negotiate the hair-raising descent of Jacobs Ladder. Your life will depend on the strength of your front brake cable. Once at the bottom, cycle to Launceston first through national park then through pastoral land. In summer this ride is not practical as the 1500 m climb will be quite tiresome with a bike.

DATA TABLE: Ben Lomond National Park

Size: 16 457 ha (plus a 2665 ha Conservation Area)
Enactment: Scenic Reserve on 23 July 1947
National Park in 1970
Animals: Wombats, possums, devils, Bennett's wallaby, pedemelons
Plants: Cushion plants, stringybark, tanglefoot beech
Attractions: Rocky alpine with tremendous views from the edge
Camping: On the slopes at the base of the plateau
District Office: (003) 90-6279

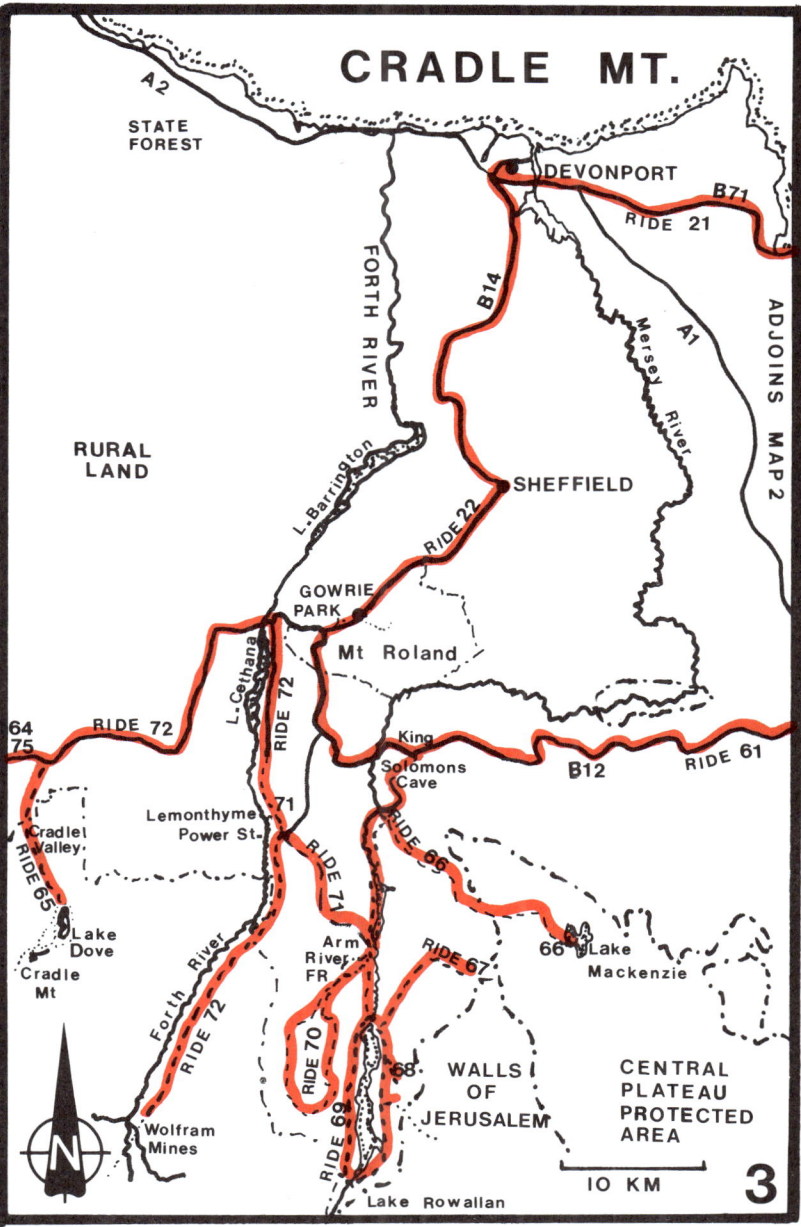

CRADLE MT.

A2

STATE FOREST

DEVONPORT

B71

RIDE 21

ADJOINS MAP 2

FORTH RIVER

B14

Mersey River

A1

RURAL LAND

L. Barrington

SHEFFIELD

RIDE 22

GOWRIE PARK

Mt Roland

64 75

RIDE 72

L. Cethana

RIDE 72

King

Solomons Cave

B12

RIDE 61

Cradle Valley

RIDE 65

Lemonthyme Power St.

71

RIDE 71

RIDE 66

Lake Dove

Cradle Mt

Forth River

RIDE 72

Arm River FR

RIDE 67

RIDE 66

Lake Mackenzie

RIDE 70

RIDE 68

WALLS OF JERUSALEM

CENTRAL PLATEAU PROTECTED AREA

N

RIDE 69

Wolfram Mines

Lake Rowallan

10 KM

3

RIDES AROUND DEVONPORT

With a population of 26 500, Devonport is the third largest city in the state. It is located almost in the exact centre of the north coast straddling the mouth of the Mersey River and is the destination for the 800 passenger *Abel Tasman*, the principal car ferry that mainlanders take to the island state. It is also Tasmania's principal cargo port.

Attractions include:

Tiagarra—An aboriginal cultural and art centre.
Home Hill — The residence of Tasmania's only Prime Minister and Dame Enid Lyons, the first female member of the House of Representatives.
Serendipity—Amusement park

Bicycle hire is available from Mersey Bluff during the holiday season. The city has a good network of bicycle paths.

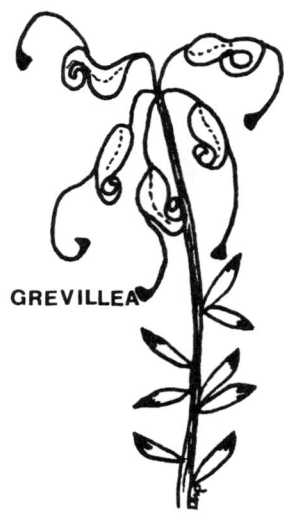

GREVILLEA

RIDE 21: ASBESTOS RANGE

FROM: Devonport
TO: Launceston
VIA: Asbestos Range National Park
LENGTH: Day 1: 39 km, Day 2: 60 km
TIME: 2 days (plus optional days exploring national park)
RIDE/TRACK GRADE: 4/4
WALKING: Optional walk to Archers Knob
HEIGHT VARIATION: 370 m
TRANSPORT: Bus services to Devonport and from Launceston
FACILITIES: Several camping and picnic areas in Asbestos Range National Park with toilets, picnic tables, fireplaces, water
SPECIAL GEAR: Knobbly tyres for traction in sandy sections. Binoculars for waterfowl observation.
MAPS: BP Touring Map of Tasmania and Asbestos Range 1:25 000 (See Map 3: *CRADLE MT* and Map 2: *TAMAR*)

From Devonport take the Frankford Main Road (B71) across the Rubicon River Bridge. Two kilometres later, cross the Franklin Rivulet Bridge and 250 m after turn left onto Bakers Beach Road. An alternative but longer and hillier route is to choose from the network of state forestry trails to the right in Branches Creek Plantation.

The C740 takes one into the park past the rangers' headquarters and main camping area to some picnic areas just behind the beach. The bikes will have to be walked along the sandy access track but once on the firm sand, one can cycle again. The beach is extremely wide. At low tide, one almost needs overnight camping gear just to reach the water!

Watch out for the strong rip.

DATA TABLE: Asbestos Range National Park

Size: 4281 ha
Enactment: July 1976
Aboriginal Sites: Middens
Animals: Forester kangaroos, Bennett's wallaby, soldier crabs
Plants: Salt marshes to dry eucalypt forest
Attractions: Observation station
Camping: Bakers Beach, Griffiths Point. Tent site $4.00 for 2 persons, $1 per extra person
District Office: (004) 28-6277

A walk from the end of the back road to the right takes you to a freshwater lagoon where you can observe black swans and native hen among others from a waterfowl observation hide. The trail also continues east up to Archers Knob (110 m) which allows one to survey the coast and western zone of the park. The cyclist can then choose from one of three campsites: Griffiths Point or Bakers Point accessed from the Bakers Point Road, or the main camp ground near the park headquarters and visitor information. The day's ride with no detours will have been 39 km. There is also an eastern section behind the Asbestos Range accessed by the Badger Head Road to Badger Beach.

Launceston is a day's ride away via Flowers Hill (370 m) and the Asbestos Road through some scenic forests to Beaconsfield and then the A7 following the Tamar up the western bank.

RIDE 22: MOUNT ROLAND

FROM: Devonport
TO: Mt. Roland Protected Area [RETURN]
VIA: Sheffield
LENGTH:
 Day 1: 40 km
 Day 2: 14 km (4 cycling, 10 walking)
 Day 3: 40 km
 Total distance is 84 km cycling, 10 walking
TIME: 3 days (includes 1 day walking)
RIDE/TRACK GRADE: 4/2
WALKING: Walk to summit of Mt. Roland (1233 m)
HEIGHT VARIATION: 1230 m
FACILITIES: Caravan park at Devonport, shops at Sheffield
SPECIAL GEAR: Walking boots
MAPS: RACT Touring Map and Mt. Roland Day Walk Map or Cethana & Wilmot 1:25 000 topographicals. (See Map 4: *CRADLE MT*)

Mount Roland is a huge dolerite plateau over a kilometre in the air that dominates the mid north-west. There is no definite peak, but the fact that no trees grow on top allow superb views. It was on these tops that Gustav Weindorfer, on his famous camping-honeymoon, first saw Cradle Mountain in 1906, which he later devoted his life to preserving.

From Devonport head south. The B14 and C150 takes you to Sheffield with its unsally large and colourful murals. From this quiet township the bulk of Mt. Roland is clearly visible. Its dolerite rock changes colour in accordance to weather and light changes. Locals at Sheffield see the plateau a pale pink or deep purple, covered in snow, and sometimes mist prevents them from seeing it at all.

From Sheffield the C136 takes you south with

relatively flat cycling to Gowrie Park 16 km away.

A popular well developed walk takes you up from the quiet township Gowrie Park (300 m) into the Protected Area and onto the plateau. Take O'Neils Road left for 2 km to the signposted start of the 10 km walk. The cyclist can actually take the track a kilometre further and 200 m higher. Another shorter alternative (6.5 km) begins from near the locality of Claude Road back towards Sheffield, although this isn't as scenic.

Return to Devonport via the same route.

RIDES AROUND GEORGE TOWN

Those cyclists alighting the Sea Cat will find themselves in a quaint administrative centre dubbed the oldest town in Australia. Since Sydney, Hobart, and Launceston have been elevated to 'city' status, that makes George Town technically the oldest, a cunning device of publicity employed by the local tourist authorities. Lying at the mouth of the Tamar River, its population of 7050 consists mainly of workers for the heavy industrial region of Bell Bay. It was named after King George in 1811 by Governor Macquarie. From here one can sail to Flinders Island (see Rides 95–98).

North of the town is Low Head where a series of old semaphore signal stations relayed messages in a 215-bit code to Launceston about boating activities in the Tamar. These were relayed at Mt. Direction.

RIDE 23: BELL BAY

FROM: Sea Cat Terminal, George Town
TO: Bell Bay [RETURN]
VIA: Comalco Aluminium Smelter
LENGTH: 13 km
TIME: 1 easy day
RIDE/TRACK GRADE: 2/1
WALKING: Tour of Comalco Aluminium Smelter (Wednesday 2 pm)
HEIGHT VARIATION: 20 m
TRANSPORT: None
FACILITIES: Caravan parks near Low Head
SPECIAL GEAR: Long-sleeved and ankle-length clothing and solid enclosed footwear is required by the tour organisers. Safety goggles and helmets provided by Comalco
MAPS: BP Touring Map of Tasmania. (See Map 2: *TAMAR*)

This free tour is only possible on Wednesdays. It is therefore ideal for people catching the Tuesday Sea Cat from Port Welshpool. One should contact the Tasmanian Government Tourist Bureau on (003) 82-5111 for booking details.

Directions are simple. Follow the A8 to Bell Bay then loop back via the Tamar to Low Head where you can check out a Pilot Station and Museum containing an old deep-sea diving suit, wreck memorabilia, and old shipping flags.

The Bell Bay Thermal Station, commissioned in 1971, has two 120 000 kW generators to top up the HEC's hydroelectric power output during peak, emergency, and drought times. Other industries located here include APPM mills.

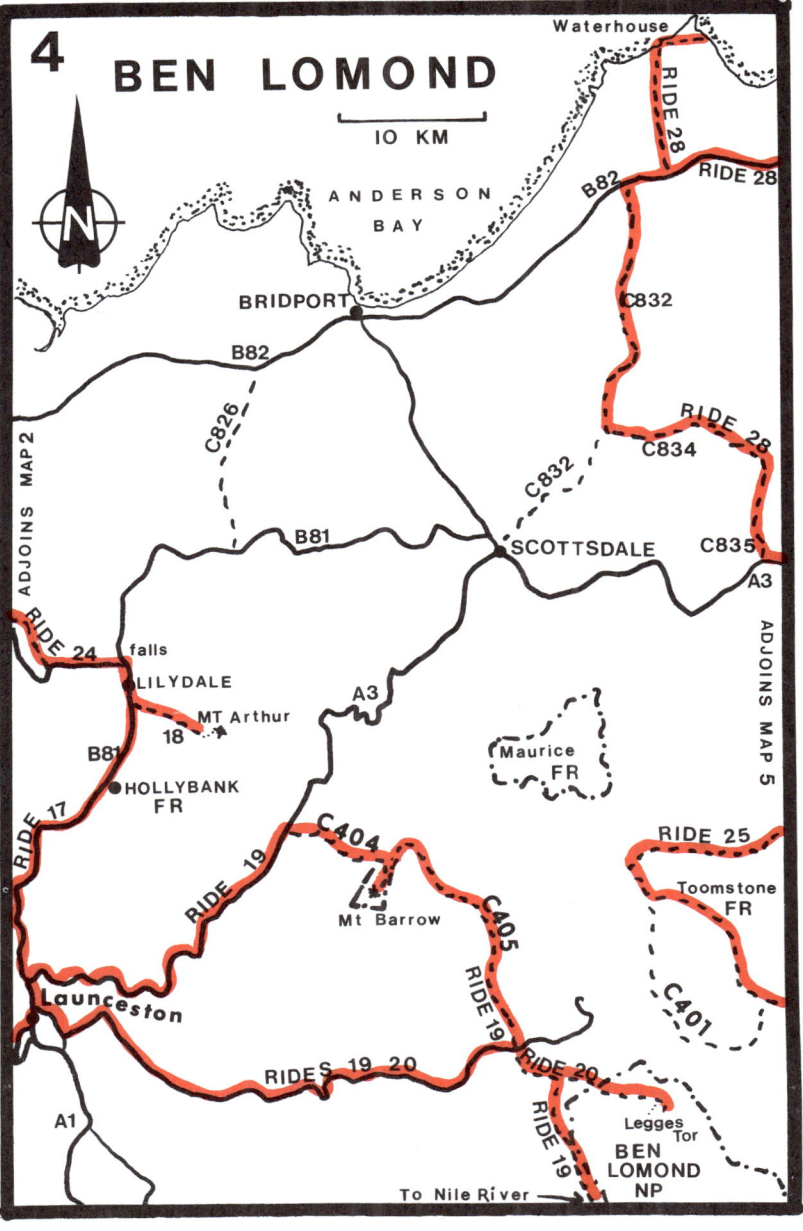

RIDE 24: LILYDALE

FROM: Sea Cat Terminal
TO: Launceston
VIA: Lilydale and Pipers River Valley
LENGTH:
    Day 1: George Town to Lilydale 51 km
    Day 2: Lilydale to Launceston 29 km
    Total distance is 80 km
TIME: 1–2 days
RIDE/TRACK GRADE: 4/3
WALKING: None
HEIGHT VARIATION: 400 m
FACILITIES: Tourist requirements at Lilydale
                Camping area at Lilydale Falls Reserve
MAPS: BP Touring Map. (See Map 2: *TAMAR* and
Map 4: *BEN LOMOND*)

This ride presents a longer but substantially more scenic route for Sea Cat passengers wishing to cycle to Launceston.

Take the Bridport Road as far as the Pipers River Road 23 km east from George Town. Follow the Pipers River Road south for 2 km until you come to a T-intersection with Baxters Road. Head right keeping the river on your left. This area is Tasmania's premium wine-grape growing region. The road is very flat here keeping between 60 and 80 m in altitude. Seven kilometres after passing the prominent and isolated conical Sugarloaf (140 m) on your left, turn left to Bangor. There are four bridges along this back-road which curves around south from west to meet with Second River Road 5 km later. Head left for 6 km to an intersection with Golcando Road. Lilydale (170 m) is 2 km to the right (south). At the falls reserve, picnic tables, shelters, and barbecues are provided. The day's distance will have been 51 km. It is a further 29 km to Launceston past the lovely Hollybank Forest

Reserve (see Ride 17) rising to 400 m altitude. One can stay at Lilydale (motel and units) or the fit cyclist can press on to Launceston. For accommodation one can also rough it in the nearby state forest at the base of Mt. Arthur to the west (see Ride 18 for details).

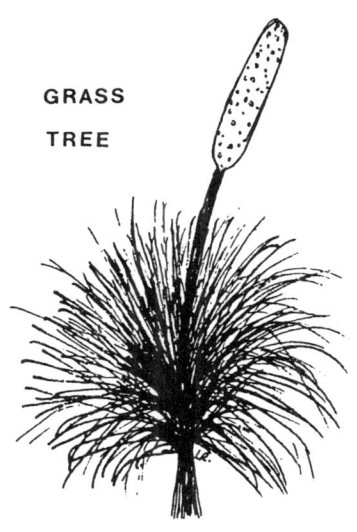

GRASS

TREE

OTHER RIDES

There remain several areas near the major population centres that the more adventurous cyclist can explore. The Wellington Range can also be accessed south from New Norfolk and further west one can explore the upper Plenty River Valley. The range extends right into the great south-west area and many trails cover the tops, slopes, and valleys as far west as the Russell River and the 1200 m Snowy Range. North of the Derwent are the state forests of Platform Peak and Mt. Dromedary.

Launceston's hinterland offers less in mountain ranges then in vast forested areas. The state forests surrounding Mount Arthur, Mount Barrow, and Ben Lomond are riddled with trails of all grades. Not many are marked on the maps or signposted so the pioneering mountain cyclist might confront some interesting navigational problems. On the western side of the Tamar are the eucalypt forests in the hills south of Asbestos Range. The road network through here is a little more developed, and a large variety of options exists for the mountain cyclist wanting to choose an interesting route between Devonport and Launceston.

5
THE NORTH-EAST

Good touring cycling conditions due to minimum of altitudinal fluctuations. Most of the coastal plains are very flat and averages of 15-20 km/h can easily be maintained for an hour or two.

While the main attractions are definitely on the coast, there are little known mountainous tiers located inland to challenge any mountain cyclist's skills. The mildest climate Tasmania has to offer enables cyclists to tour here all year round. The following rides give a cross-section of both these terrains.

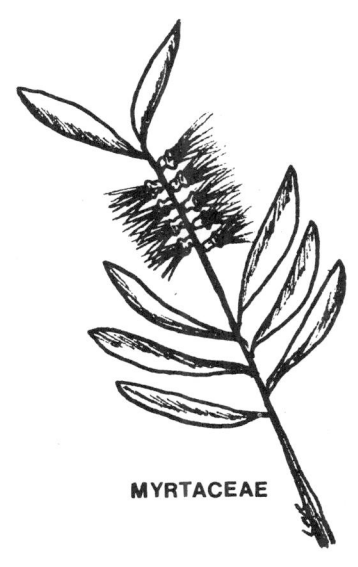

MYRTACEAE

RIDE 25: NORTH-EAST FOREST RESERVES

(SOUTH ESK RIVER WATERSHED)

FROM: St. Marys
TO: Upper South Esk River catchment
VIA: Tower Hill, Upper Esk
LENGTH:
   Day 1: St. Marys to Evercreech FR 63 km
   Day 2: Evercreech FR to Mathinna Falls FR 25 km
   Day 3: Mathinna Falls FR to Victoria FR 30 km
   Day 4: Victoria FR to Tombstone FR 38 km
   Day 5: Tombstone FR to Griffin FR 31 km
   Day 6: Griffin FR to St. Marys 62 km
   Total distance is 249 km
TIME: 6–7 days
RIDE/TRACK GRADE: 9/7
HEIGHT VARIATION: 1110 m
TRANSPORT: Coach to and from St. Marys
FACILITIES: None, camping allowed anywhere in state forests
SPECIAL GEAR: Complete self-sufficiency, one night away from water
MAPS: Mangana, Stacks, Giblin, Mathinna, and Saddleback 1:25 000 topos. (See Map 4: *BEN LOMOND* and Map 5: *ST. HELENS*)

Several wet and dry forest reserves exist in the upper catchment area of the South Esk River. These have been developed by the Forestry Commission so that people can enjoy portions of state forests for an indefinite period as logging operations are not permitted. The trails that link these reserves are fairly rough and steep. Therefore I recommend this ride only for experienced cyclists with overnight equipment ensuring self-sufficiency.

Start early. From St. Marys hit the A4 west for 21 km to Fingal. Turn right onto the B42 crossing the South Esk River. Head right again after the

152

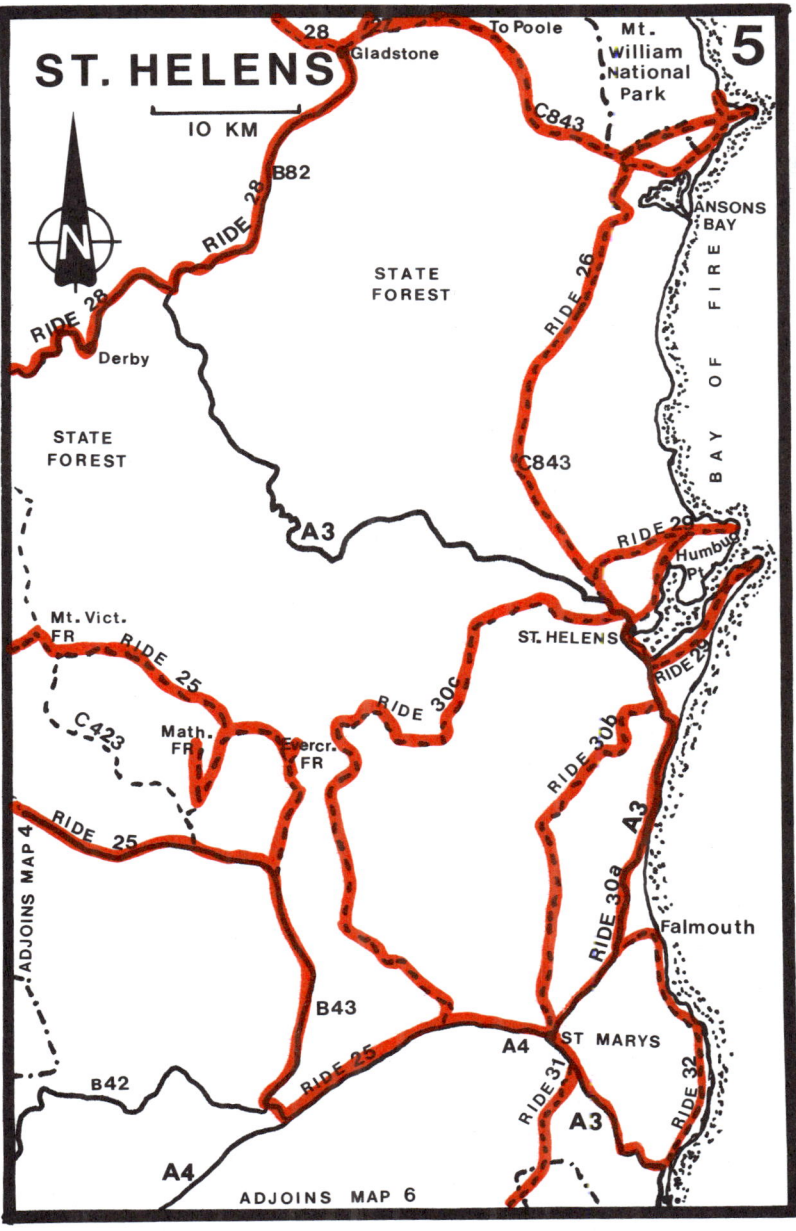

bridge onto Mathinna Road (B43) at 240 m altitude which follows the river's western shore north. 22 km from Fingal head back down to the river, crossing it via Evercreech Road (C430). As you start ascending you leave the agricultural land behind. The trees close in to eventually become state forest. A turnoff on the right leads to Evercreech Forest Reserve centred on Evercreech Rivulet. Here the cyclist can see the White Knights, a cluster of huge white gums almost 100 m tall and estimated to be about 300 years old.

The next day, continue up Hauler Ridge and turn left at Symonds Road leading down to Mathinna. Near here the large steam-powered gold mine was located. A track on the right on the way down leads to Mathinna Falls Forest Reserve.

On the third day, start early as 600 m of climbing is involved. Backtrack up to the Mt. Victoria plateau via Dilgers Hills Road (800 m). This leads into the Mt. Victoria Forest Reserve where you cycle amongst tall callidendrous rainforest. This becomes Mt. Albert Road which passes to the south of the huge pinnacle of Mt. Victoria. Camp anywhere along here where suitable. The next morning it is relatively flat cycling at this altitude before arriving at an intersection with Mathinna Plains Road (C423). Left exits the plateau leading down to Mathinna again. Head right to the Ben Ridge Road and turn left. Head left onto Telopea Road and left yet again into the Tombstone Creek Forest Reserve, set on one of the tributaries of the South Esk River.

After five days, you deserve a late start the next morning as it is nearly all downhill following the upper South Esk River from 800 m to 400 m. The roads to take are Cohens and then Griffin leading to the riverside Griffin Forest Reserve. The next day continue east joining Eton Road crossing the river to get to the B43 again. From here it's 27 km to Fingal and another 22 km to St. Marys.

RIDE 26: MOUNT WILLIAM
NATIONAL PARK
(South)

FROM: St. Helens
TO: Gladstone
VIA: Ansons River, Eddystone Lighthouse
LENGTH:
　　Day 1: St. Helens to Ansons Bay 43 km
　　Day 2: Ansons Bay to Groves Creek Camp
　　　　Ground 15 km
　　Day 3: Groves Creek to Gladstone 41 km
　　Total distance is 99 km
TIME: 3 days
RIDE/TRACK GRADE: 5/5
HEIGHT VARIATION: 120 m
TRANSPORT: Coach to St. Helens and own transport from Gladstone
FACILITIES: Camping area at Groves Creek
MAPS: Binalong, The Gardens, Ansons Bay, Eddystone 1:25 000 topographical. (See Map 5: *ST. HELENS*)

Mt. William contains some truly beautiful beaches with clear unpolluted water and the mildest most protected climate in the state. In fact, if it's too cold to swim at Mt. William, it's too cold to swim in the state.

From St. Helens head north along the Tasman Highway (A3) and then right onto the C843. Once over the Georges River, the vegetation closes as you climb gently up to a flat low-lying plateau. This descends again into the Anson River valley. One can either camp by this exquisite river or continue for 6 km to Ansons Bay. This area is frequented by Peregrine Adventure's mountain cycling tours so don't be surprised to see a group of cyclists who've paid a few hundred dollars to tour this area.

155

The next day is an easy cycle from Ansons Bay to Eddystone Point and then the camping site at Groves Creek just to the north. Along the rough track that meets up with Eddystone Point Road you pass through low heath and the occasional grass tree. Watch out for sand patches. You come out at an intersection. To the right leads to the lighthouse while straight ahead leads to the camping ground.

Built in 1889, Eddystone Lighthouse is atypical of lighthouses in that it is not white. The headlands are also different, being rounded granite, unlike the dolerite cliffs of the south-east.

If you do not feel like camping with the masses at Grove Creek you can rough it in one of the many clearings that line the beach edge.

DATA TABLE: Mount William National Park

Size: 13 899 ha
Aboriginal Sites: Middens
Animals: Devils, wallabies, seabirds, kangaroos, echidnas
Plants: Largest dry eucalypt forest in Tasmania
11 of Tasmania's 37 heath communities are reserved here
Attractions: Isolated beaches, fishing
Camping: Developed camp sites to the north and south
District Office: (003) 57-2108

RIDE 27: MOUNT WILLIAM NATIONAL PARK

(North)

FROM: Gladstone
TO: Boulder Point [RETURN]
VIA: Mt. William
LENGTH: 78 km (39 km each way)
TIME: 2 days
RIDE/TRACK GRADE: 4/5
WALKING: To summit of Mt. William
HEIGHT VARIATION: 216 m
TRANSPORT: Own to and from Gladstone
FACILITIES: Campgrounds in Mt. William National Park
MAPS: Naturalsite and Eddystone 1:25 000 topographical

Mt. William National Park contains some truly beautiful beaches with clear unpolluted water and the mildest most protected climate in the state. In fact, if it's too cold to swim at Mt. William, it's too cold to swim in the state. The route descriptions for this ride are simple. Two kilometres north-east of Gladstone cross Bells Bridge over the Ringarooma River, ignoring the left turn to Cape Portland. Follow this to Poole in the north of the Mt. William National Park. This was named after Charles Edward Lane Poole (1885-1970), a prominent forester who helped establish the Australian Forestry School.

The next day or two can be spent relaxing and exploring this end of the park. There is a walk up to the summit of Mt. William giving views to Cape Barren Island to the south of Flinders. On the beach at Great Musselroe Bay are Aboriginal middens, and there is also another coastal camping area just north of Boulder Point in the park. The route from the Poole camping area south to the national park camp ground via Mt. William is about 30 km.

RIDE 28: NORTH-EAST COAST

FROM: Derby [RETURN]
TO: Waterhouse Protected Area, Mt. William National Park
VIA: Gladstone
LENGTH:
    Day 1: Derby to Waterhouse Point 60 km
    Day 2: Waterhouse Point to Poole 76 km
    Day 3: Poole to Stumpys Bay via Mt. William
      30 km
    Day 4: Stumpys Bay to Derby 60 km
    Total distance is 226 km
TIME: 4-5 days
RIDE/TRACK GRADE: 8/6
WALKING: Optional walk to Mt. William summit
HEIGHT VARIATION: 250 m
TRANSPORT: Coach service to and from Derby
FACILITIES: Basic camping at Waterhouse Point and Poole. Supplies at Gladstone
SPECIAL GEAR: Swimming gear, insect repellent
MAPS: Pearly Brook, Oxberry, Waterhouse, Naturalsite 1:25 000 topographical. (See Map 4: *BEN LOMOND* and Map 5: *ST. HELENS*)

This ride not only encompasses some fabulous beaches and secluded coastal inlets, but in addition the cyclist can enjoy the least difficult riding in the state amongst huge dry sclerophyll (hard-leaved) forest as well as exploring a large protected area, a national park, and a coastal reserve.

Follow the A3 8 km back to Branxholm turning off to Forester via Winnaleah. Head north via the C832 to Waterhouse Point. This is flat easy cycling and a good average can be maintained. There is a well developed camping area and some short educational coastal walks. The cyclist/camper can also rough it at a selection of more isolated coastal campsites following any one of the 4WD tracks to the water around the peninsula. Mosquitoes can be a problem here. Consult the Waterhouse 1:25 000 topographical.

The next day cycle back down the 15 km to Waterhouse and then east to Gladstone. Two kilometres north-east of Gladstone cross Bells Bridge over the Ringarooma River, ignoring the left turn to Cape Portland. Follow this to Poole in the north of the Mt. William National Park. The next day or two can be spent relaxing and exploring this end of the park. There is a walk up to the summit of Mt. William giving views to Cape Barren Island to the south of Flinders. On the beach at Great Musselroe Bay are Aboriginal middens, and there is also another coastal camping area just north of Boulder Point in the park. The route from the Poole camping area south to the national park camping ground via Mt. William is about 30 km.

The return journey to Derby via the C843 and A3 is 60 km.

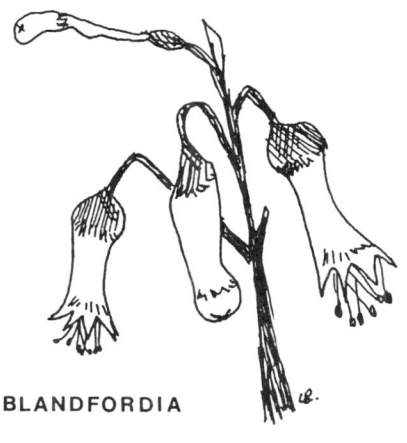

BLANDFORDIA

RIDE 29: ST. GEORGES BAY

FROM: St. Helens
TO: Humbug Point State Recreation Area, St. Helens Point
State Recreation Area
VIA: Bayview, Stieglitz
LENGTH: Ride 29a 32 km
Ride 29b 42 km
TIME: 2 x 1 day
RIDE/TRACK GRADE: 3/4
HEIGHT VARIATION: 110 m
TRANSPORT: Coach to St. Helens
FACILITIES: Camping grounds in State Recreation Areas. Caravan parks in St. Helens
MAPS: St. Helens 1:25 000 topographical. (See Map 5: *ST. HELENS*)

Those touring Tasmania and staying in St. Helens for a while might like to consider a pleasant ride to one of two places by the open sea. The first, lining George Bay to the north is the Humbug State Recreation Area accessed by the Binalong Bay Road (C850).

From Binalong Bay, minor roads take you into the reserve to various points of interest around the Humbug Peninsula making enjoyable cycling, despite the occasional hill. There are picnic facilities located here beside sheltered bayside beaches. The total return distance is 32 km taking C849 out through eucalypt state forest to avoid backtracking.

The second alternative is to the St. Helens Point State Recreation Area via the St. Helens Point Road (C851) for a swim at Maurourand Beach if the weather is suitable. The return distance is 42 km.

There are also developed camping grounds with all the usual facilities in both recreation areas but they are very popular during weekend summer holidays.

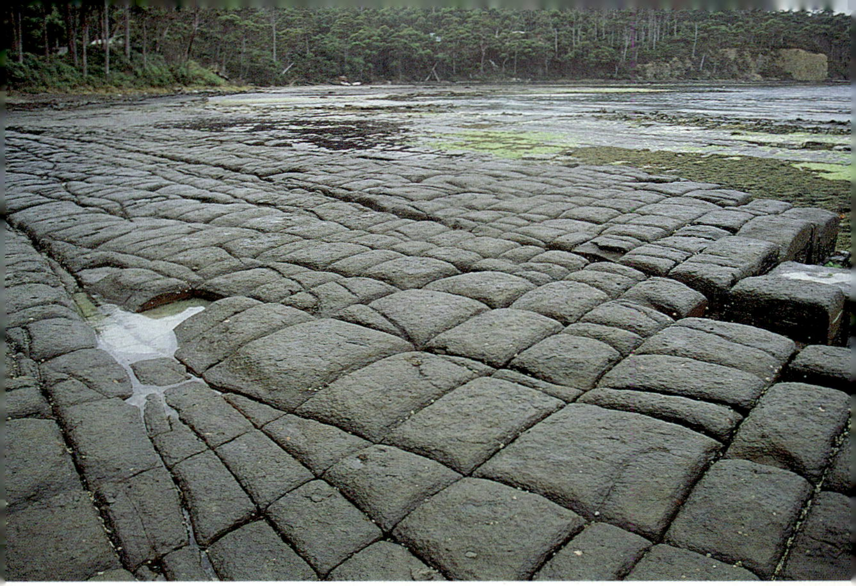

Tesselated Pavement, near Eaglehawk Neck

Arve Falls, Hartz Mountains National Park (Ride 47)

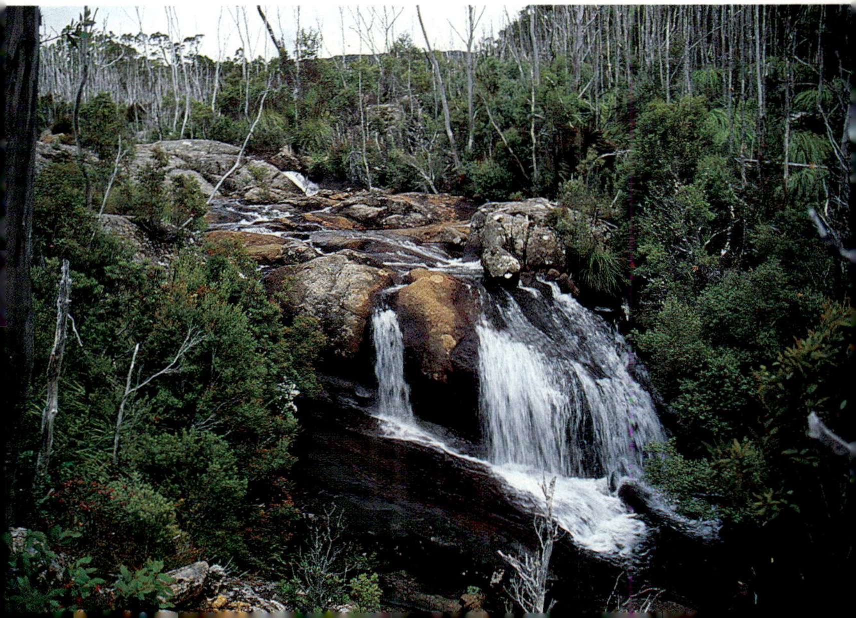

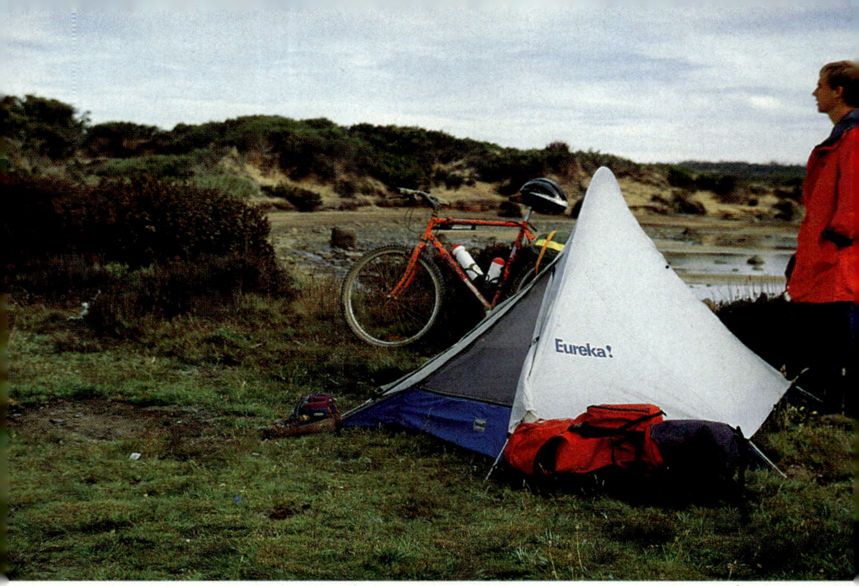

Double Lagoon, Central Plateau Protected Area (Ride 58)

Franklin River (Ride 59)

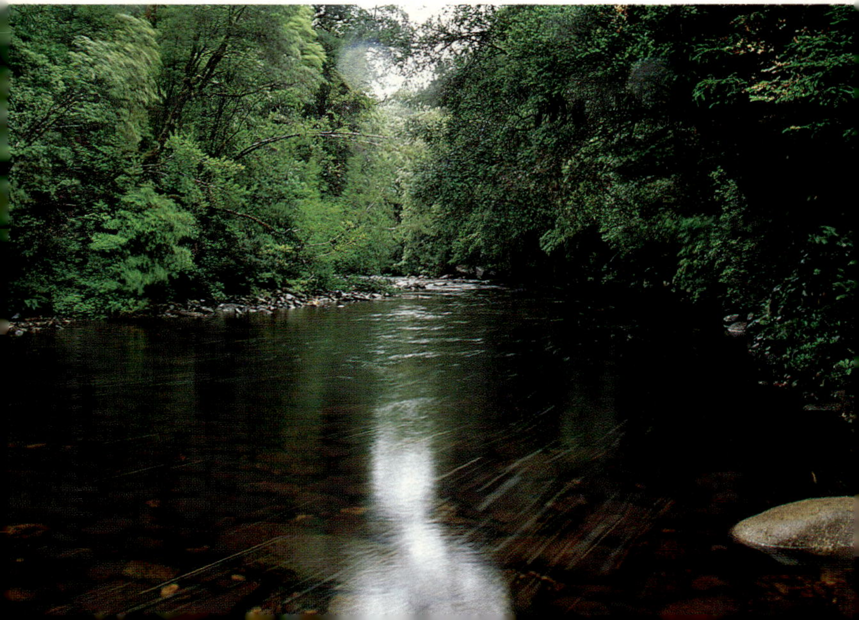

RIDE 30: ST. HELENS—ST. MARYS HINTERLAND

FROM: St. Helens
TO: St. Marys
VIA: Scamander River watershed ridges, Nicholas Range
LENGTH:
    Ride 30a 35 km (1 day)
    Ride 30b 49 km (1-2 days)
    Ride 30c 81 km (3 days)
RIDE/TRACK GRADE: 9/7
HEIGHT VARIATION: Up to 830 m
TRANSPORT: Coach to St. Helens and from St. Marys
FACILITIES: Caravan park in St. Helens
SPECIAL GEAR: Complete self-sufficiency
MAPS: Pyengana, Brilliant, Dublin Town, St. Marys 1:25 000 topographical. (See Map 5: *ST. HELENS*)

There are a variety of state forestry trails that the keen mountain cyclist can take between St. Helens and St. Marys. Tracknotes and spot heights are given only for the most challenging of the three alternatives suggested. The shortest way obviously is the Tasman Highway (35 km). More scenic, less traffic, and a moderate amount of climbing is through Upper Scamander (49 km). The Nicholas Range has to be negotiated and great views are obtainable from the detour up to South Sister (831 m). However the gradient is far too steep here and the bike has to be laboriously pushed or left behind.

    Another route is onto the Mt. Victoria plateau via Beahrs Creek and C430 through the saddle between Mt. Nicholas (857 m) and Mt. Durham. This is a tiring 81 km climbing to 650 m with some never-ending uphills and terrifying rocky downhills.

    TRACKNOTES: The third alternative (30c) is

ONLY FOR EXPERIENCED MOUNTAIN CYCLISTS. Maps are definitely needed and navigational expertise is essential. We got lost around the high ridges here due to a lack of adequate signposting. From St. Helens head west on Argonaut Road and turn left onto Trafalgar Track, and then onto Hogans Road (250 m). Cross the upper Scamander River and follow Beahrs Creek valley west through some pleasant forest. The track climbs steeply to 620 m. Keep left on the middle of the ridge ignoring the many turn-offs. Sugarloaf Road then connects into Mt. Nicholas Road for the big climb over the range. The Esk Highway then leads 7 km east to St. Marys.

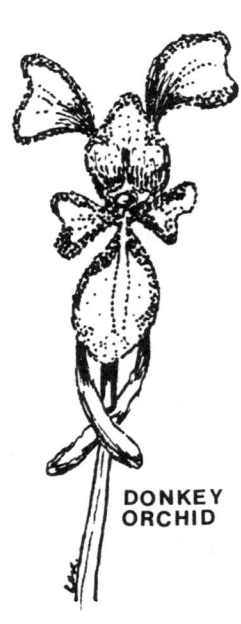

DONKEY ORCHID

RIDE 31: EASTERN TIERS

FROM: St. Marys
TO: Little Swanport
VIA: Douglas-Apsley National Park, Meetus Falls
Forest
Reserve, Tooms Lake.
LENGTH: 160 km
TIME: 6–8 days (camping where suitable)
RIDE/TRACK GRADE: 9/8
HEIGHT VARIATION: 800 m
TRANSPORT: Coach service to St. Marys, own from
Little Swanport
SPECIAL GEAR: Spare tubes, water, thick knobbly
tires and gear to ensure complete self-sufficiency
MAPS: Break O'Day, St. Pauls, Little Swanport
1:100 000 topos (See Map 5: *ST. HELENS* and Map
6: *FREYCINET*)

This ride is one of the most challenging on the
east coast as it negotiates some rough trails through
some remote highland terrain only suitable for
strong mountain bikes. The maps, full provisions,
extra precautionary days, water, and experience
are all necessary. The eastern tiers are isolated but
mountain bikers are becoming increasingly aware
of it and the national parks authorities encourage
cycling around the Tooms Lake area so as to relieve
pressure from other more significant and sensitive
areas. The trail follows the four-wheel-drive track
called MacKays Road that follows the spine of the
Eastern Tiers at about 550-650 m altitude. Along
the way is the Meetus Falls Forest Reserve, the
Tooms Lake Protected Area, and a section of the
Douglas-Apsley National Park.
　　The total distance is 160 km and camping is
possible in a selection of areas including the picnic
area at Meetus Falls, and by the shores of Lake
Leake and Lake Toom.

It was through territory like this that Governor Arthur sent his 2000 armed civilian troops in an infamous attempt to round up the Aborigines, driving them down to the Tasman peninsula. Called the Black Line, the campaign cost £60 000 and just two prisoners were taken, a woman and child.

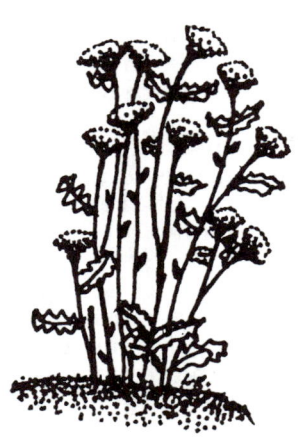

Meetus Falls, which fall a considerable distance in half a dozen stages, are difficult to access directly due to the dense vegetation and the nature of the steep gorge they fall into. However good views can be obtained from a lookout located directly opposite and higher than the Cygnet River.

Entry onto MacKays Road is also possible through Avoca and Royal George. The last part of this route down the spur to Little Swanport following Bresnehans Road is the same as Ride 36. On the other side of the Little Swanport River is the Buckland Military Training Area (entry prohibited).

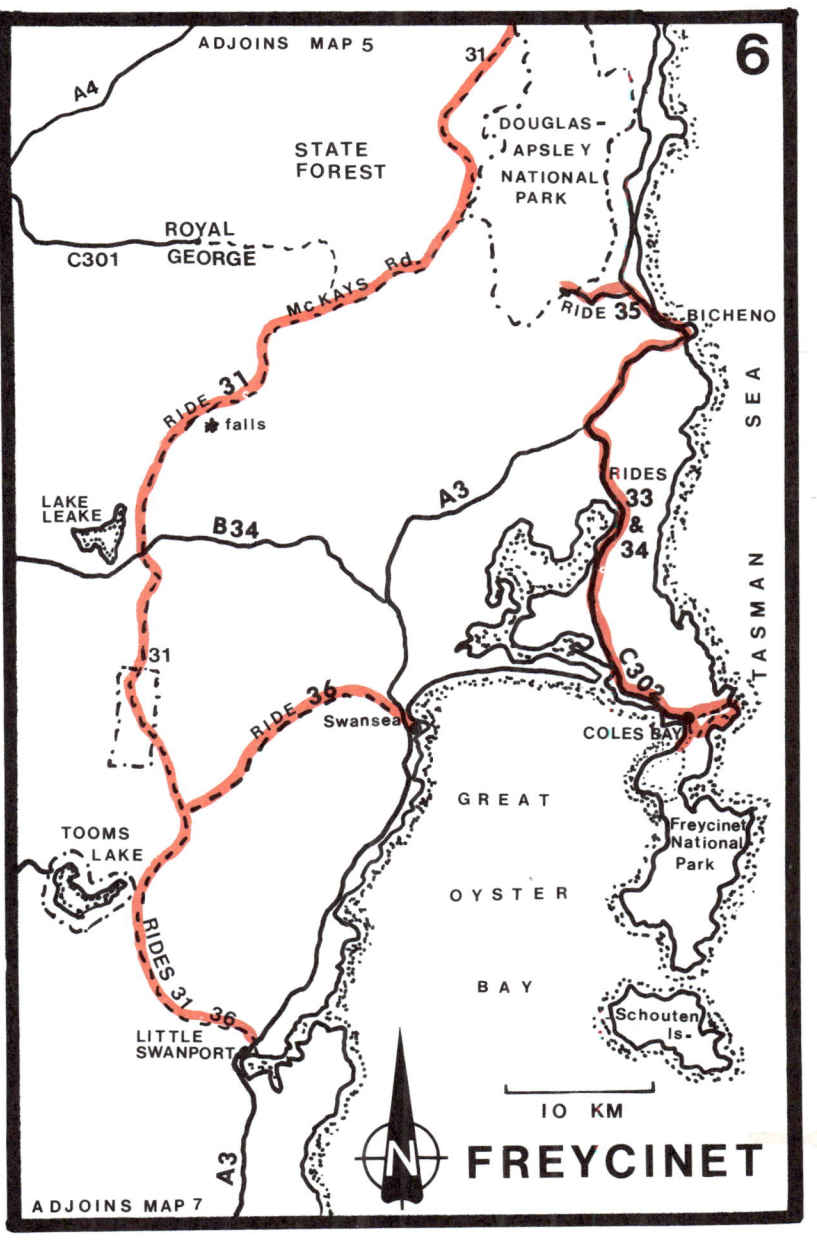

RIDE 32: ST. MARYS COASTAL LOOP

FROM: St. Marys [RETURN]
VIA: Four Mile Creek
LENGTH: 54 km
TIME: 1 day
RIDE/TRACK GRADE: 3/4
HEIGHT VARIATION: 396 m
TRANSPORT: Coach service to and from St. Marys
MAPS: Gray 1:25 000 topographical. (See Map 5: *ST. HELENS*)

St. Marys is located 10 km inland. Those visiting the city can do a round loop along a relatively unknown portion of Tasmania's mild eastern coast. Head north and up the St. Marys Pass (305 m) before descending 300 m to the flat coastal plains. Turn right off the Tasman Highway onto the C411 to Falmouth. Head right to Four Mile Creek and continue south where the newly developed road meets the A3 again just north of Chain of Lagoons. It is 16 km to St. Marys climbing Elephant Pass (396 m).

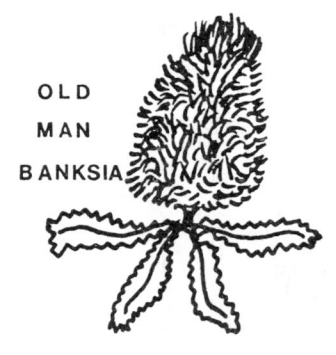

OLD
MAN
BANKSIA

RIDE 33: FREYCINET PENINSULA

FROM: Bicheno
TO: Freycinet National Park
VIA: Coles Bay
LENGTH: 96 km
TIME: 2-4 days (excludes extra days for walking)
RIDE/TRACK GRADE: 3/3
WALKING: 25 km circuit track of Wineglass Bay, Mt. Freycinet
HEIGHT VARIATION: 100 m cycling, 600 m walking
TRANSPORT: Coach service to Bicheno
FACILITIES: Youth Hostel at Parsons Cove (key needed from Hobart), stores at Coles Bay, camping grounds have toilets. There's also a Youth Hostel at Bicheno.
MAPS: Freycinet National Park 1:50 000 and Freycinet 1:100 000 topographic. (See Map 6: *FREYCINET*)

Freycinet Peninsula was originally named 'Vanderlyn Island' in 1642 by Abel Tasman who didn't realise it was part of the mainland. The French explorer Baudin changed the name in 1802 after a member of his party. The national park is known for its clear water and white beaches being the result of erosion of the crystalline granite that dominates local geology. Swimming conditions are ideal at Hazards Beach: if it wasn't for the temperature you could almost believe you were on the Great Barrier Reef!

Start from Bicheno on the Tasman Highway (A3) extending from Burgess Street. From this township, with its unusual granite outcrops, whalers once kept a lookout for waterspouts. It has been a fishing port for 180 years, commencing with sealing but now dominated by oysters and abalone. Today it hosts a Sea Life Centre opened in 1979. It's worth inspecting for its unique display of marine life endemic to Tasmania. There are 28 separate tanks containing hundreds of species including the largest crabs in the world. Docked near by is the ketch *Enterprise*.

Bicheno Beach is also a particularly attractive venue. Take the C302 to Coles Bay 39 km from Bicheno. This town is dominated by the Hazards which are formed from granite coloured pink-red with lichens which give good contrast to the very blue water. Other colours of lichen are also common, ranging from bright yellow to pale green. Coles Bay is not just a tourist town as a small fishing fleet operates from here.

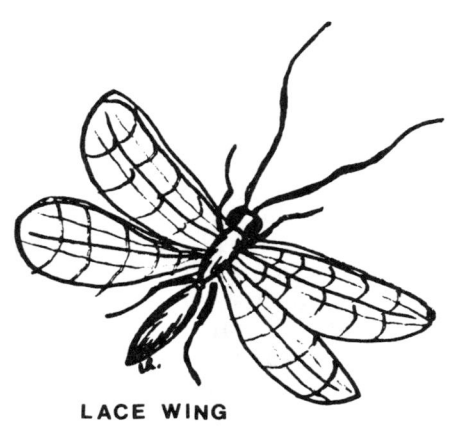

LACE WING

Camp at the ground here and do a tour of the park heading south parallel to Richardsons Beach and then left to the Cape Tourville lighthouse. Take the short-cut via the powerlines to Coles Bay if wishing to purchase supplies.

To see the rest of the national park, your wheels must be left behind. In fact it is strongly recommended that you do the popular hike around the Hazards to the famous Wineglass Bay. From the vantage points along the way, one commands views over dry low open eucalypt woodland looking south to Schouten Island. One will notice that Schouten Island is divided by an obvious fault line. On the right, dolerite supports forests, while left of the fault the poorer granite supports only stunted heath.

One can also do longer overnight walks to Bryans Beach in the far south of the peninsula.

Walk	Distance	Time (return)
Wineglass Bay	9 km	2 hours
Cooks Beach circuit	30 km	2 days

When leaving Coles Bay, it is also possible to proceed direct to Swansea via a small boat to Nine Mile Beach.

DATA TABLE: Freycinet National Park

Size: 10 010 ha (including Schouten Island)
Enactment: 29 August 1916 (first Tasmanian National Park)
Aboriginal Sites: Middens
Animals: 146 species of birds, red-necked wallaby, devils
Plants: Heath, Oyster Bay pines, banksias, tea trees, wattle. Sixty varieties of ground orchid have been identified. Vegetation is recovering from two severe 1980 fires
Attractions: Wine Glass Bay, the Hazards
Camping: Bookings required in summer and at Easter.
District Office: (002) 57-0146

RIDE 34: BLUESTONE BAY

FROM: Bicheno
TO: Cape Tourville
VIA: Coles Bay
LENGTH: 98 km (48 each way)
TIME: 2-3 days
RIDE/TRACK GRADE: 4/6
HEIGHT VARIATION: 120 m
TRANSPORT: Coach service to and from Coles Bay
FACILITIES: Basic camping area at Bluestone Bay
Stores at Coles Bay
MAPS: Freycinet National Park 1:50 000 and
Freycinet 1:100 000 topographical. (See Map 6:
FREYCINET)

Bluestone Bay is a very secluded inlet located just
to the north of the Freycinet National Park. There
are two nice flat campsites available. A watercourse
exists but it is too small to be relied upon as a
regular source. The bay was formerly unoccupied
Crown Land but now has been incorporated into
the Friendly Beaches extension to Freycinet
National Park.

Make your way to Coles Bay from Bicheno. Cross
the bridge over Mosquito Creek and turnoff the
road left. It passes a ranger depot and follows power
lines climbing briefly. It's easy cycling along this
debilitated road. It joins the Tourville Road but
head immediately left again through thicker bush.
This trail follows the Ranger Creek gully up to a
saddle and thereafter it's easy cycling. Keep left.
A hairpin corner announces the short steep descent
down to the water. It is reasonably popular but
firewood is plentiful. Another campsite exists: cross
the rocky creek and follow the road to its very
end. A walking track heads along the southern bank
to another inlet containing a rocky beach around
to the right.

Another variation is to access the Friendly Beaches to the north via Coles Bay. It is also possible to proceed direct to Swansea via a small boat to Nine Mile Beach.

RIDE 35: DOUGLAS-APSLEY NATIONAL PARK

FROM: Bicheno
TO: Apsley River [RETURN]
LENGTH: 18 km
TIME: 1 day (plus time for swimming)
RIDE/TRACK GRADE: 3/3
WALKING: Walking opportunities throughout park
HEIGHT VARIATION: 90 m
TRANSPORT: Coach to and from Bicheno
FACILITIES: None
MAPS: Break O'Day 1:100 000 topo. (See Map 6: FREYCINET)

To see this little known recently declared national park head north from Bicheno and left at the signpost. The road passes through rural land at the base of a low range before coming to a carpark. Your bikes can be wheeled a short distance to the Apsley River where there is a popular swimming hole. For the walker, one can venture further to the interior of the park. The cliffs that line the Apsley River are formed by blocks so regular they look as if sculpted by a stonemason. Camping is permitted as long as you pitch your tent well away from the river.

DATA TABLE: Douglas-Apsley National Park

Size: 16 080 ha
Animals: Unusual distribution and concentrations of marsupials, mammals, and birds for a dry eucalypt forest.
Plants: 14 species of eucalypt
Attractions: Largest unaltered dry forests and intact river catchments in Tasmania. Swimming in pristine gorge. Wilderness walk to Nicholls Cap
Camping: Small site near Waterhole, toilets, tables, shelter
District Office: (003) 75-1236

OTHER RIDES

The north-east contains the largest single block of state forest in Tasmania. Consequently cycling pioneers have an infinite range of opportunities to explore old and new trails, discover fantastic downhills and beautiful camping spots on their way from Launceston to St. Helens.

There are also areas of public land along the coast, in particular Cape Portland and the Bay of Fires around The Gardens. The latter area is covered in Peregrine Adventures' mountain biking tours.

6
THE SOUTH-EAST

Considerable variety makes the south-eastern part of Tasmania a delight for cyclist. Because Hobart is contained within this quadrant many of these rides can be attempted using the capital as a base. The south-east offers cyclists an extension of the eastern tiers for mountain cyclists, large eucalypt state forests of trees over 100 m in height, the Tasman Peninsula with its famous penal colony ruins and unusual coastal formations, and magnificent forest reserves and river valleys of the far south. There are caves. There are beaches. There are mountains.

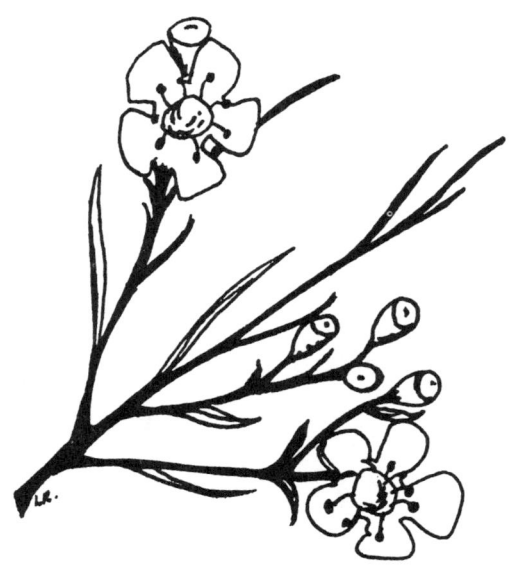

RIDE 36: SWANSEA—LITTLE SWANPORT HINTERLAND

FROM: Little Swanport (or Swansea)
TO: Swansea (or Little Swanport)
VIA: White Grass Ridge
LENGTH: 52 km (plus 12 km detour to Tooms Lake)
TIME: 2 days
RIDE/TRACK GRADE: 7/6
HEIGHT VARIATION: 620 m
TRANSPORT: Coaches to/from Swansea and Triabunna
FACILITIES: None
SPECIAL GEAR: Self-sufficient
MAPS: Little Swanport 1:100 000 topo. (See Map 6: *FREYCINET*)

Those circumnavigating Tasmania around the coastal highways can break up the monotony of the traffic by taking an eventful rocky detour between Swansea and Little Swanport. Over 600 m of height must be gained as you take Bresnehans Road left 1 km north of Little Swanport. Most of the height is gained on this long climb. Once on top it becomes flatter and much easier pedalling.

Turn right at McKays Road travelling north over the plateau top with the terrain here consisting of swamps and marshes. The map listed is essential for negotiating your way through the maze of dead-end tracks that branch off regularly on either side. For a camping detour make your way left down 6 km to the shore of Tooms Lake (464 m). This location conveniently divides the ride into two.

Head back to MacKays Road the next day, head north through more marshes. McNeills Road to the right takes you off Tom Legges Tier and down White Grass Ridge back to the coast to Swansea. Very good brakes are needed for this descent to be successful.

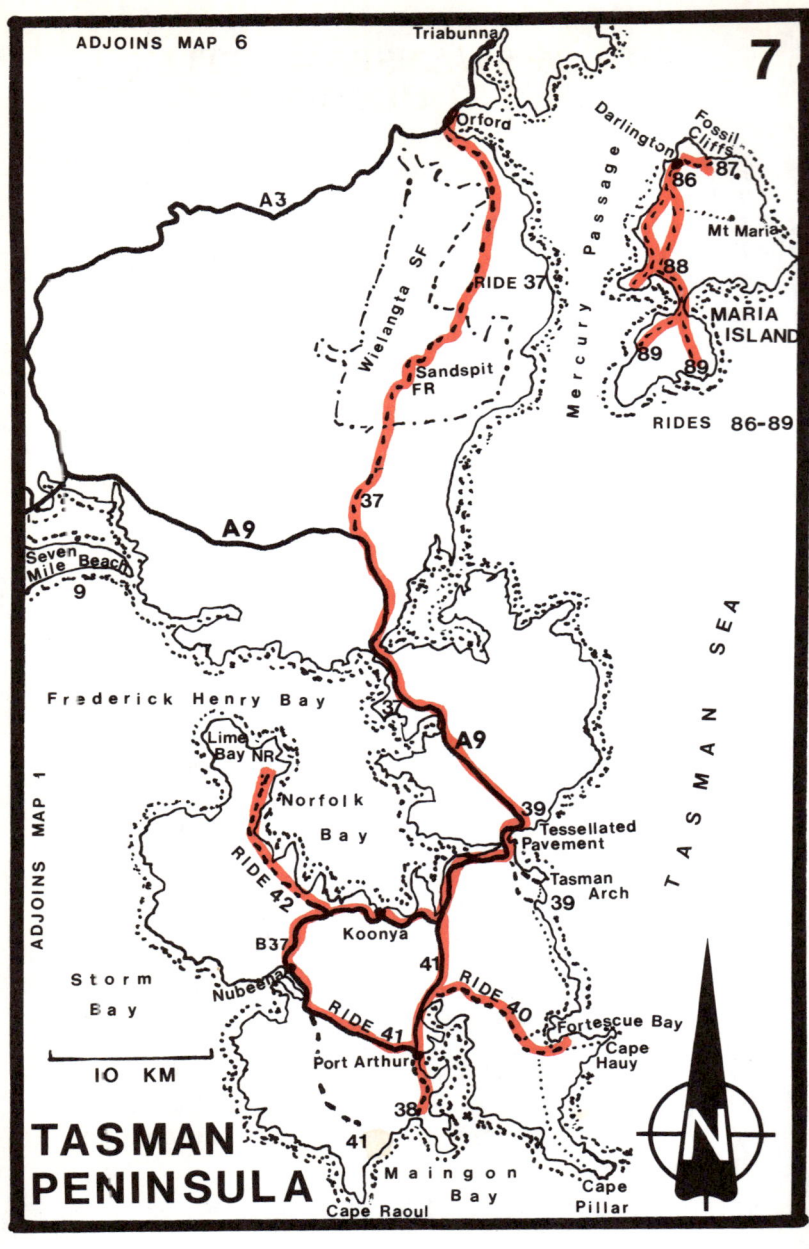

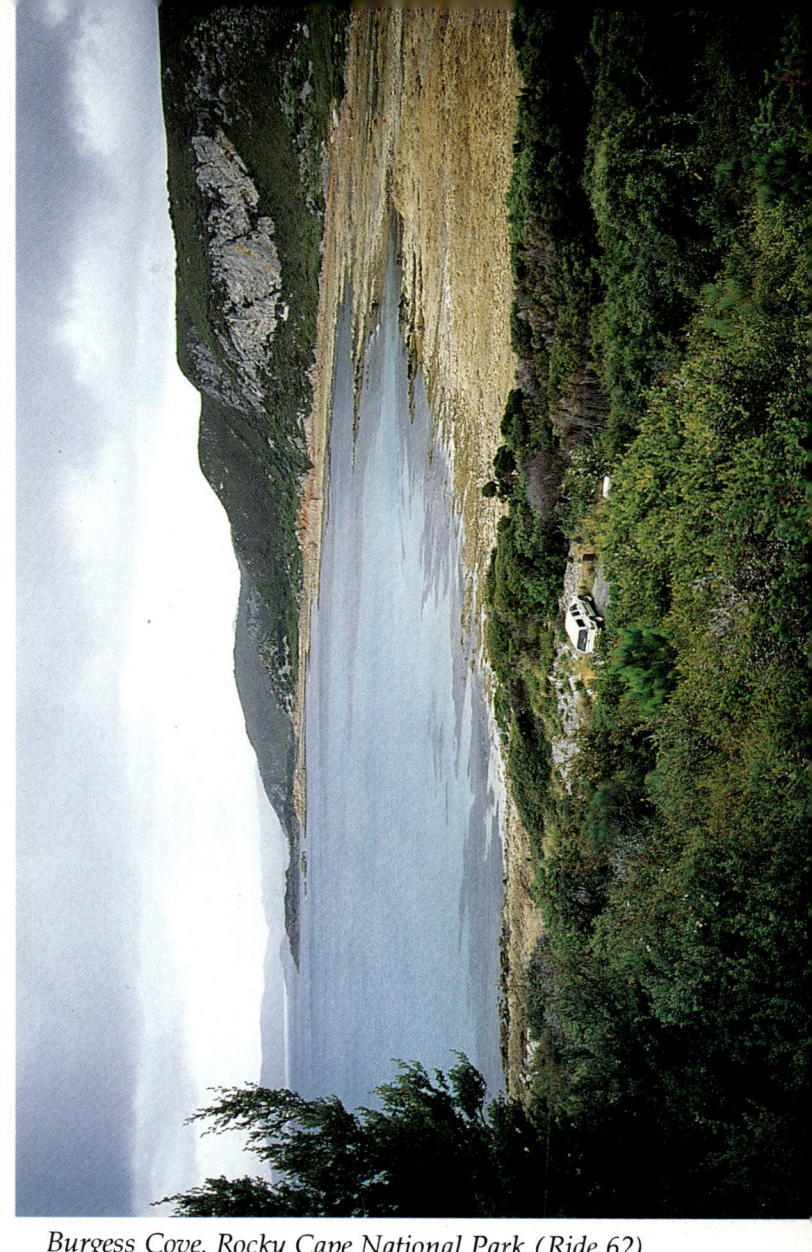

Burgess Cove, Rocky Cape National Park (Ride 62)

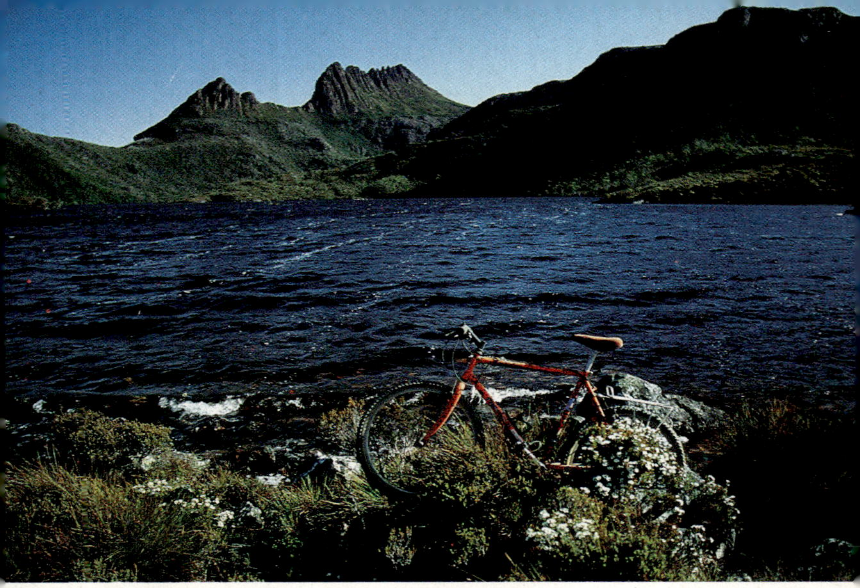

Cradle Mountain and Lake Dove (Ride 64)

Waldheim, Cradle Valley (Ride 65)

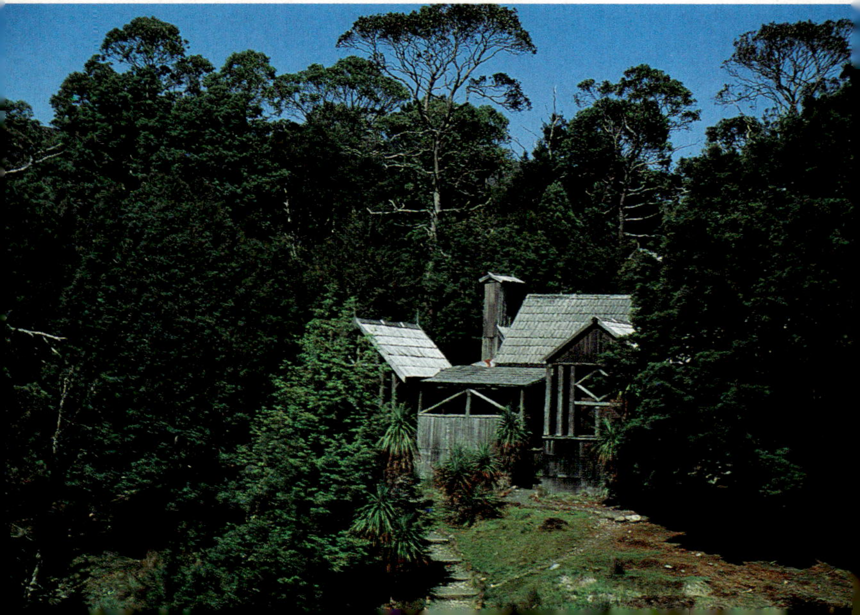

RIDE 37: WIELANGTA STATE FOREST

FROM: Triabunna
TO: Port Arthur (or reverse)
VIA: Wielangta State Forest, Sandspit Forest Reserve
LENGTH:
  Day 1: Triabunna to Sandspit Forest Reserve 32 km
  Day 2: Sandspit Forest Reserve to Port Arthur 73 km
  Total distance is 105 km
TIME: 2 days
RIDE/TRACK GRADE: 5/4
WALKING: Short rainforest walk
HEIGHT VARIATION: 480 m
TRANSPORT: Bus service to Triabunna and from Port Arthur
FACILITIES: Picnic, barbecue, shelters, toilets
MAPS: Kellevie, Sandspit, and Orford 1:25 000 topographical (See Map 6: *FREYCINET* and Map 7: *TASMAN PENINSULA*)

Those cyclists attempting a clockwise tour of Tasmania need look no further for a pleasant scenic short-cut from Triabunna to the Tasman Peninsula without having to negotiate the heavy traffic through Sorell. The Wielangta Road starts at Orford on the Tasman Highway. The road, which cost $2 million, paid for by Associated Pulp and Paper Mills, goes through the 12 650 ha Wielangta State Forest within which lies the newly developed Sandspit Forest Reserve (232 ha). The reserve is set in a rare patch of relict rainforest amid the dry tall forests that dominate the state forest since this is the driest part of Tasmania, receiving less than 100 mm rain per year. There is also a patch of 175-year-old tall blue gums. A signposted educational discovery walk winds through this patch. It takes 10 minutes.

When ready to leave continue south through forests that have been logged since 1911. Once on the Arthur Highway simply head south to Port Arthur on the scenically spectacular Tasman Peninsula. On the way are various historical monuments, unique coastal formations, and dramatic sea-cliffs. The southern headland of Pirate Bay is a typical example of the rugged nature of the eastern coastline. Ride 38 includes notes on Port Arthur.

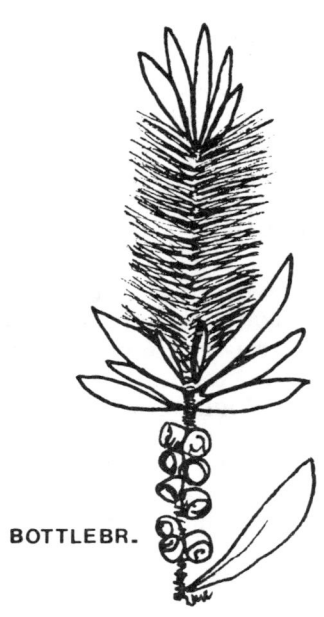

BOTTLEBR.

RIDE 38: PORT ARTHUR

FROM: Port Arthur
TO: Remarkable Cave, Devil Park
LENGTH: 36 km
TIME: 1 day
RIDE/TRACK GRADE: 4/3
WALKING: Around convict ruins
FACILITIES: Youth Hostel at Champ Street, Port Arthur
SPECIAL GEAR: None
MAPS: RACT Touring Map. (See Map 7: *TASMAN PENINSULA*)

A pleasant half-day ride can be taken to Remarkable Cave 16 km return from Port Arthur. The youth hostel is located by keeping on the Tasman Highway and turning left on the Stanley Cove Road. There are 42 beds in 7 dormitories and the cost of a bed is about $10. To get to the cave cycle up Champ St back to the Stanley Cove Road and head left. It's located to the south and signposted, with views to Cape Raoul. Another similar distanced half-day ride is to the Tasmanian Devil Park to the north. This is a wildlife park containing not only devils but eagles, pademelons, wombats, emus, peacocks, etc. Be warned: there is a hefty entrance fee.

To see the ruins from the Roseview youth hostel, just head a few hundred metres down the other end of Champ St. It is better to walk as the structures can only be explored on foot. However the youth hostel will mind the bikes.

PORT ARTHUR: HISTORY

Crossing the narrow Eaglehawk Neck it is easy to see why Port Arthur was chosen as a penal settlement. Any land escape was made impossible by stationing guards and ferocious dogs across this narrow strip of land in the last century.

These very popular ruins inspired Marcus Clarke's classic, *For the Term of his Natural Life*. 30 000 convicts passed through the prison here, making it at one stage the third largest town in Tasmania when population peaked at 2200. It was established in 1830 as a sawmilling outpost, intended for the hard-core criminals amongst the convicts.

The first 'community' consisted of 150 prisoners who clearfelled the immediate vicinity erecting huts. Across Carnarvon Bay the teenage convicts were stationed. The officers and their families, while not living in luxury, enjoyed a comfortable lifestyle.

A decade after establishment, all other convicts around Australia were sent here, and it wasn't until 1853 that transportation ceased. However, the settlement was not abandoned until 1877, during which time the model prison housed a variety of lunatics and ex-convict derelicts. Almost immediately after abandonment, tourists started visiting the buildings as myths evolved concerning past conditions. Many of the Gothic style buildings were demolished by contractors for their bricks and those surviving were damaged in the great bushfires of 1895 and 1897.

CHIEF ATTRACTIONS

1. CHURCH. The large church was co-designed in the Gothic Revival tradition by a convict named Henry Laing. It was built in 1837 and could accommodate 1200 people during the weekly services. The Chaplains included Wesleyans, Anglicans, and Catholics. It has been gradually restored over the last four decades. Location: Church St, off Jetty Rd.

2. MODEL PRISON. The architecture copied the infamous Pentonville Plan in England in 1842 where one warder could look into all cells simultaneously. In theory prisoners were supposed to be rehabilitated by solitary religious contemplation in total silence and anonymity. The building was constructed by Royal Engineers in 1848 and has also been restored. Location: off Old Safety Cove Road.

3. PENITENTIARY. This is the largest structure at Port Arthur and the first you see as you cycle along the entrance road. Four storeys high when constructed in 1844, it was claimed to be the largest building in Australia. Originally a flour-mill built on reclaimed land, it was converted to a penitentiary in 1853 to house the prisoners sent from the penal settlement on Norfolk Island. It could accommodate well over 600 convicts, as well as housing other facilities such as kitchen, blacksmith, and a foundry. A timbered walkway has been built right through the building so tourists need not touch anything. Last decade saw the completion of an extensive stabilisation program.

4. DEAD ISLAND. In the calm waters of Carnarvon Bay lies the aptly named Isle of the Dead (*Ile des Morts*) on which are 1769 graves. This is the final resting place of every convict and official who died at Port Arthur. Only 180 graves are marked: principally officials and the occasional convict. The majority, however, were buried in unmarked multiple graves. The ferry *Bundeena* allows one to visit the island on regular tours.

RIDE 39: EAST TASMAN PENINSULA

FROM: Port Arthur
TO: Tesselated Pavement, Tasman Arch
VIA: Oakwood
LENGTH: 56 km
TIME: 1 long day
RIDE/TRACK GRADE: 4/2
WALKING: Waterfall Bay
HEIGHT VARIATION: 210 m
TRANSPORT: Hobart bus service to and from Port Arthur
MAPS: RACT Touring Map. (See Map 7: *TASMAN PENINSULA*)

This ride is divided into three covering the outstanding natural and historical attractions east of the Arthur Highway with your base being the camping ground at Port Arthur. From the historic site, head north along the A9 to the Tesselated Pavement just on the northern side of Eaglehawk Neck. The short walk is largely rideable before steps lead down to the formation. A sign on the way explains their unusual formation.

It's then 9 km back to the Tasman Arch, over 50 m above the sea. Another walking track leads over the arch to a lookout over the rugged coast to the south. Also located here is the Devil's Kitchen formation and just to the north is the Blowhole. A 10 km return walking track amongst coastal heath and stunted eucalypts leads along cliffs to Waterfall Bay. It starts from the Devil's Kitchen. One can also cycle inland by returning to Penzance and following Waterfall Bay Road.

Yet another overnight walk leads north along the Tasman track. Camping is in an isolated cove at Bivouac Bay and along the way are waterfalls and lookouts.

From Penzance and Eaglehawk Neck travel west

and then south along the Arthur Highway. If this is just to be a one-day trip returning to Port Arthur head back along the A9, the day being 56 km. You will pass Australia's oldest railway track, a wooden man-powered 8 km line built in 1833 by Port Arthur Commandant O'Hara Booth.

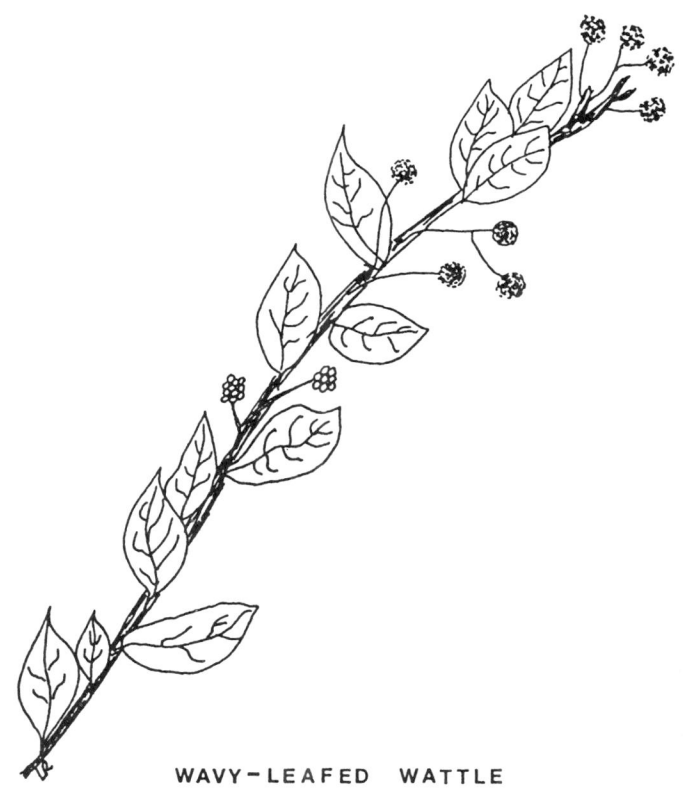

WAVY-LEAFED WATTLE

RIDE 40: FORTESCUE BAY

FROM: Port Arthur
TO: Fortescue Bay Forest Reserve
VIA: Murdunna
LENGTH: 34 km
TIME: 1-2 days (plus additional days for walking)
RIDE/TRACK GRADE: 5/4
WALKING: Tasman Coast Trail (29 km return). (Overnight camping at Canoe Bay.) Cape Hauy walking track (8.6 km return). Cape Pillar walking track (24 km return)
HEIGHT VARIATION: 250 m
TRANSPORT: Bus service from Port Arthur and to Triabunna
FACILITIES: Shelter, picnic tables, barbecues, toilets, at camping grounds in Fortescue Bay Forest Reserve
SPECIAL GEAR: None
MAPS: RACT Touring Map of Tasmania, Hippolyte 1:25 000 topographical or Storm Bay 1:100 000 topographical. (See Map 7: *TASMAN PENINSULA*)

Cycle north again and just after Oakwood turn right onto Fortescue Road to the Fortescue Bay Forest Reserve (1482 ha). It should take you about 1½–2 hours each way leaving you plenty of time for walking along the coast. The bay was originally named Dolomieu Bay by French explorer Nicolas Baudin in 1802 but was changed in 1824 after Hugh Fortescue, a British scientist and member of Parliament. At Mill Creek a sawmill once operated before WW1, employing about 20 men. It was closed in 1940. The two camping grounds are set amongst brown top stringybarks and big swamp gums.

Fishing opportunities here include tuna (yellowfin, southern blue fin, and albacore). On the way is a 4WD turnoff that leads 2.3 km down to Canoe Bay.

The 10 km (3 hour return) track to Cape Hauy gives good views over the spectacular dolerite coastline that the Tasman Peninsula is famous for. The last section is quite steep, and gives excellent views as it is raised above the rest of the area. Just off the tip are the steeply sloping Lanterns rising to 135 m and separated by needle-like spires. One feature is appropriately named the Candlestick (120 m).

Those prepared to walk a full day to Cape Pillar will be rewarded with views over the spectacular fluted columnar dolerite coastal cliffs dotted with hardy vegetation. Like Cape Hauy, the walking track to Cape Pillar ends on a pronounced peak above the cliffs commanding views not only of the water but of the Tasman Peninsula as well.

The most prominent feature is the fortress-like formation of Tasman Island. It is a stark flat plateau surrounded completely by sheer cliffs, on top of which is a lighthouse and half-a-dozen buildings including the lightkeeper's residence. Supplies can only be flown in by helicopter.

The start of the walk is about 4 km back along the Fortescue Road on the left.

This ride can be completed as an extension to Ride 39. From Eaglehawk Neck when travelling back from Waterfall Bay, turn left about 9 km from Waterfall Bay onto Pirates Road. Turn right 8 km further at Allans Road and then left onto Coronation. This meets up with Fortescue Road. It is 16 km from Allans Road to the Fortescue Bay Forest Reserve and camping grounds. From here Port Arthur is 19 km away.

RIDE 41: WEST TASMAN PENINSULA

FROM: Port Arthur [RETURN]
VIA: Premaydena, Nubeena, and Cape Raoul
LENGTH: 65 km
TIME: 1-3 days (optional overnight detour to Cape Raoul)
RIDE/TRACK GRADE: 4/3
HEIGHT VARIATION: 150 m
WALKING: Optional detour to Cape Raoul
TRANSPORT: Hobart bus service to and from Port Arthur
FACILITIES: Youth hostel, camping ground at Port Arthur
MAPS: Storm Bay 1:100 000 topo. (See Map 7: *TASMAN PENINSULA*)

Despite not being as well visited, the western half of the peninsula has just as much to offer as the east. This circuit can be completed in one day with a little bit of time left to relax at Roaring Beach.

Take Nubeena Road to Nubeena (11 km) and then Roaring Beach Road to Roaring Beach (10 km). Dam Road (B37) then takes you through idyllic country to Saltwater River. It is then less than an hour to Premaydena a further 24 km back to Port Arthur via Oakwood.

An overnight south detour from Nubeena leads to Highcroft and Stormlea to Cape Raoul. Cyclists prepared to walk 14 km (return) can view some more of the outstanding rock formations that dot the peninsula. This time it's the classic dolerite columnar extrusion where towering 'organ pipes' 165 million years old jut out of the Southern Ocean. Water is needed if staying and walking here. If one asks for permission to pass through the farm, one can then cycle down an abandoned trail to Tunnel Bay.

RIDE 42: LIME BAY

FROM: Port Arthur
TO: Lime Bay Nature Reserve (1 310 ha)
VIA: Saltwater River
LENGTH: 80 km (40 km each way)
TIME: 2 days
RIDE/TRACK GRADE: 3/3
WALKING: Around Lime Bay
HEIGHT VARIATION: 150 m
TRANSPORT: Hobart bus service to and from Port Arthur
FACILITIES: Developed swamp grounds at Lime Bay Nature Reserve and less developed site at Saltwater River
MAPS: Storm Bay 1:100 000 and Cremone 1:25 000 topographicals. (See Map 7: *TASMAN PENINSULA*)

This ride's destination is the nature reserve located on the north-western extension of the Tasman Peninsula. There are two pleasant camping grounds relatively close to the ocean. Along the way are the large convict ruins north of Saltwater River.

From Port Arthur, cycle to Premaydena via Nubeena (21 km). It's a further 19 km to the Nature Reserve via the Coal Mines Historic Site. The 45 m deep mines had their heyday in 1838 when 200 convicts kept the mine operating 24 hours a day. Buildings located here include the convicts' barracks, officers' quarters, a chapel, and bake house.

The most scenic natural area on the peninsula's tip is that at Lagoon Beach accessed by a rough 3.5 km trail from Lime Bay cutting north then west across the peninsula.

RIDE 43: SNUG TIERS

FROM: Hobart
TO: Cygnet
LENGTH:
   Day 1: Hobart to Snug 29 km
   Day 2: Snug to Cygnet 37 km
   Total distance is 66 km
TIME: 2 days
RIDE/TRACK GRADE: 8/6
HEIGHT VARIATION: 725 m
WALKING: None
FACILITIES: Youth hostel at Cygnet
SPECIAL GEAR: None
MAPS: Cygnet 1:25 000 topographical or D'Entrecasteaux 1:100 000 topographical. (See Map 1: *DERWENT* and Map 8: *SOUTH COAST & BRUNY ISLAND*)

Like the Mt. Wellington Range, this ride offers good remote mountain bike riding opportunities relatively close to Hobart.

Take the Channel Highway to Margate via Kingston. One can camp at the Snug Caravan Park. The next day head north 6 km again to Margate and then left onto the Van Morey Road up onto the Margate and Snug Plains levelling out at about 700 m amidst swamp marches dominated by Grey Mountain at 831 m. We were suddenly in the clouds here after leaving the sunny D'Entrecasteaux Channel. After a very steep descent on the other side, Slab Road then takes you to Cygnet. Be careful to avoid polluting the water on the plateau as it is the catchment area for the local population's drinking water.

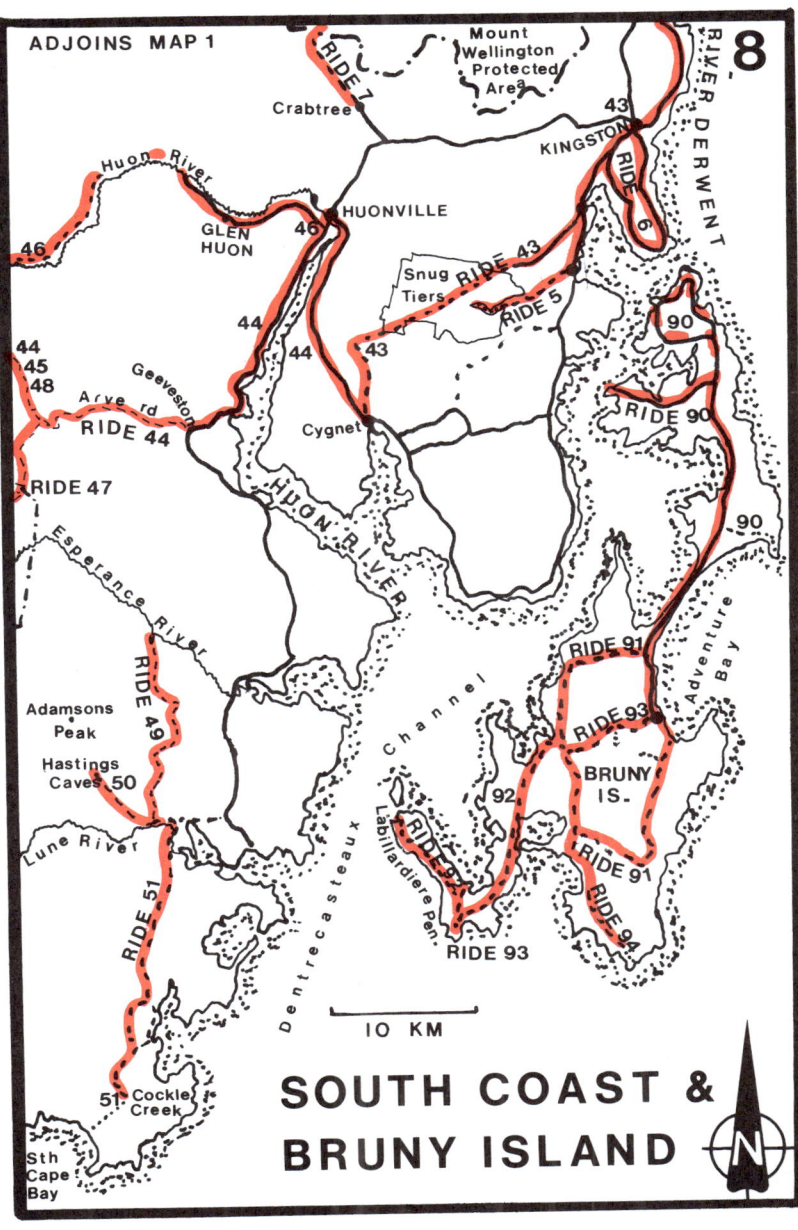

SOUTH COAST & BRUNY ISLAND

RIDE 44: HUON VALLEY

FROM: Cygnet
TO: Geeveston
VIA: Huonville, Tahune Forest Reserve
LENGTH:
   Day 1: Cygnet to Port Huon 35 km
   Day 2: Port Huon to Tahune Forest Reserve 35 km
   Day 3: Tahune Forest Reserve to Geeveston 29 km
   Total distance is 99 km
TIME: 3 days (plus extra days for exploration)
RIDE/TRACK GRADE: 5/5
HEIGHT VARIATION: 200 m
TRANSPORT: Own transport to start and from end
FACILITIES: Shelter, picnic tables, barbecues, toilets, wood, official camp ground.
SPECIAL GEAR: Self-sufficiency
MAPS: Glen Huon, Geeveston, Picton 1:25 000 topographical. (See Map 8: *SOUTH COAST & BRUNY ISLAND* and Map 1: *DERWENT*)

The most popular and developed picnic and camping area in the south-coast hinterland is the Tahune River Forest Reserve (102 ha) located on the mid-Huon River. Although this route is detailed as an extension of the previous ride, access to the reserve is shorter direct from Huonville or Geeveston.

Cycle the 19 km from Cygnet to Huonville. Take the Huon Highway south through apple orchards to Port Huon where one can camp. Then follow the signs from Geeveston past the Hartz Mountain National Park turnoff along the C632 and C631 down to the forest reserve. The vegetation here included millennia old huon pines and 500-year-old celery-top pines. Tahune is what the Aborigines called the Huon. The river was discovered by the

French Admiral d'Entrecasteaux in 1792 who named it after his second in command, Huon deKermadec.

It was in the Huon Valley that the Huon Pine *(Dacrydium franklinii)* was first discovered just after settlement and was studied scientifically in 1818 by Allan Cunningham. Despite attempts by the CSIRO to synthesise its properties, it remains one of the most unique timbers in the world. Needing 500 years to mature, a substance in its aroma resists worms that cause rot, making it the ideal ship-building timber, and some century-old vessels can still be seen on the Derwent. The first development of the west coast occurred due to pine extracters led by James Kelly and Thomas Birch as resources in the Huon became quickly exhausted.

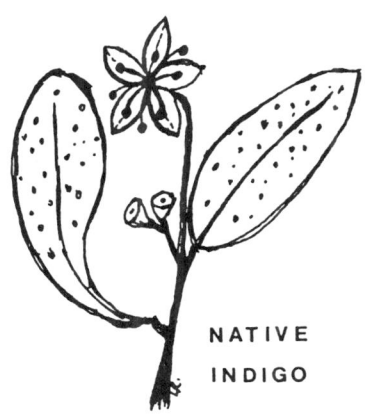

NATIVE INDIGO

One can also return direct to Huonville by means of the Arve Lidgerwood, Bermuda, and Glen Huon Roads. This involves significant height climbs as the Scotts Divide has to be negotiated. Total distance is about 60 km.

191

RIDE 45: REUBEN FALLS

FROM: Tahune Forest Reserve
TO: South Weld Forest Reserve
VIA: South Weld Road
LENGTH: 30 km (15 km each way)
TIME: 1 day
RIDE/TRACK GRADE: 5/4
WALKING: Short walk to see falls
HEIGHT VARIATION: 350 m
TRANSPORT: Own transport to Tahune Forest Reserve *or* as extension to Ride 44
FACILITIES: Camp ground at Tahune Forest Reserve. Usual rest area facilities
SPECIAL GEAR: Tripod for photographing falls
MAPS: Picton and Weld 1:25 000 topographical. (See Map 8: *SOUTH COAST & BRUNY ISLAND* and Map 1: *DERWENT*)

Those wishing to extend the previous ride can continue from the Tahune Forest Reserve crossing the Huon and climbing gradually up 350 m to the South Weld Forest Reserve (46 ha). Here a short walking track leads to the very impressive Reuben Falls located about 170 m above the Weld River.

All throughout the day you will be touring the tallest hardwoods in the world. Some of the early pioneer loggers here claim they removed trees *taller* than the 112 m record set by a tree in the Californian redwood forest, but no-one will ever know. It was by logging the forests of the south coast that Australia surpassed the United States in becoming the largest exporter of woodchips in the world, primarily supplying Japanese mills.

RIDE 46: WELD RIVER

FROM: Huonville
TO: Fletchers Eddy
VIA: Weld Road
LENGTH: 52 km (26 km each way)
TIME: 2 days
RIDE/TRACK GRADE: 5/7
WALKING: Short walks through rainforest on Huon River
HEIGHT VARIATION: 200 m
TRANSPORT: Own to and from Huonville
FACILITIES: None
SPECIAL GEAR: Complete self-sufficiency
MAPS: Weld, Glen, Huon 1:25 000 topographical. (See Map 8: *SOUTH COAST & BRUNY ISLAND* and Map 1: *DERWENT*)

The tallest forests in the southern hemisphere grow in the Weld and Picton River valleys, dominated by the mountain ash (up to 100 m), the largest flowering plant in the world.

This ride follows an old four-wheel-drive track to the northern bank of the river where flat banks offer isolated camping set in a tremendous wilderness atmosphere miles from any sign of civilisation. Clean drinking water flows permanently, much purer than the world's major cities' official stores.

From Huonville head west along the C619 to Judbury 15 km upstream. Follow the northern bank west turning left at Russell Rd, left at Denson Rd, and left onto Weld Rd. Follow this through dense green bracken to the end at a prominent bend in the Weld marked as Fletchers Eddy (a name for the rapids). The river was named after F. A. Weld, Tasmanian Governor (1875-1880).

RIDE 47: HARTZ MOUNTAINS

FROM: Geeveston
TO: Hartz Mountains National Park
VIA: Arve River
LENGTH: 50 km (25 km each way)
TIME: 2-3 days
RIDE/TRACK GRADE: 7/4
WALKING: Numerous
HEIGHT VARIATION: 840 m
TRANSPORT: Own to and from Geeveston
FACILITIES: Picnic facilities
SPECIAL GEAR: Warm clothing wind & waterproof
MAPS: Hartz Mountains Day Walk Map and RACT Touring Map of Tasmania. (See Map 8: *SOUTH COAST & BRUNY ISLAND*)

The Hartz Mountains were advertised in the *Mercury* on 20 September 1938 as a tourist attraction that awaits development.

> *Looking to the south-west from Geeveston . . . one sees a solitary mountain peak—the Hartz . . . In lavishness of scenic attraction the Hartz makes a particular appeal to tourists, with its extensive and beautiful stretches of plain, its rugged escarpments, and hidden lakes. At present . . . it is accessible only by pack-horse or by foot. It is an area calling loudly for development*

The area was proclaimed a year later but since there was no development apart from forestry concessions this led to revocations in 1943, 1952, 1958 and 1979 totalling over 4000 ha. Today the cyclist willing to endure a steep kilometre climb through rainforest to the range can enjoy this interesting area.

Signposts from Geeveston lead the way via the C632. Along the way is a picnic area on the Arve

River. Originating from the slopes of the range, this river was named by Surveyor Frankland after a river flowing through France and Switzerland.

At the top of the escarpment is another picnic area with shelter and toilets opposite Waratah Lookout and Keoghs Falls. One can use this as a rest area.

The next day is flat cycling across the upper Arve River and past a closed walking trail to Lake Osbourne and Lake Perry. At the car-park at the end are excellent views over the south-west. A four hour walk leads to the top of Hartz Peak (1 254 m) for even better panoramic views to the south-west including Precipitous Bluff, the mighty Federation Peak, and big Mt. Anne. In the foreground is Lake Hartz and the vast Picton River valley.

DATA TABLE: Hartz Mountains National Park

Size: 6470 ha

Enactment: Scenic Reserve 1939
    National Park 1971
    Revocations 1979

Animals: Nocturnal mammals, echidnas, wallabies, cuckoos

Plants: Main community is alpine moorland with slopes supporting dense rainforest

Attractions: Hartz Peak (1254 m) and glacial lakes

Camping: No official sites

District Office: (002) 98-3198

RIDE 48: PICTON RIVER

FROM: Geeveston
TO: Farmhouse Creek [RETURN]
VIA: Tahune Forest Reserve
LENGTH:
    Day 1: Geeveston to Tahune Forest Reserve
       30 km
    Day 2: Tahune Forest Reserve to Farmhouse
       Creek 25 km
    Day 3: Farmhouse Creek to Tahune Forest
       Reserve 25 km
    Day 4: Tahune Forest Reserve to Geeveston
       30 km
    Total distance is 110 km
TIME: 4–5 days
RIDE/TRACK GRADE: 6/6
WALKING: Short walks through rainforest on Huon River
HEIGHT VARIATION: 500 m
TRANSPORT: Own to and from Geeveston
FACILITIES: Clearing at Farmhouse Creek. Shelters, picnic tables, BBQs, toilets, camp ground at Tahune Forest Reserve.
SPECIAL GEAR: Wide knobbly tires for potentially muddy conditions, complete self-sufficiency
MAPS: Geeveston, Picton, Burgess 1:25 000 topographicals (See Map 8: *SOUTH COAST & BRUNY ISLAND*)

The south coast hinterland contains some of the most attractive forests in Australia. Cyclists can access some particularly impressive stands along logging roads following the Picton River upstream from its confluence with the Huon.

For track-notes, consult Ride 44's descriptions to the Tahune Forest Reserve.

The lower Picton River was bridged in 1977 which facilitated forestry operations westward along the southern bank of the Huon River and up the Picton Valley. A popular walking track starts here leading to the Western Arthurs, Federation Peak, Scotts Peak Dam, and the Port Davey Track.

Camp at the Tahune Forest Reserve on the first night and then backtrack slightly turning right onto Picton Road. Follow this upstream amidst extensive logging operations to the confluence with Farmhouse Creek 25 km from the turnoff. On the way you cross the river via an old bridge. A track keeps left leading to some rapids at the base of the Hartz Mountain range. Much of the vegetation here is young regrowth less than a decade old that has been seeded from the air. The road then diverges away from the river and several kilometres later is a major turnoff leading up the Cook Creek valley in the South Picton Range. Cross Cook Creek, heading gradually back to the Picton River at the confluence with Farmhouse Creek. Choose any suitable clearing for a campsite. Water here is pure and drinkable. Firewood, too, is plentiful, although often wet.

Logging operations of the majestic *eucalypt regans* here have been particularly controversial. Clear felling has resulted in a gross wastage of wood and erosion and the construction of hundreds of kilometres of trails has encroached upon the great south-west wilderness so much that vistas from spectacular summits such as Federation Peak now include visual scars from forestry operations. The confluence of Farmhouse Creek and the Picton River valley was the scene of protests by conservationists led by Dr Bob Brown in early March 1986 against Risbys Forest Industries sawmillers in relation to the many rainforest trees left rotting on the ground or burnt. The confrontation made national headlines when they turned violent. The Forestry Commission claimed that the trees were unusable, while conservationists countered that the waste was putting pressure on opening up other protected areas. To the west, where Farmhouse Creek begins, a stream disappears underground in Judds Cavern, a strange phenomenon peculiar to karst areas.

The Picton River was named by Surveyor-General George Frankland after the military leader Sir Thomas Picton (1758-1815).

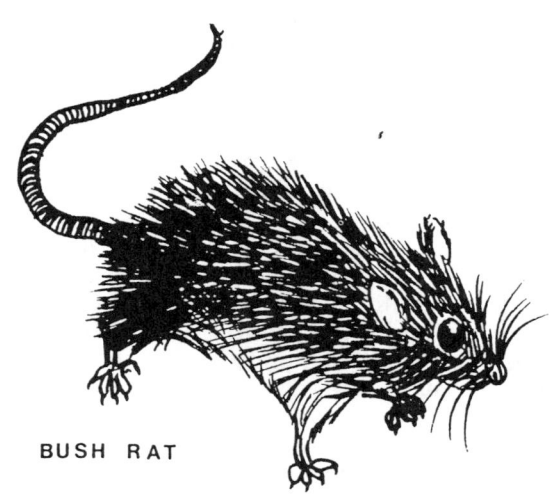

BUSH RAT

RIDE 49: ESPERANCE RIVER

FROM: Lune River Youth Hostel
TO: Esperance River Forest Reserve [RETURN]
VIA: Thermal Pool
LENGTH: 68 km (34 km each day)
TIME: 2 days
RIDE/TRACK GRADE: 4/4
WALKING: None
HEIGHT VARIATION: 450 m
TRANSPORT: Wilderness Transport Network to and from Lune River.
FACILITIES: Camp ground on Esperance River
MAPS: Leprena, Hastings, Raminea, Waterloo 1:25 000 topos are essential. (See Map 8: *SOUTH COAST & BRUNY ISLAND*)

The south coast hinterland contains some of the most attractive forests in Australia. Cyclists doing this ride will visit a particularly diverse mixed forest in the picturesque Esperance River Forest Reserve (150 ha). An arboretum is being developed by the Forestry Commission where species are on display that existed during the Gondwanaland period of about 150 million years ago when all southern continents were joined.

Head north across the Lune River (named after the Aboriginal word for woman). The prominent conical peak in the background on the left is Adamsons Peak (1226 m). Named by Captain John Hayes in 1794, it has been likened to Mt. Fujiyama in Japan. A rough walking track leads up to its summit.

Turn left at Hastings Road and then onto Tughanah Road, Creekton Road crossing Halfway Creek. Two successive left turns gets you onto Rivulet Road leading down to meet with the Esperance River Road. Cross the river and continue upstream for 8 km rising to an altitude of 460 m when entering the forest reserve.

199

RIDE 50: HASTINGS CAVES

FROM: Lune River Youth Hostel
TO: Hastings Cave and Thermal Pool [RETURN]
LENGTH: 22 km (11 km each way)
TIME: 1 easy day
RIDE/TRACK GRADE: 2/3
WALKING: Cave tour
HEIGHT VARIATION: 180 m
TRANSPORT: Wilderness Transport Network to and from Lune River
FACILITIES: General catering for tourists
MAPS: RACT Touring Map. (See Map 8: *SOUTH COAST & BRUNY ISLAND*)

Tasmanian caves are unarguably the best in Australia. The island state has older, more decorated, deeper, and longer caves than any on the mainland. The Khan in the Xanadu Chamber of the Kubla Khan Cave near King Solomon's Cave (Ride 60) is the largest stalagmite in the world. The Exit Cave system south of Hastings Caves, with its concentration of glow-worms, has been charted for 19 km underground.

Anyway, getting back to Hastings. While the others mentioned above are closed to the general public, with permits needed, Newdegate at Hastings is a simple tourist cave with some truly beautiful decorations. The caves were discovered in 1917 and reserved two years later, being subsequently developed for tourists in the 1930s and they now attract tens of thousands of visitors a year. The formations are made of dolomite which is calcium carbonate (limestone) with a high magnesium content. This adds a lot of colour variation and makes it more soluble.

The Thermal Pool entrance fee is $2.00. Cave tours run several times a day usually at a quarter past the hour. Phone (002) 98-3198 for details.

Endemic to Newdegate is a gigantic spider known as *Hickmania troglotytes* which has adapted solely to underground conditions. But they are very shy and you'd be very (un)lucky to see one.

Access is via C635 and is well signposted. Return by the same route.

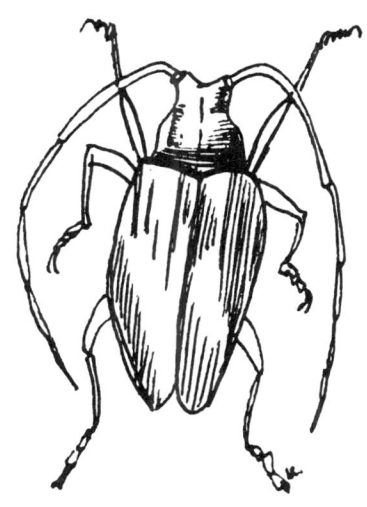

RIDE 51: COCKLE CREEK

FROM: Lune River Youth Hostel
TO: D'Entrecasteaux Watering Place, Recherche Bay State Recreation Area
VIA: Catamaran
LENGTH: 42 km (21 km each way)
TIME: 1-2 days (3 days including walking to South-Cape Bay)
RIDE/TRACK GRADE: 4/4
WALKING: 16 km boarded South-Coast Track to South-Cape Bay
HEIGHT VARIATION: 110 m
TRANSPORT: Wilderness Transport Network to/from Lune River. (The service also operates from Cockle Creek)
FACILITIES: Developed camping ground including phone at Recherche Bay State Recreation Area
SPECIAL GEAR: Self-sufficiency
MAPS: Recherche 1:25 000 or South-East Cape 1:100 000 (available with South-West Cape 1:100 000 for $8.58). See Map 8: *SOUTH COAST & BRUNY ISLAND*

To get to the most southerly place accessible by bike in Australia take the C636 south. It's 10 km to the D'Entrecasteaux River and a further 11 km to Cockle Creek. Located here are some exquisite sheltered beaches that rival that of Wineglass Bay.

The sawmill that operated here in the nineteenth century burnt down. Felling was an art. Two axemen would first cut the platform whereby planks could be inserted so the cross-sawers could get up to a more practically sized trunk. The wedge and main cut would be sawn and when the first creaking of wood occurred, they had to be very agile in order to jump off for cover before the tower crashed down. There were countless accidents where falling trunks kicked back killing men instantly. The trees were then hauled by steam engines across carefully constructed tracks to the mill where they were trimmed, barked, and sorted for quality. Lubrication for the bearings in the sawmills was mutton bird oil, extracted from rookeries along the coast and on the many islands off the eastern and northern coasts.

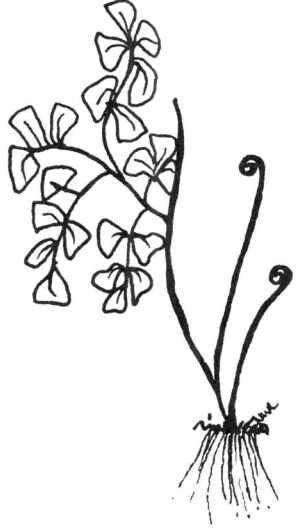

MAIDENHAIR FERN

A new boarded track leads 8 km from the Cockle Creek camping ground to South Cape Bay. A steady balance is needed to cycle this flat open track to the long clean beach, but unfortunately pushbikes are not permitted, even though there exists plenty of warning to walkers due to the low stunted heath. This is the start of the marathon South Coast walking track to Port Davey and Lake Pedder.

The second of a three day trip here can be spent on the most southerly beach in Australia. Also here is the D'Entrecasteaux Watering Place Historical Site opposite Evoralls Point.

203

OTHER RIDES

The south-east represents perhaps the most scenic area in Tasmania for intermediate and advanced mountain cycling, if not the best in Australia. The combination of state forests containing some of the tallest and oldest trees in the world and interlaced with many trails that lead from the coast to the alpine mountain ranges is almost irresistible. From Judbury on the Huon River, trails lead up the Russell River valley to the Snowy Range. Fortunately TASMAP have recently produced a complete 1:25 000 topographical series for the area showing the vast majority of logging roads and minor trails. This area also allows the walker to access wild places such as Federation Peak, described as Australia's most spectacular mountain.

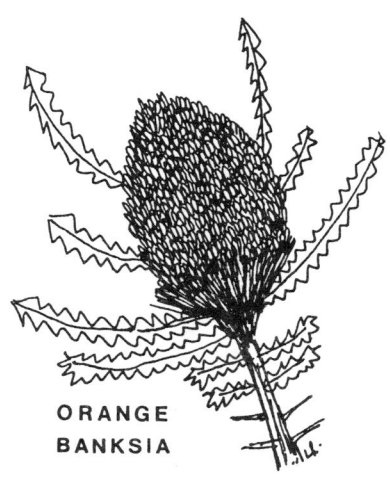

ORANGE
BANKSIA

7

THE CENTRAL HIGHLANDS
(Land of Three Thousand Lakes)

Actually over 4000 lakes exist on the 'Roof of Tasmania' but this chapter details rides to only a selection of the major ones, their primary attraction being trout fishing, especially fly fishing.

The plateau was ice-covered in Pleistocene times and the lakes were formed by glaciers eroding depressions in the hard Jurassic dolerite surface rock or deposited morainic material that dammed run-off of melted ice and snow. The deepest of these is Lake St. Clair formed by massive glacial excavation activity that gouged a 161 m depression. Other lakes, such as Great Lake, on the plateau have been enlarged artificially, while others, for example Lake King William, are entirely man-made.

Fish include brown trout *(Salmo trutta)*, rainbow trout *(Salmo gairdneri)*, and brook trout *(Salvelinus fontinalis)*, introduced from English ova in the 1860s. These lakes were used as a source to stock mainland Australia and New Zealand.

The highlands are the source of all of Tasmania's major rivers: Arthur, Tamar, Derwent, Gordon, Franklin, Pieman, Forth, and Mersey. The plateau was used last century for grazing and the Aboriginals were quickly dispersed. It has now been radically altered by erosion due to over grazing, rabbits, burning, hydro-electric developments, weeds, roads, and the introduction of exotic fish.

FISHING

People travel from around the world to fish in Tasmania's Central Plateau lakes. The abundant brown trout is renowned for its fighting qualities and can grow up to 6 kilograms and can be caught using dry and wet flies as well as spinning or baiting.

A licence is required (about 30 000 are issued yearly), the price depending on the duration. These can be purchased at service stations, sports stores, and police stations. You'll then be given information on what type of gear is permissible. Certain lakes are reserved for only certain types of fishing, such as artificial lures or fly fishing. The fisherman must be aware of legal minimum sizes, bag limits, bait regulations, and protected species.

For trout (brown, rainbow, and brook), the minimum size permitted is 22 cm.

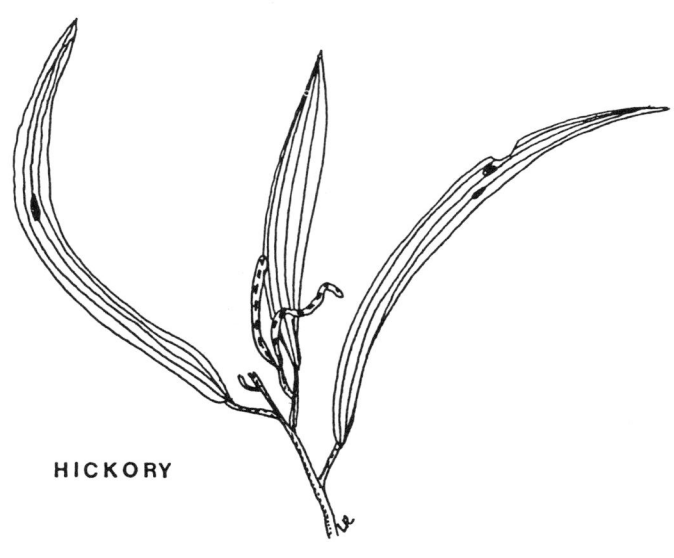

HICKORY

RIDE 52: LAKE SORELL

FROM: Oatlands
TO: Lake Sorell [RETURN]
VIA: C527
LENGTH: 65 km (Silver Plains a further 18 km return)
TIME: 3 days (optional days for fishing)
RIDE/TRACK GRADE: 7/3–4
HEIGHT VARIATION: 800 m
TRANSPORT: Redline coach service to and from Oatlands
FACILITIES: Youth hostel at Oatlands. Camping grounds at Dago Point, Interlaken, and Silver Plains as well as rough spots all around lake shore
SPECIAL GEAR: Fishing, cold weather gear
MAPS: Central Tasmania 1:150 000. (See Map 9: *CENTRAL PLATEAU*)

There are many access routes to the Central Plateau (98 000 ha). This ride climbs the most easterly one via the C527. Lake Sorell (55 km²) is at 823 m altitude and ranks in the top three trout fishing lakes in Tasmania. Fishing is by artificial lure only. Extensive shallow marshes provide good feeding grounds and catches are frequent averaging 1–2 kg.

The starting point is Oatlands (pop. 2000), a regular stopping point for Hobart-Launceston coach services. It was once a notorious refuge for bushrangers and serves as the district centre for cattle and sheep grazing. Bordering Oatlands on the eastern perimeter is Lake Dulverton, which easily dries up when rainfall fails to make the average of 560 mm. An interesting tourist attraction is the historic Carrington Flour Mill (1937).

Head east along the C527 rising steadily up to Interlaken which separates Lake Crescent from Lake Sorell. Here you can make your choice as

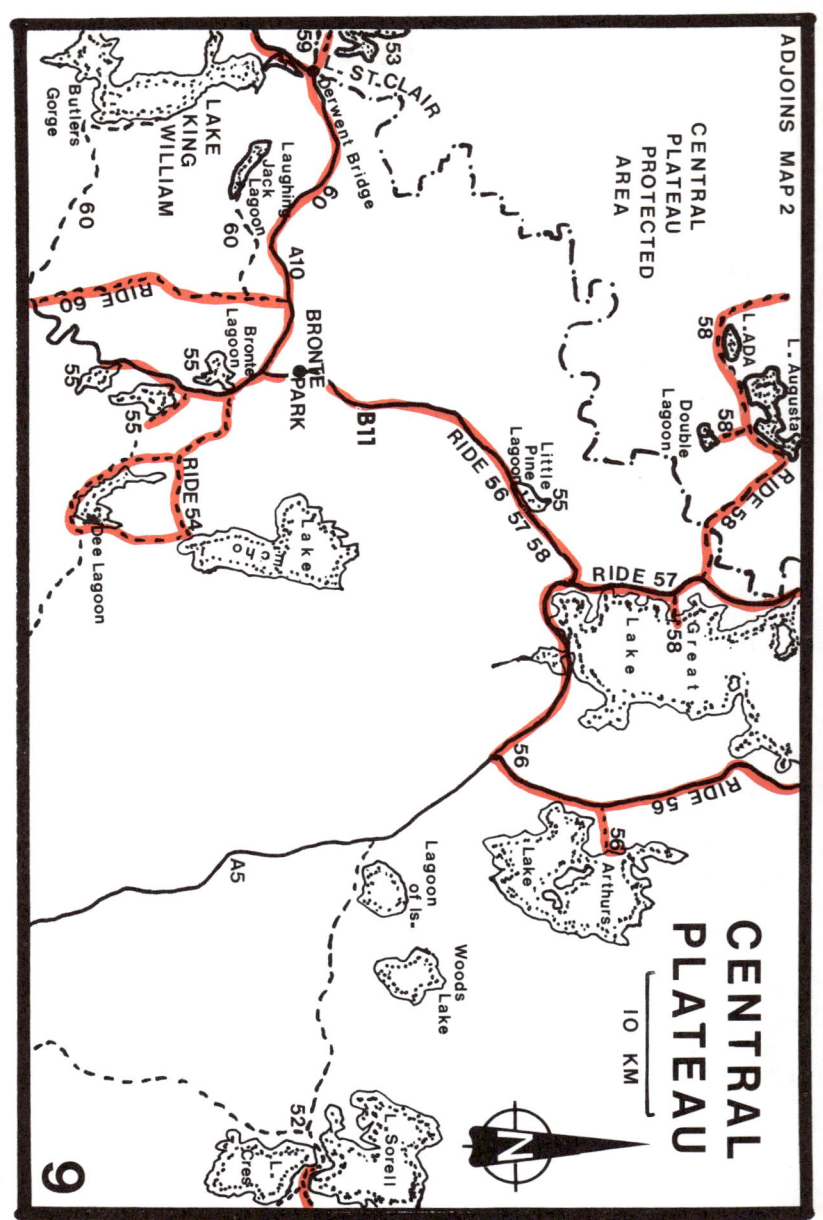

CENTRAL
PLATEAU
PROTECTED
AREA

Butlers
Gorge

LAKE
KING
WILLIAM

ST. CLAIR

Derwent Bridge

Laughing
Jack
Lagoon

60

60

410

RIDE 60

55

55

Bronte
Lagoon

BRONTE
PARK

B11

RIDE 54

Dee Lagoon

Echo
Lake

L. ADA

Double
Lagoon

L. Augusta

RIDE 58

58

58

58

Little
Pine
Lagoon

55

RIDE 56
57 58

RIDE 57

58

Great
Lake

56

RIDE 56

A5

Lagoon
of Is-

Lake
Arthurs

56

Woods
Lake

521

L.
Crest

L. Sorell

CENTRAL
PLATEAU

10 KM

N

9

to where to camp. Consult the locals as to where fish are biting. Many potential rough spots for camping can become very windy due to exposure. Please note artificial lures only are permitted.

This ride can also be done from Derwent Bridge or Bronte Park. Lake Sorell is about 45 km from Arthurs Lake. In addition a 122 km circumnavigation of the lake from Oatlands can be done involving some rough muddy trails. Fish are protected in the inflowing watercourses, especially within the boundaries of the Lake Sorell Wildlife Sanctuary.

RIDE 53: LAKE ST. CLAIR

FROM: Derwent Bridge
TO: Cynthia Bay [RETURN]
LENGTH: 16 km
TIME: 1 day (extra days for walking)
RIDE/TRACK GRADE: 2/3
WALKING: Curvier River, Lake Marion, The Acropolis, Mersey River falls, Mt. Ossa, Mt. Pelion East, Shadow Lake
HEIGHT VARIATION: Cycling 20 m, walking up to 880 m
TRANSPORT: Redline coach service to and from Derwent Bridge
FACILITIES: Well developed camp ground at Cynthia Bay
SPECIAL GEAR: Walking gear
MAPS: Cradle Mountain-Lake St. Clair National Park 1:100 000 (See Map 9: *CENTRAL PLATEAU*)

Discovered in 1826 by Jorgen Jorgenson, and named by Surveyor-General George Frankland in 1835 after the St. Clair family of Loch Lomond, Lake St. Clair (737 m) is the source of the Derwent River and the deepest lake in Australia at 161 m (its Aboriginal name is *Leeawuleena* meaning 'The Sleeping water'). Mt. Olympus (1430 m) dominates the 17 km western shore on which the walking track to Cradle Mountain starts. The first of the many features along the way is the mighty Du Cane Range.

From the drop-off point at Derwent Bridge, simply head north along the C193 (built in 1934) to boat launching area, rangers' station, and camping area where a number of walking tracks start from. A small detour to the pumping station and dam exists on the right. This was built in 1937 and raised the height of the lake by 3 m.

A shuttle boat leaves from the jetty near the

camping area to Narcissus Bay on the very northern shore of the lake saving a considerable distance for walkers heading to the Du Cane Range. An 11 km walk also leads to Shadow Lake.

DATA TABLE: Cradle Mountain-Lake St. Clair National Park (Southern Section)

Size: 131 915 ha
Enactment: 1947
Aboriginal Evidence: Vegetation affected by regular burning
Animals: Bennett's wallaby, platypus, echidna
Plants: Myrtle beech, mountain ash, 27% montane grass
Attractions: Lake St. Clair, Shadow Lake, The Acropolis, Du Cane Range, Pelion area
Camping: Well developed camp ground at Cynthia Bay
District Office: (002) 89-1115

RIDE 54: LAKE ECHO

FROM: Bronte Park
TO: Lake Echo [RETURN]
LENGTH: 54 km (27 km each way)
TIME: 2 days
RIDE/TRACK GRADE: 4/4
HEIGHT VARIATION: 120 m
TRANSPORT: Wilderness Transport Network to/from Bronte Park. Coach services to Derwent Bridge
FACILITIES: Bronte Park Highland Village hostel has 52 bunks in 9 rooms.
SPECIAL GEAR: Fishing, cold-weather clothing
MAPS: Central Tasmania 1:150 000. (See Map 9: *CENTRAL PLATEAU*)

Fishing restrictions are very relaxed at Lake Echo (846 m) and one can use any type of lure one wishes. This was the first lake stocked in Tasmania. All the trout types are available in addition to English perch.

From Bronte Park head down to the Lyell Highway and south for 2 km to the Echo Dam turnoff (C173). The best camping areas are around the southern areas. Rougher spots are available along the eastern shore.

RIDE 55: SOUTHERN LAKES TOURS

FROM: Derwent Bridge
TO: Little Pine Lagoon
VIA: London Lakes, Bradys Lake, Lake Binney, Dee Lagoon
LENGTH: See below
TIME: 1 day each (extra days for fishing)
RIDE/TRACK GRADE: 5/4
HEIGHT VARIATION: 300 m
TRANSPORT: Redline coach service to Derwent Bridge. Wilderness Transport Network to/from Lake St. Clair
FACILITIES: Bronte Park Highland Village hostel has 52 bunks in 9 rooms. Basic camping grounds on lake shores
SPECIAL GEAR: Camping for self-sufficiency, fishing
MAPS: Central Tasmania 1:150 000. (See Map 9: *CENTRAL PLATEAU*)

Those not wishing to travel to remote wild places to fish can tour around the southern lakes, all relatively close to Bronte Park.
   On offer are:

Lake	Distance from Bronte Park	Altitude
1. Bronte Lagoon	9 km	666 m
2. Bradys Lake	15 km	651 m
3. Lake Binney	18 km	651 m
4. Dee Lagoon	25 km	656 m
5. Tungatinah Lagoon	21 km	651 m
6. Big Jim Lake	17 km	674 m
7. Lake Samuel	14 km	669 m
8. Pine Tier Lagoon	14 km	671 m
9. Little Pine Lagoon	20 km	1007 m

Little Pine Lagoon is Tasmania's most famous fly fishing water. Located two hours ride north of Bronte Park via the B11, there are several camping areas around the shore. Across the shallow lake are usually dozens of fishermen here standing waist deep for hours in the cold water. Firewood is scarce. Please note the other lagoons and lakes are reserved only for artificial lures.

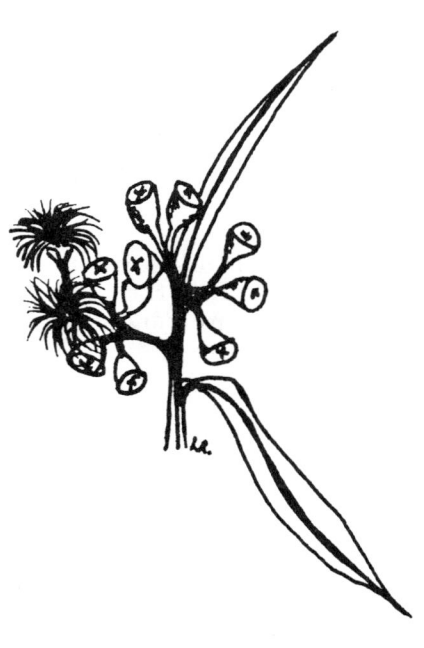

RIDE 56: ARTHURS LAKE

FROM: Bronte Park
TO: Launceston
VIA: Arthurs Lake [RETURN]
LENGTH:
    Day 1: Bronte Park to Miena 33 km
    Day 2: Miena to Cowpaddock Bay 38 km
    Day 3: Cowpaddock Bay to Mother Lords Plains
        33 km
    Day 4: Mother Lords Plains to Bracknell 32 km
    Day 5: Bracknell to Launceston 40 km
    Total distance is 176 km
TIME: 5–7 days
RIDE/TRACK GRADE: 6/4
HEIGHT VARIATION: 220 m
TRANSPORT: Wilderness Transport Network to Bronte Park
FACILITIES: Bronte Park Highland Village hostel has 52 bunks in 9 rooms. Supplies, bait and tackle at Miena, Great Lake
SPECIAL GEAR: Fishing, self-sufficiency, cold-weather clothes
MAPS: Central Tasmania 1:150 000. (See Map 9: *CENTRAL PLATEAU*)

An alternative fishing spot is Arthurs Lake (952 m). Average winter temperatures here are about 2 degrees while in summer it can get up to a sizzling 12. Follow the B11 to Miena where accommodation is available either in camping form or sheltered cabins. Next day head east along the A5 then take the Poatina Highway (B51) to the turnoff to Jonah Bay. Several camping areas exist around this part of the lake all the way north to Cowpaddock Bay.

When you've caught every fish and are ready to move on, head out to the Poatina Highway again and north to the second boat-launching ramp on the left. About 2 km past this turnoff an old track heads left following the picturesque northern part of the lake. This section is completely undeveloped and not frequently visited. The track can get muddy here after rain. Select a place on the shore at Sandbanks Bay for your next fishing venue.

Once again, when ready to move on take the hair-raising pass down using a trail that branches off to the left where the Protected Area boundary is crossed. Make your way via Blackwood Creek to the camping area outside of Bracknell on the Liffey River. Next day simply head into the hustle and bustle of Launceston, a seemingly different world from the serenity of the cold highland lakes.

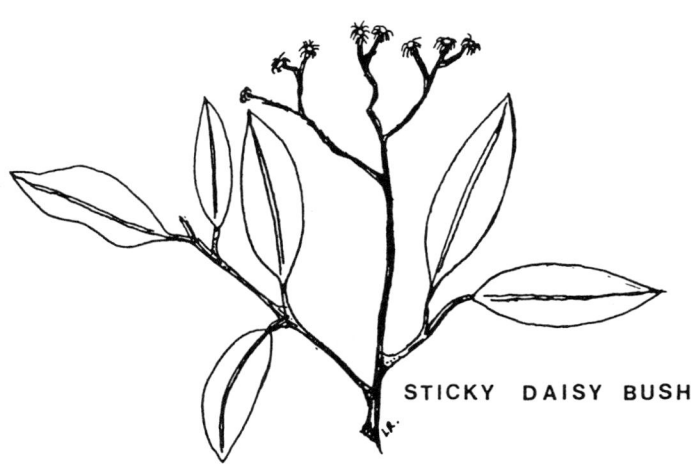

STICKY DAISY BUSH

RIDE 57: GREAT LAKE

FROM: Bronte Park
TO: Launceston
VIA: Pine Lagoon
LENGTH:
    Day 1: Bronte Park to Duck Point 40 km
    Day 2: Duck Point to Little Lake Bay 23 km
    Day 3: Little Lake Bay to Deloraine 49 km
    Day 4: Deloraine to Launceston 48 km
    Total distance is 160 km
TIME: 4–5 days
RIDE/TRACK GRADE: 6/4
WALKING: Pine Lake walk amongst pencil pines
HEIGHT VARIATION: 1200 m
TRANSPORT: Wilderness Transport Network to Bronte Park. Various coach services from Launceston
FACILITIES: Bronte Park Highland Village hostel has 52 bunks in 9 rooms. Supplies and accommodation at Miena, Great Lake
SPECIAL GEAR: Fishing
MAPS: Central Tasmania 1:150 000. (See Map 9: *CENTRAL PLATEAU*)

Great Lake is the largest of the central plateau lakes. In 1911 its run-off was blocked by the Miena Dam, part of the first hydro-electric scheme in Tasmania. In 1982 the height of the dam was raised by 6 m at a cost of $12 million enlarging the catchment area. Today it is one the world's best trout fishing grounds, with its season extending from August to May.

    From Bronte Park head north to Great Lake (1039 m). Supplies can be bought at Miena just to the right. There are two alternative routes to Launceston. One can continue right along the A5 and then the B51 up the eastern side of the lake and over the Great Western Tiers to Poatina.

Alternatively, and this is the route recommended, head north along the Lakes Highway to camp at Ducks Point and again on the lake shore at Little Lake Bay, Breona. Then continue north to the Pine Lake where a scenic short walk takes you amongst the hardy pencil pines. They were once the most common tree on the plateau, and in fact covered southern Australia four million years ago. Like the Huon Pine they are slow growing, the first metre taking over half a century. A very steep climb takes one up to the maximum altitude along the way (1209 m) giving new meaning to the term *highway*. Descend via hairpin corners through the rainforest of the Liffey Forest Reserve under the prominent Quamby's Bluff to Deloraine. You lose 500 m of altitude in under 10 km.

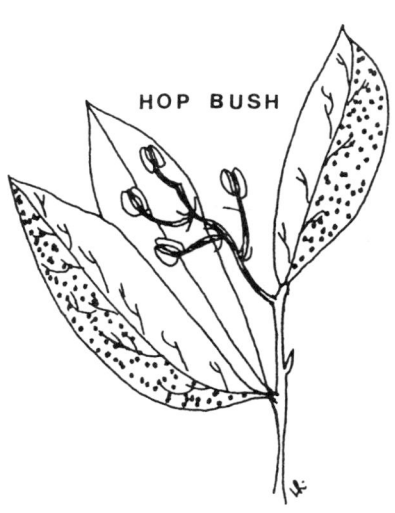

HOP BUSH

RIDE 58: LAKE ADA

FROM: Bronte Park
TO: Lake Ada
VIA: Double Lagoon, Lake Augusta
LENGTH:
    Day 1: Bronte Park to Duck Point 40 km
    Day 2: Duck Point to Lake Ada 29 km
    Day 3: Lake Ada to Duck Point 29 km
    Day 4: Duck Point to Bronte Park 40 km
    Total distance is 138 km
TIME: 4 days cycling days fishing
RIDE/TRACK GRADE: 5/6
HEIGHT VARIATION: 411 m
TRANSPORT: Wilderness Transport Network to/from Bronte Park
FACILITIES: Bronte Park Highland Village hostel has 52 bunks in 9 rooms
SPECIAL GEAR: Camping for self-sufficiency, fishing
MAPS: Central Tasmania 1:150 000. (See Map 9: *CENTRAL PLATEAU*)

Lake Ada is the most remote of the western lakes accessible by road. Take the A10 to Bronte, then the B11 to Great Lake. Follow the A5 up the western shore towards Liawenee. Camp at Duck Point just before the road curves left away from the water. The next day head left at the Inland Fisheries Commission depot and 14 km later you'll come to Lake Augusta. The large modern solid multi-storeyed building is a training centre for scientists visiting Antarctica. Along the way you enter the Protected Area. There are good views of the plateau's plains and cycling is quite easy due to the complete lack of vertical undulation and hard-surface roads. Cross the weir and follow Lake Augusta's southern shore below a very long thin earth bank to Lake Ada. Camping is available anywhere. Please note artificial lures only are permitted.

Beyond Lake Ada, a sandy four-wheel-drive track leads from the southern shore north to Lake Pillans and Julian Lakes. This is the start of tarn country: thousands of small natural lakes formed by glaciation. An extra day or two can be spent here in remote isolation but trout generally do not exist except in the larger western lakes such as Lake Meston.

Another variation is to take the turnoff to Double Lagoon where hard-core fly-fishermen brave the inclement weather in their on-going love-affair with the brown trout.

RIDE 59: FRANKLIN RIVER
'THE LAST WILD RIVER'

FROM: Derwent Bridge (6 km from Cynthia Bay)
TO: Franklin River (return)
VIA: Lyell Highway
LENGTH: 54 km (27 each way)
TIME: 2 days
RIDE/TRACK GRADE: 6/1
WALKING: Short nature trail at bridge. Optional overnight walk to Frenchmans Cap
HEIGHT VARIATION: 470 m
TRANSPORT: Redline coach service to Derwent Bridge. Wilderness Transport Network to/from Lake St. Clair
FACILITIES: Rest areas include toilets. Unlimited fresh water
SPECIAL EQUIPMENT: Salt to combat leeches
MAPS: RACT Touring Map of Tasmania, Frenchmans Cap 1: 50 000

One of Australia's most famous rivers, the Franklin is also the wildest. In fact the Lyell Highway is the only public road that crosses the very upper reaches of this pristine beautiful river. In the early 1980s, thousands of protesters clashed with HEC dam builders and police in a desperate effort to prevent yet another river from being flooded. The proposal was to dam the Gordon just downstream of its confluence with the Franklin thereby preventing the free flow of untamed water. The federal government intervened with authority granted it by a historic High Court constitutional law case therefore putting a stop to development.

From Derwent Bridge head west towards Queenstown. Take note of the topography change. You are entering the great south-west: a primitive turbulent land where volcanoes, earthquakes, glaciers of three ice ages, and rapid erosion from fierce winds have sculpted the terrain into one of utmost beauty.

A total of 355 m is lost as you freewheel through the dense rainforest of the World Heritage Area. The views are incredible along the mountain passes. The point at which the highway crosses is very scenic. This is the starting point of dozens of kayak or rafting expeditions down through the ravines to the Gordon River. There is a clearing here with toilets, tables, and shelters. A baptism in the pure icy waters will be a long-remembered experience. The river is named after Governor Sir John Franklin who made an epic journey to Macquarie Harbour, writing of 'stupendous mountains' and 'bog and sludge'.

If there's good weather and you feel like walking, a two to four day diversion to big Frenchmans Cap will reward you with some unrivalled views of the south-west including the Franklin River ravines all the way to Lake Gordon. The peak is white quartzite rising sharply to 1433 m. The rock cairn on top was built by Surveyor-General Sprent in 1856. The start of the walk is about 3 km from the Franklin Bridge. The Frenchmans Cap 1:50 000 map is needed.

From the river crossing, Queenstown is 53 km to the west. If electing to exit the park this way, there is a short walk to Donaghys Lookout about 8 km from the Franklin.

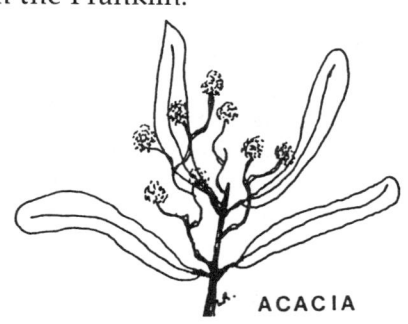

ACACIA

DATA TABLE: Franklin—Gordon Wild Rivers National Park

Size: 195 200 ha
Enactment: 1981
Aboriginal Sites: Significant archaeological caves along Franklin River
Animals: Wallabies, possums, devils, native cat, platypus
Plants: Horizontal, Huon and King Billy Pines, myrtles, snow gums
Attractions: Frenchmans Cap, white-water rafting
Camping: Unrestricted (Fuel Stove Only Area)
District Office: (004) 71-2511

RIDE 60: DERWENT RIVER VALLEY

FROM: Derwent Bridge
TO: Hobart
VIA: Butlers Gorge, Hamilton, New Norfolk
LENGTH: 168 km
TIME: 5 days
RIDE/TRACK GRADE: 7/5
HEIGHT VARIATION: 736 m
TRANSPORT: Redline coach service to Derwent Bridge. Wilderness Transport Network to Lake St. Clair
FACILITIES: Supplies from townships along the way
MAPS: Central Tasmania 1:150 000 and BP or RACT Touring Map of Tasmania. (See Map 9: *CENTRAL PLATEAU* and Map 1: *DERWENT*)

This ride approximately follows the course of the Derwent that starts from the dark waters of Lake St. Clair and flows for 180 km to Hobart. The following is a running counter of the route:

Place	*Route*	*Distance*	*Height*
Cynthia Bay		0 km	740 m
Derwent Bridge	C193	6 km	730 m
Turn-off to 14 Mile Rd	A10	27 km	700 m
Lyell Highway	C601	48 km	640 m
Ouse	A10	82 km	60 m
Hobart	A10	170 km	4 m

There is also a 20 km sidetrip to Laughing Jack Lagoon (C602) and a 40 km round trip to Butlers Gorge from Tarraleah (C603) Both allow access to lake shores for potential rest areas. For other nights, camping is available in the caravan parks in the townships along the way or one can rough it by heading along one of the dozens of private HEC access roads to a suitable area on the lakes' foreshores.

OTHER RIDES

As large stretches of the Central Plateau are protected wilderness, there are not many further avenues to investigate regarding mountain cycling. The inclement weather, isolation, and flat bleakness further contribute to this.

Trails of a very minor nature exist around the foreshore of the main lakes and some longer tracks exist in the Ouse River valley and to the north of Arthurs Lake. However the northern base of the Great Western Tiers is accessible by a multitude of tracks accessed from Deloraine via Meander.

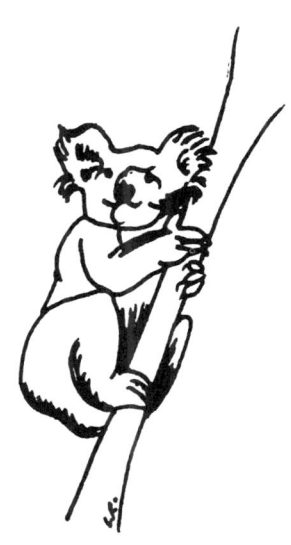

8
THE NORTH-WEST

When people refer to Tasmania resembling the English countryside, it's usually after visiting the north-west. The agricultural greenness is derived from rich dark volcanic soils that support a wide range of crops. There are a particularly wide range of graded rides available through a variety of topography: rainforest, mountain scenery, pristine rivers, coastal dunes and headlands, plains, highland plateaux, and steep gorges.

Some of the longest and most difficult rides in this guide are detailed in this chapter. Cyclists undertaking these should prepare themselves in regard to tours and boat cruises. Prices for supplies in remote townships and developed camping grounds are significantly higher. The longer rides along the central western coast will appeal to those with a longing to access extremely remote places.

Tracks are invariably rough and strong westerly winds are forever present. THE MAPS LISTED FOR EACH TOUR IN THIS AREA (RIDES 73-78) ARE COMPULSORY IF NO LOCAL KNOWLEDGE IS OBTAINABLE.

RIDE 61: KING SOLOMON'S CAVE

FROM: Devonport
TO: Launceston
VIA: Mole Creek Cave Reserves
LENGTH: Day 1: Devonport to Gowrie Park 48 km
Day 2: Gowrie Park to Mole Creek 39 km
Day 3: Mole Creek to Launceston 63 km
Total distance is 150 km
RIDE/TRACK GRADE: 6/3
WALKING: Cave tours (optional walk to Mt. Roland summit)
HEIGHT VARIATION: 700 m
TRANSPORT: Bus service to Devonport and from Launceston
FACILITIES: Camping at Gowrie Park & Mole Creek
MAPS: RACT Touring Map. (See Map 3: *CRADLE MT* and Map 2: *TAMAR*)

From Devonport (10 m) to Gowrie Park (300 m) via Sheffield (280 m) is 48 km. There is a camping ground here where the cyclist can leave his bike behind and take the popular walk up to the Mt. Roland plateau which overlooks a lot of north-west Tasmania including the Great Western Tiers and Cradle Mountain.

The next day head west along the C136 and then turn south (C138) and up a 500 m hill crossing over into the Mersey River valley. Keeping on the 138, head left and 2.5 km later left again for a wild descent down to the Liena bridge. Push up the narrow road on the other side through some pleasant forest to reach the King Solomon's Cave State Reserve. This will have been a tiring 23 km since Gowrie Park. Tours are at 10.30 am, 11.30 am, 12.30pm, 2.00pm, 3.00pm and 4.00pm. The Mole Creek camping ground is 16 km away. Cycle along the B12 to Deloraine (240 m) and then the A1 to Launceston, a total of 63 km.

RIDE 62: ROCKY CAPE NATIONAL PARK

FROM: Wynyard
TO: Smithton
VIA: Sisters Beach, Rocky Cape
LENGTH:
    Day 1: Wynyard to Sisters Beach 21 km
    Day 2: Sisters Beach to Rocky Cape 36 km
    Day 3: Rocky Cape to Smithton 37 km
    Total distance is 94 km
TIME: 3 days
RIDE/TRACK GRADE: 4/5
WALKING: To Aboriginal archaeological caves, Sisters Hills lookouts and coast
HEIGHT VARIATION: 188 m
TRANSPORT: Redline coach service to and from Wynyard
FACILITIES: Supplies from Sisters Beach and Boat Harbour
SPECIAL GEAR: Torch
MAPS: RACT Touring Map of Tasmania and Rocky Cape National Park 1:30 000 topographical. (See Map 10: *ARTHUR*)

This ride tours one of the most interesting but little known coastal parks in Tasmania. Featured within Rocky Cape National Park's boundaries are several Aboriginal caves which were occupied for about 8000 years.

From Wynyard (171 km from Launceston) head west along the Bass Highway to the turnoff to Boat Harbour Beach. Then turn left along Irbys Road 1 km before reaching the sea. This winds its way through eucalypt forest descending to Lake Llewellyn and then to Sisters Beach. Keep right making your way to the ocean. A dirt trail heads east parallel with the water. There are numerous

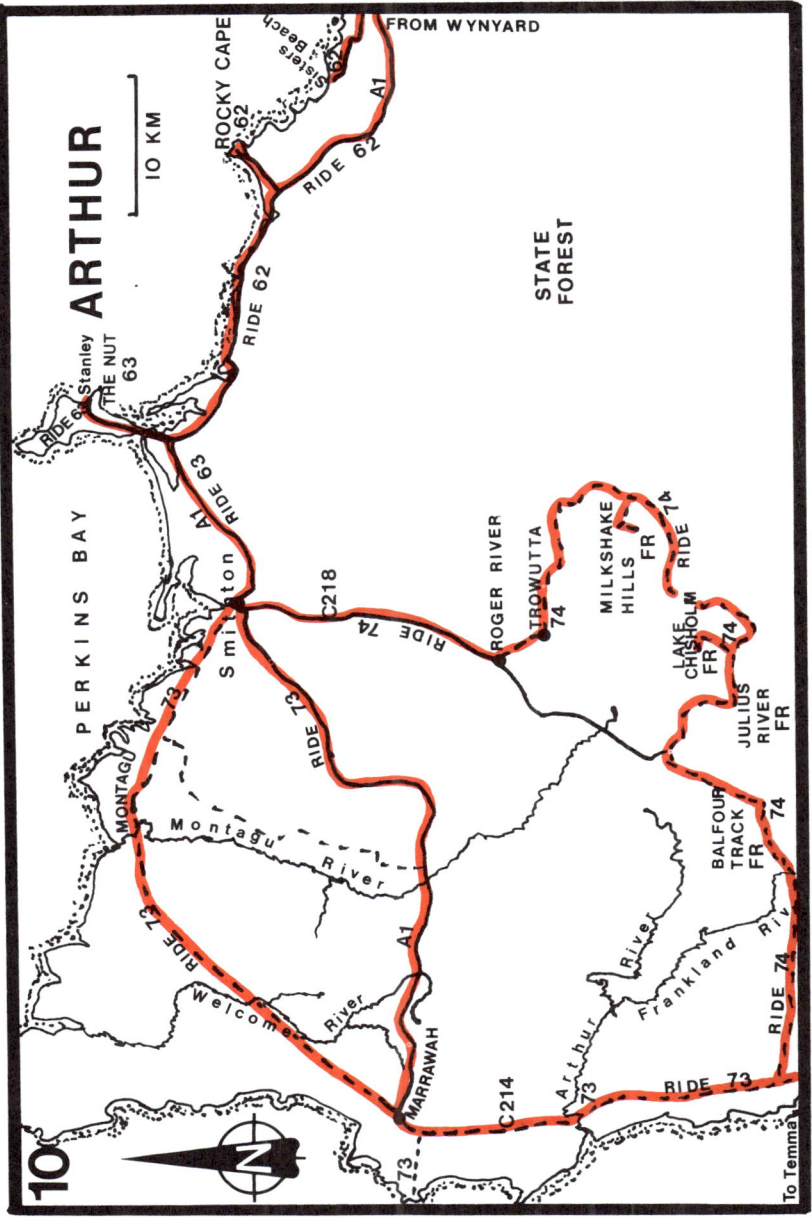

ARTHUR

10 KM

10

N

FROM WYNYARD

Sisters Beach

ROCKY CAPE
62
RIDE 62
A1
RIDE 62

Stanley
THE NUT
63
RIDE 63

RIDE 63
A1
RIDE 63

PERKINS BAY

Smithton

C218

RIDE 74

MONTAGU
73

Montagu River

RIDE 73

STATE FOREST

ROGER RIVER
TROWUTTA
74

MILKSHAKE HILLS FR
RIDE 74

LAKE CHISHOLM FR
74

JULIUS RIVER FR

BALFOUR TRACK FR
74

Welcomes River

A1

MARRAWAH

C214

73

Arthur River

Frankland River

RIDE 74

RIDE 73

To Temma

camping spots here, some unfortunately very frequently used for car-camping.

If there's time in the afternoon or the next day head back to the township which consists mainly of holiday homes, cross the creek, and head west to Wet Cave Point where one can do a number of walks to Lee Archer Cave and Wet Cave, with signs explaining the background to the Aboriginal occupations. A longer inland walk leads to Broadview Hill (241 m) for magnificent views of the coast, down to Anniversary Point via Doone Falls and along the bay back to Sisters Beach. Rocks of red-banded quartzite that characterise the park have been tilted almost 90 degrees.

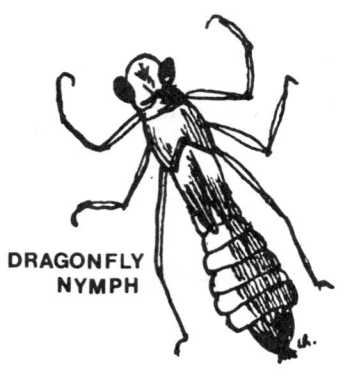

DRAGONFLY NYMPH

Head back out to Boat Harbour and then east along the Bass Highway to the slightly obscured turnoff to the Rocky Cape Lighthouse. At the end is a junction set amidst windswept heath. The lighthouse to the left offers good views of Rocky Cape's dramatically folded red quartzite. A walking track shortly before the lighthouse leads to the grand arch of the North Cave.

The right option at the junction leads to South Cave where a short steep walking track leads up to the crevice entrance. A torch is recommended as the fissure is quite deep. Camp down at Burgess Cove, which is unfortunately beachless. There is no official camping area. There are walking tracks from the junction south inland to the highest point of the Sisters Hill Range, Tinkers Lookout (291 m) and to Cathedral Rocks. All are well signposted.

Upon reaching the Bass Highway again, both Wynyard and Smithton are 37 km to the east and west respectively. Turning right to Smithton not only avoids backtracking but allows a 14 km sidetrip to Stanley and the famous Nut (see Ride 63 for details).

DATA TABLE: Rocky Cape National Park

Size: 3000 ha
Enactment: 21 June 1967
Aboriginal Sites: Sisters Hills caves
Animals: Marine life, 90 species of birds including sea eagles
Plants: Peppermint eucalypts, stringybark, paperbark, and 300 other flowering plants including 50 orchids. Heath is well represented on quartzite hills. Rocky Cape is only habitat of saw banksia in Tasmania.
Attractions: Aboriginal caves, coastal views, wildflowers
Camping: Sisters Beach
District Office: (003) 41-5312

RIDE 63: STANLEY AND THE NUT

FROM: Smithton
TO: Stanley
VIA: Bass Highway
LENGTH: 48 km
TIME: 2 days
RIDE/TRACK GRADE: 2/1
WALKING: To/from summit of the Nut (140 m)
HEIGHT VARIATION: 30 m
TRANSPORT: Redline Coach service to and from Smithton
FACILITIES: Tourists catered for at Stanley
MAPS: RACT Touring Map of Tasmania. (See Map 10: *ARTHUR*)

This short ride to one of Tasmania's most popular natural tourist attractions involves no complicated navigation. Simply follow the Bass Highway to the turnoff to Stanley. The one-way distance is 24 km.

The Nut was first seen by Matthew Flinders in 1798. He named it Circular Head.

Stanley was the headquarters of the Van Diemen's Land Company from 1827 onwards at Highfield, its aim being to make Britain independent of foreign countries for wool. Located here are stables, convict barracks, and a chapel.

Also at Stanley is the cottage of Joseph Lyons, the only Prime Minister from Tasmania.

A chairlift offers you single or return trips to the flat summit for a fee. The whole peninsula becomes visible and the ascent is recommended whether by foot or cable. A kiosk at the bottom provides food, drinks, and souvenirs. For those wishing to continue cycling a small track continues to North Point.

RIDE 64: HELLYER GORGE

FROM: Burnie
TO: Cradle Valley
VIA: Ridgley, Hellyer Gorge, Waratah
LENGTH:
  Day 1: Burnie to Hellyer Gorge 59 km
  Day 2: Hellyer Gorge to Waratah 34 km
  Day 3: Waratah to Cradle Valley 66 km
  Total distance is 159 km
TIME: 3 days
RIDE/TRACK GRADE: 7/3
HEIGHT VARIATION: 1000 m
WALKING: Short track along river through old myrtle-beech rainforest containing epiphyte orchids
TRANSPORT: Redline coach service to Burnie and from Wynyard
FACILITIES: Ridgley, Waratah, Cradle Valley
SPECIAL GEAR: Self-sufficiency
MAPS: Hellyer 1:100 000 topographical. (See Map 3: *CRADLE MT*)

The shoreline of Burnie (pop. 20 000) is dominated by the giant Associated Pulp and Paper Mill (APPM) factory, the site of bloody industrial disputes during mid-1992. The first paper factory at Burnie was built in 1937. A tour of the mill starts at 2 pm on Monday to Thursday and lasts 90 minutes covering the Pulp Mill, Bleaching Plant, Paper Machine Rooms, and Paper Finishing area. Phone (004) 30-7426 for details.

Take the B18 to Ridgley, then to Highclere, right to Tewkesbury and joining the Murchison Highway near Oonah. A short fast descent leads to the Hellyer Gorge State Reserve (569 ha), named after the Van Diemen's Land Company explorer-surveyor, Henry Hellyer, who is noted as the first European to climb Cradle Mountain in March 1831.

A memorial to him exists upon the summit.

When ready to leave, a long uphill push south to Parrawe leads to relatively flat cycling again. 20 km later a signposted turnoff right leads to Waratah. Mt. Bischoff north of Waratah was once the world's largest tin mine. The next day head back east to the A10 and then south. 20 km later a turnoff to the left leads to Cradle Valley.

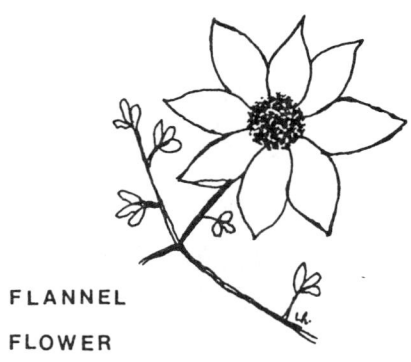

FLANNEL FLOWER

DATA TABLE: Cradle Mountain-Lake St. Clair National Park (Northern Section)

Size: 131 915 ha
Enactment: Scenic Reserve 1922
           National Park 1947
           World Heritage 1982
Animals: 20 species of mammals including Bennett's Wallaby, pademelons, potoroos, possums, and tiger cats.
Plants: Antarctic Beech, King Billy Pine, Huon Pine
Attractions: Waldheim, Cradle Mountain, Barn Bluff
Camping: P&O Camping Ground north of Cradle Lodge
District Office: (003) 63-5187

RIDE 65: CRADLE MOUNTAIN

FROM: Cradle Valley
TO: Lake Dove Car Park [RETURN]
VIA: Sheffield
LENGTH: 22 km
TIME: 1 day cycling plus extra days walking
RIDE/TRACK GRADE: 2/2
WALKING: Numerous short and extended walking tracks from Lake Dove carpark. Suggested is to the summit of Cradle Mountain
HEIGHT VARIATION: 50 m
TRANSPORT: Wilderness Transport Network to/from Cradle Valley Also: Cradle Mountain Coaches, Mountain Stage Line
FACILITIES: Developed camp ground and supplies at Cradle Valley
SPECIAL GEAR: Walking boots
MAPS: Cradle Mountain National Park and/or Day Walk Map (See Map 3: *CRADLE MT*)

The main camping ground at this most popular national park is a significant distance from all 'the action'. The bicycle is the best way of exploring the scenery between the camping ground and the Lake Dove car park. Along the way are scenic flights, horse riding, the visitor centre, short nature walks, and Waldheim. The route-notes are simple: take the C132 south, making a detour right to Waldheim just past the ranger station.

Waldheim is a reconstruction of the picturesque Tyrolean hut built by Gustav Weindorfer. Born in 1874 in Spittal, Austria, he devoted his whole life to the preservation of Cradle Mountain. Educated as a botanist, he was fascinated with the mountain scenery of Tasmania as it reminded him of the Carinthian alps back home. He first saw Cradle Mountain on his honeymoon camped up on Mount Roland in 1905 but didn't visit Cradle Valley itself until a break in farmer duties allowed him a walking expedition with friend Charlie Sutton in 1909.

On a later expedition, they climbed the summit with several friends and the legendary vision was born. Weindorfer is claimed to have stated with outstretched hands the immortal words: 'There must be a national park for the people for all time. It is magnificent, and people must know about it and enjoy it'. Having witnessed the opening of the Mount Buffalo National Park in Victoria, he adopted the campaign strategy. First he built an alpine chalet, then petitioned the government for a road. Upon descending the mountain, they chose a site for the proposed chalet, to be called Waldheim, which translates as 'forest home'. They purchased 600 acres of land, classified as third-class Crown Land—today it's World Heritage. Construction began in March 1912, from the slow-growing King Billy pine near by. Most of the work was carried out by Weindorfer himself and by the end of the year the first visitors where arriving.

He commuted from Cradle Mountain to his farm in Roland Lea by bicycle on some very rough roads. Improvements were made to the area: a bath house, a chapel, an animal pen, and further accommodation. Despite trouble with locals when Austria fought Australia in World War I and the death of his wife, Weindorfer continued to promote Cradle Mountain throughout Australia and succeeded in establishing the northern part as a national park in 1922, then Australia's largest at 64 000 ha. Improvements in the access road, transport, and the blazing of walking trails led to hundreds of people enjoying the wilderness. A lot of places in the area are named after his family, friends, and visitors.

A weak heart led to his death in 1932. Waldheim was destroyed by the National Parks and Wildlife Service in 1976 but protests from all around Australia led to a hasty apologetic reconstruction.

Today the replica is a museum where you can learn about life in the 1920s in Cradle Valley, when Waldheim enjoyed its heyday. Weindorfer is buried just outside and one can see the monument erected to him. There is also a short nature track where one can see the grand King Billy Pines.

From Waldheim it is a little over 2 km to Lake Dove. From here one can do a number of walks:

Walk	Distance	Time (return)
Twisted Lakes	5 km	2 hours
Marions Lookout	5 km	3 hours
Lake Dove Circuit	7 km	3 hours
Lake Rodway	10 km	4.5 hours
Cradle Mountain summit	12 km	4.5 hours
Barn Bluff	25 km	10 hours

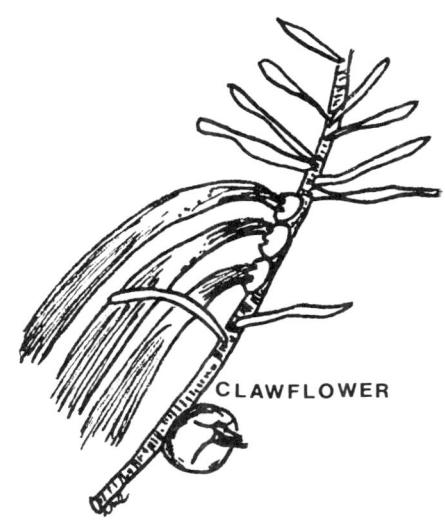

CLAWFLOWER

RIDE 66: LAKE MACKENZIE

FROM: Launceston
TO: Devonport
VIA: Mole Creek, Lake MacKenzie
LENGTH:
    Day 1: Launceston to Mole Creek 72 km
    Day 2: Mole Creek to Lake MacKenzie 42 km
    Day 3: Lake MacKenzie to Gowrie Park 44 km
    Day 4: Gowrie Park to Devonport 48 km
    Total is 206 km
TIME: 4–6 days
RIDE/TRACK GRADE: 8/4
HEIGHT VARIATION: 1 110 m
WALKING: Optional walk of King Solomon's Cave and Mt. Roland summit
TRANSPORT: Coach services to Launceston and from Devonport
FACILITIES: Mole Creek and Gowrie Park have camping grounds. No facilities at Lake MacKenzie
SPECIAL GEAR: Fishing
MAPS: Central Tasmania 1:150 000 (optional Lake MacKenzie 1:25 000 topographical). (See Map 2: *TAMAR* and Map 3: *CRADLE MT*)

Lake MacKenzie (1120 m) is the highest lake in the Mersey-Forth development comprising seven power stations and utilising four rivers. Water from the storage generates electricity as it falls on its way to Lake Barrington, location of the 1990 World Rowing Championships. This ride takes you along the base of the Great Western Tiers, through the karst area of King Solomon's Cave, into the Mersey River valley, and up onto the Central Plateau.

It is 48 km from Launceston to Deloraine (A1) at 240 m. Continue west for another 24 km to Mole Creek (B12). On the way is the Tasmanian Wildlife Park and the capital of leatherwood honey. The next day, leave very early and head west for 13 km before turning left onto the C138 signposted to Lake Rowallan. You can also take a detour to King Solomon's Cave, only another 2 km up the B12. See Ride 61 for details.

Six kilometres later along the Mersey Forest Road at 400 m altitude turn left onto Lake MacKenzie Road. The lake is 20 km to the south-east and 700 m higher. Towards the end you'll cycle past evidence of the HEC's all-pervading presence: gravel pits, tunnels, siphons, quarries, weirs, and flume canals. The vegetation changes markedly in response to the higher altitude and increased exposure. Once on top of the plateau, the trees become stunted and give way to low shrubs and alpine grasses. This is the start of the 'Land of three thousand lakes'. When in the clouds, as is often the case, the atmosphere created is one of total separation from the planet.

When ascending, ignore the turnoff right (780 m) to Snake Creek 8.5 km from the turnoff at Mill Creek. You'll pass Western Bluff (1420 m) to its south, one of the highest points on the Central Plateau, and there'll be some good views over the beautiful tree-lined Lake Parangana. The cliffs up here converge to form Devils Gullet, the middle catchment for the Fisher River.

At the top, a road leads left to a boat launching area. Head right across the river and slightly downstream to some old rough tracks that again meet the water at 1000 m altitude. This is not an official camping area so you'll have to find the spot that suits you most. The total day's distance will have been 42 km.

The next day can be spent either fishing in the lake (licence required) or walking north to the edge of the Great Western Tiers for tremendous views over northern Tasmania or a short walk slightly downstream to Parsons Falls. Overnight walking tracks lead south to some of the remote glacial tarns in the Walls of Jerusalem National Park. Please note that this area is for fuel stoves only.

When ready to descend back down to earth, backtrack to the Mersey River, head north and cross over following the C138 to Gowrie Park 44 km from the lake. Here one can climb Mt. Roland on foot (see Ride 22 for details) and stay at the quiet township with its large hydro-electric theme mural. Devonport is less than 50 km away.

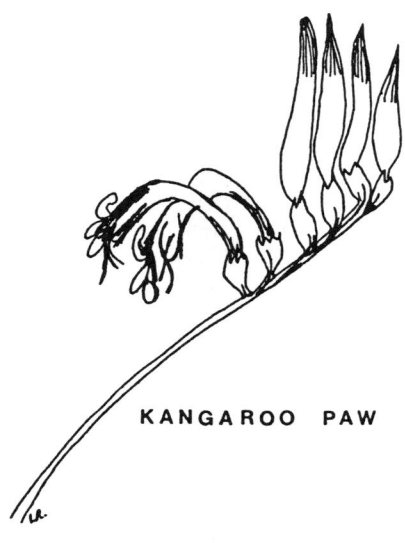

KANGAROO PAW

This ride can also be performed from the Fish River Carpark using the Wilderness Transport Network service. From the drop-off point to the lake is 51 km and involves only half the height variation.

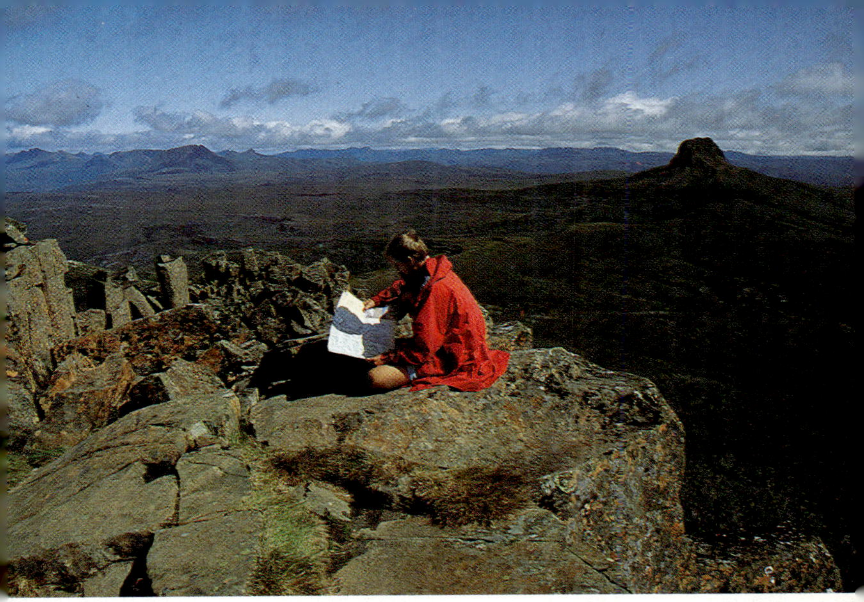

Summit of Cradle Mountain with Barn Bluff to right

Repairs in the Mersey River valley (Ride 70)

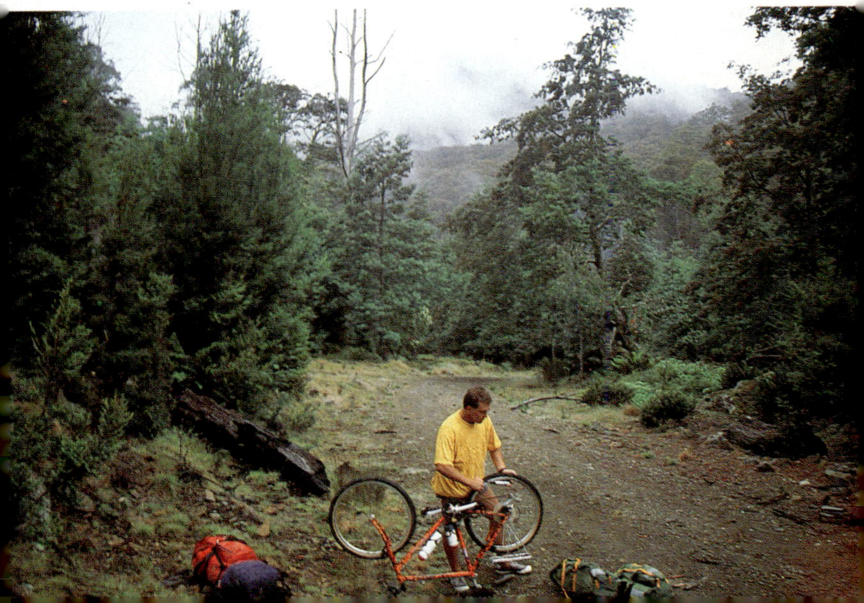

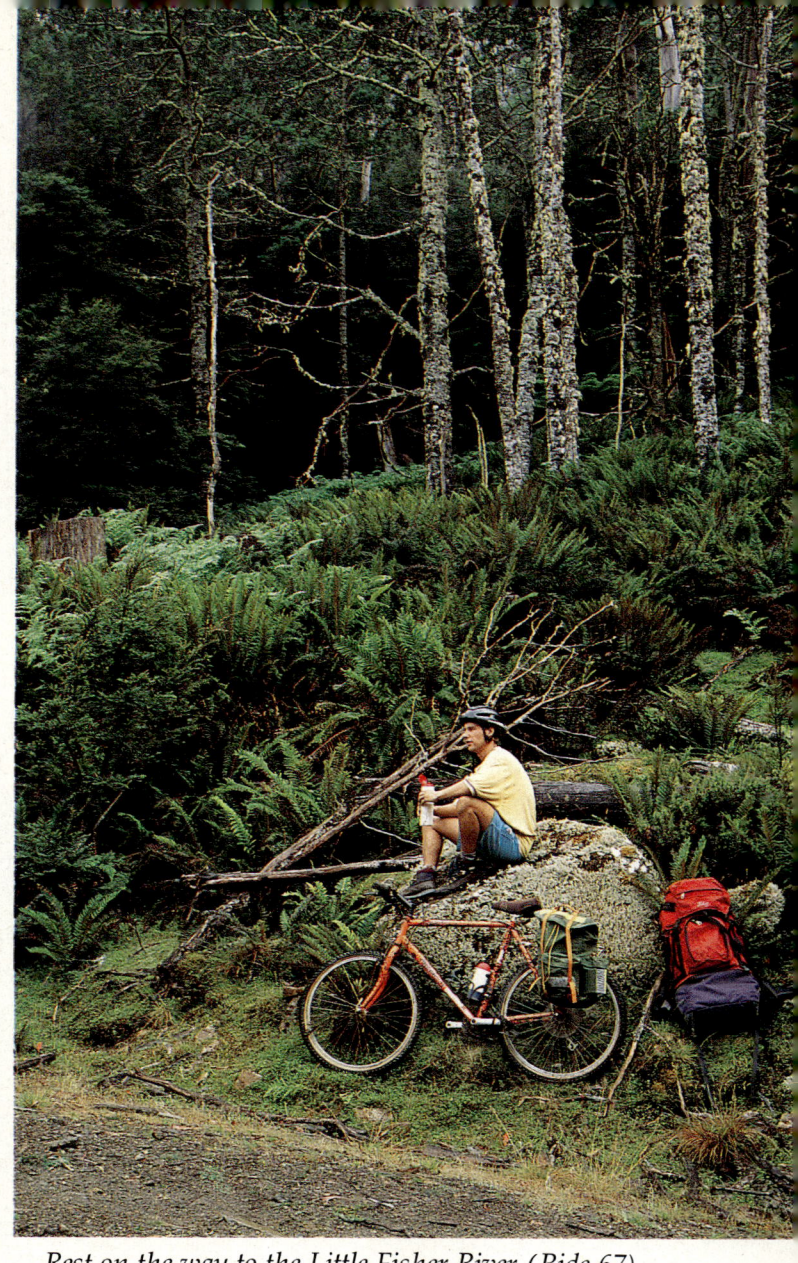

Rest on the way to the Little Fisher River (Ride 67)

RIDE 67: LITTLE FISHER RIVER

FROM: Fish River Carpark
TO: Upper Little Fisher River [RETURN]
VIA: Little Fisher Road and logging trails
LENGTH: 36 km
TIME: 1 or 2 days (each day 18 km)
RIDE/TRACK GRADE: 5/6–7
HEIGHT VARIATION: 250 m
TRANSPORT: Wilderness Transport Network to/from Lake Rowallan
FACILITIES: None
SPECIAL GEAR: Complete self-sufficiency
MAPS: Rowallan, Borradaile, Lake MacKenzie, Pillans Lake 1:25 000 topographicals plus RACT Touring Map of Tasmania. Optional are the Central Tasmania 1:150 000 and Walls of Jerusalem National Park 1:25 000. (See Map 3: *CRADLE MT*)

The upper Little Fisher River valley has seen extensive logging operations over the last 20 years. The mountain cyclist can use these logging trails to access the headwaters of a scenic river at the base of the Walls of Jerusalem. From the drop-off point at 700 m, head down to the river and north 7 km to Dublin Road. A five kilometre climb will take you to Little Fisher Road. Follow this around and down to the river. Cross over and rise about 30 m before following the river upstream for 3 km until you cross it again. To the west looms the craggy Deception Point at 1400 m. The rock around here is fine-grained blue-grey dolerite, one of the largest deposits in the world and the only in Australia. By studying the alignment of ferrous materials in the rock, geologists believe that at formation Tasmania was less than 1000 km from the South Pole and connected to Antarctica about 165 million years ago.

Find a camping spot that suits you as the river

banks are very flat. Spend some time exploring the many trails around here. You might find one that goes somewhere. We didn't. Return via the same route.

RIDE 68: FISH RIVER
(WALLS OF JERUSALEM WALK)

FROM: Fish River Carpark
TO: Fish River [RETURN]
VIA: Fish River Road
LENGTH: 20 km
TIME: 1-2 days (extra days for walking to Walls of Jerusalem)
RIDE/TRACK GRADE: 3/4
HEIGHT VARIATION: 100 m
TRANSPORT: Wilderness Transport Network to/from Lake Rowallan
FACILITIES: Fireplace
SPECIAL GEAR: Self-sufficiency
MAPS: Walls of Jerusalem National Park 1:25 000 (See Map 3: *CRADLE MT*)

The Walls of Jerusalem, despite their remoteness, are a popular venue for walkers and consequently camping sites and huts can be crowded. At the drop-off point walkers also on the bus will proceed up to the plateau. This ride suggests cycling to a lonely campsite on the other bank of the Fish River and waiting a day or two before commencing the walk.

Cycle down the slope to the Mersey River Road, head north, crossing the Fish, and take the first on the right. A gradual uphill slope takes you to two small clearings where the road bends left. A sign at the back marks the boundary of the Walls of Jerusalem National Park signifying a fuel stove only area. But just before the sign is a fireplace with some wood. There is also another grassy clearing on the right. A steep slippery walking track leads down to the water where you can refresh yourself in some nice cascades. The water here cannot be purer.

DATA TABLE: Walls of Jerusalem National Park

Size: 11 510 ha
Enactment: 24 June 1981
Animals: Eels, native and introduced fish in lakes
Plants: Snow gums, yellow gums, swamp grass, heaths
Attractions: Herod's Gate, Lake Salome, Mt. Jerusalem
Camping: Trappers Hut sleeps 4, Dixons Kingdom Hut sleeps 6. Other huts in disrepair. Tent camping also by Lake Salome and Pool of Bethesda
District Office: Launceston, Bass Highway, (003) 41-5312

When you are ready to do the 20 km return walk, head back to the drop-off point and hide the bikes. The track takes you at first through gum trees to Trappers Hut an hour away. After this the track branches. The right connects with the Overland Track in the Cradle Mountain Lake St. Clair National Park. Head left and through some lakes known as Solomon's Jewels. Further climbing reveals more exposed vegetation as you enter Herod's Gate. This will remind NSW bushwalkers of Nibelung Pass into the Monolith Valley. The track peters out but head left to the Pool of Bethesda and through Damascus Gate to an ancient pencil pine forest (*Athrotaxis cupressoides*). This is believed to be the largest of its kind. Their 20 m height make them about a millennium old. The round trip from Fish River takes about 8 hours. Camping is therefore not necessary but recommended considering the scenic quality of the landscape. A walk to Mt. Jerusalem (1459 m) can then be done the next day if it is clear for some commanding views over this spectacular terrain. Reg Hall gave the features their biblical titles.

RIDE 69: LAKE ROWALLAN CIRCUIT

FROM: Fish River Carpark [RETURN]
VIA: Mersey River
LENGTH: 38 km
TIME: 1 day (recommended 2 days)
RIDE/TRACK GRADE: 4/6
HEIGHT VARIATION: 100 m
TRANSPORT: Wilderness Transport Network to/from Lake Rowallan
FACILITIES: None. Natural firewood in plentiful supply
SPECIAL GEAR: Self-sufficiency
MAPS: Central Tasmania 1:150 000 and Walls of Jerusalem National Park 1:25 000. (See Map 3: *CRADLE MT*)

Another way to spend time in the Mersey River valley while you are waiting for walkers to return from the Walls of Jerusalem is to cycle around Lake Rowallan. The circumference tour can take the fit cyclist a day, but it is recommended to break it into two to camp at one of the many places on the shore.

From the drop-off point at the Fish River, backtrack down the slope and head south (left) along the Mersey River Forest Road. At the end, where the stored water starts to back up and the water is a graveyard of trees, cross over to the West Rowallan Track, head north and take a rough track right down to the water. The maps are inaccurate here as continuing forestry operations and fluctuations in the water level have made new roads while old ones have vanished. However navigation is made easy by keeping the lake on your right.

Make camp amidst hundreds of dead trunks. Firewood is plentiful. Keep an eye out for fossils among conglomerate. Also beware of stirring thousands of mozzies when swimming near the trunks.

The Rowallan power station began operation in 1968, part of seven power stations generating a total capacity of over 300 000 kW. The largest consumers are Comalco Aluminium at Bell Bay, Electrolytic Zinc, and the Australian Newsprint Mills.

The next day head back up to the West Rowallan Track which steadily rises to a maximum of 60 m above the water. Pass the dam on the right and a canoe mustering/assembly area on the left. Cross back to the eastern bank downstream of the power station and head south to the Fish River carpark.

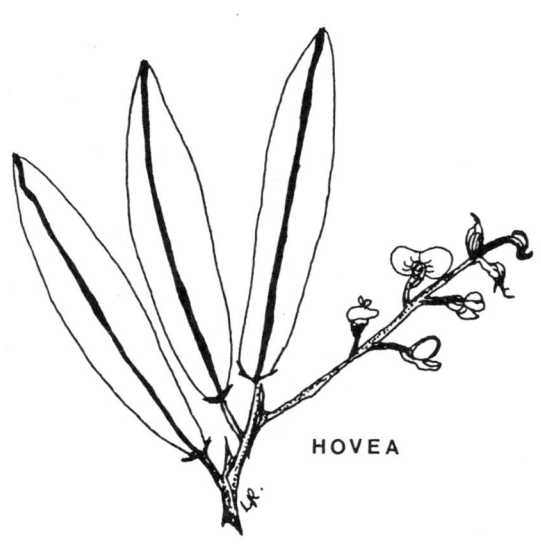

HOVEA

RIDE 70: ARM RIVER FOREST RESERVE

FROM: Fish River Carpark
VIA: Arm River Forest Reserve
LENGTH: 61 km returning to Fish River Carpark
TIME: 2 days
RIDE/TRACK GRADE: 5–6/6
HEIGHT VARIATION: 160 m
TRANSPORT: Wilderness Transport Network to/from Lake Rowallan
FACILITIES: Campground at Arm River Forest Reserve
SPECIAL GEAR: Self-sufficiency
MAPS: Central Tasmania 1:150 000, Cradle Mountain-Lake St. Clair National Park 1:100 000, and Borradaile, and Rowallan 1:25 000 topographicals. (See Map 3: *CRADLE MT*)

Quality mountain biking country exists around Maggs Mountain (840 m) via the Arm River Forest Reserve. From the Fish River carpark in the Mersey River valley, head right along the Mersey Forest Road and cross the river downstream from the dam and power station passing through the Mersey White Water Forest Reserve (239 ha). Continue north and take the Arm Road into the Arm River Forest Reserve (128 ha). This is the location of an outdoor recreation centre for school students, undergraduates, academics, conservationists, scientific institutions, and government departments studying the forests west of Lake Rowallan.

Take the Maggs Mountain Road (C172) up to the top with views east to Clumner and Howells Bluff. Once on top it stays relatively flat with views of the river valley before looping around to become the Arm Road leading back to the campground. One can either stay here at the developed accommodation or return to the Fish River (Ride 68) or connect with other rides such as the Lake Rowallan Circuit (Ride 69) or to the Little Fisher River (Ride 67).

RIDE 71: FORTH RIVER (LOWER)

FROM: Fish River Carpark
TO: Forth River
VIA: Borradaile Plains
LENGTH: 80 km (each day 40 km)
TIME: 2 days
RIDE/TRACK GRADE: 7/6
HEIGHT VARIATION: 160 m
TRANSPORT: Wilderness Transport Network to/from Lake Rowallan
FACILITIES: None
SPECIAL GEAR: Self-sufficiency
MAPS: Rowallan, Borradaile, Liena 1:25 000 topographicals, Cradle Mountain—Lake St. Clair National Park 1:100 000 (See Map 3: *CRADLE MT*)

This ride includes the place where the cover-shot was taken for this book. It is a good fishing spot on a clean river fit for drinking and swimming with a secluded campsite very close by. Along the way are some good mountain biking trails to negotiate.

From the Fish River Carpark, head north along the Mersey Forest Road (C171), crossing the Mersey and Arm Rivers. Just 2 km after the latter, turn left and climb up to the 850 m plateau comprising Borradaile Plains. Make your way through the network of logging roads across the swampy plateau. Logging operations here have been in progress since the 1970s with good examples of regeneration taking place. Good progress can be made if the trails are dry. Drop down over the western edge to Lemonthyme Power Station. Head briefly up the main C139 road but turn immediately left on a large gravel clearing. A trail to the back and right of the clearing leads to Lorinna along the Forth River. Almost immediately upon cycling along this trail, a branch heads left straight down a short slope to the water itself. A flat clearing to the right makes for a pleasant campsite (watch out for snakes though). A short track leads down to the water. Be careful when swimming here as the power station just upstream can release sudden torrents of water that could suddenly sweep you along. Return via the same route. This ride can be augmented by a 52 km round trip to the upper Forth on the border of the World Heritage Area where a walking track leads to Tasmania's highest mountain. See Ride 72.

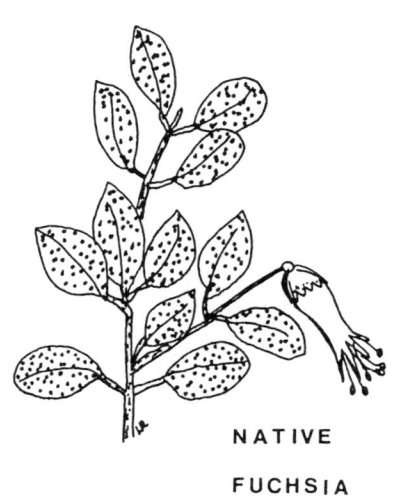

NATIVE

FUCHSIA

RIDE 72: FORTH RIVER (UPPER)
(WOLFRAM MINES)

FROM: Fish River Carpark
TO: Cradle Valley
VIA: Patons Road
LENGTH:
   Day 1: Fish River to Lemonthyme Power Station 40 km
   Day 2: Lemonthyme Power Station to Wolfram Mines 27 km
   Day 3: Wolfram Mines to Lemonthyme Power Station 27 km
   Day 4: Lemonthyme Power Station to Cradle Valley 60 km
   Total distance is 154 km
TIME: 4–6 days
RIDE/TRACK GRADE: 9/8
WALKING: Optional walking to Pelion huts, Mt. Ossa, Mt. Pelion West, Mt. Pelion East, Mt. Oakleigh
HEIGHT VARIATION: 700 m
TRANSPORT: Wilderness Transport Network to Lake Rowallan and from Cradle Valley
FACILITIES: None
SPECIAL GEAR: Complete self-sufficiency
MAPS: Rowallan, Borradaile, Will, Liena 1:25 000 topographicals. If walking, the Achilles 1:25 000 topographical will also be needed. (See Map 3: CRADLE MT)

One of the best rides in the book, this encompasses some spectacular and varied scenery and can be augmented by side cycling and walking trips into the world heritage area. A warning, the topographical maps listed above are essential as the areas listed are in remote mountain terrain and a literal maze of logging trails has to be negotiated on the opening day.

First, organise a week's supply of food and get

dropped off at the Fish River Carpark. Follow Ride 71's notes to the Forth River for the first day's camp.

The next day head back out to the Lemonthyme Power Station (210 m) and south following the river along its eastern bank along Patons Road constructed in 1908. You'll pass a hut on the right about 6 km from the station. Ignore two left turn-offs immediately to the left. Another 6 km through the Lemonthyme State Forest takes you down close to a wide bend in the river. You then leave the river for another 5 km before rejoining when the bank is flat making for perfect camping. Along the way are glimpses of Barn Bluff. In all the location of the abandoned Wolfram Mines at the edge of the World Heritage Area is 26 km from the power station and you'll have gained about 300 m. Camp anywhere you want on the flat banks in the Oakleigh Creek Conservation Area (proclaimed in 1981).

HISTORY James Smith and other fossickers, reacting to rumours of rich deposits of minerals in the Pelion area, explored the upper Forth river around 1900. Silver, lead, gold, and wolfram were found and an access road built in 1908. The most significant deposit, discovered by Paddy Harnett, was wolfram from which tungsten is produced. The mines began operating during WW1. The largest was located about 1500 m south of Oakleigh Creek and extracted wolfram and tin until 1985 long after the others were abandoned.

A walking track leads to the famous Overland Track connecting some of the most spectacular mountain scenery along the way. The Old Pelion Hut which sleeps 8 is 8 km to the south. It's named after the home of the Centaurs in Greek mythology. The Will and Achilles 1:25 000 topographicals will assist you if you're planning to do any short segments of the Overland Track from here. One possible walk is to the highest peak in Tasmania,

Mt. Ossa (1617 m). The Wolfram Mines site is the closest the mountain cyclist can get to the summit. It would be a 36 km return walk camping at Pelion Hut (sleeps 12) on the return.

When ready to leave, backtrack to the Lemonthyme Power Station. The gradual downhill makes for easy fast cycling. Camp again by the Forth River as on Day 1 or continue on the Lorinna track which contours around Lake Cethana. At first it winds around about 30 m above the water. The track is in a state of disrepair but this is where mountain bikes come into their own. Rough camping is also available when suitably flat and near the water. This spot is the historic crossing location that Henry Hellyer used when exploring the Forth River valley in 1826.

To get to Cradle Mountain, rise early and continue north through Lorinna and across the bridge 1 km downstream of the Cethana Power Station. This is where Bert Nicholas lived who blazed the famous 85 km Overland Track. A colourful character, he seemed to defy the weather by never wearing a coat even in the bleakest of conditions.

Across the other side of the Forth River the road steeply rises to 700 m but cycling is then flat and comfortable for most of the way to Cradle Valley.

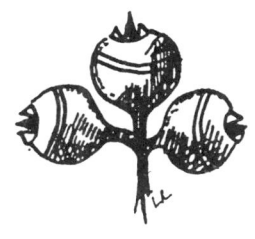

RED STRINGYBARK

RIDE 73: ARTHUR-PIEMAN PROTECTED AREA

FROM: Smithton
TO: Temma
VIA: Arthur River
LENGTH:
   Day 1: Smithton to Montagu 16 km
   Day 2: Montagu to Marrawah 33 km
   Day 3: Marrawah to Arthur River 16 km
   Day 4: Arthur River to Temma 25 km
   Day 5: Temma tour 20 km
   Day 6: Temma to Marrawah 42 km
   Day 7: Marrawah to Smithton 51 km
   Total distance is 203 km
TIME: 7–8 days
RIDE/TRACK GRADE: 9/8
HEIGHT VARIATION: 120 m
TRANSPORT: Redline coach service to Smithton
FACILITIES: Camp ground at Green Point, Marrawah. Picnic area at West Point Lighthouse, developed camp ground at Arthur River
SPECIAL GEAR: Complete self-sufficiency, windbreaker
MAPS: RACT Touring Map of Tasmania, Studland, Bluff, Sundown, and Temma 1:25 000 topographicals. (See Map 10: *ARTHUR*)

Encompassing the very north-west of the island, this tour for experienced cyclists explores some lonely coast that is the first place reached by winds from South America after 20 000 km of ocean. The highlight is the Arthur River. A cruise is available here aboard the licensed *MV George Robinson* upstream to the confluence with the Frankland River.

From Smithton take the straight flat C215 to Montagu. Along the way are views of Duck Bay and Perkins Island. The north-west coastal tip is dominated by poorer soils derived from sandstone and supporting mostly heath and open woodland. At low tide it's even possible to cross to Robbins Island.

Head to West Montagu where the road deteriorates into a track. The wind will pick up as you approach Marrawah. This is the service centre of a rich dairying district. On the way to the Arthur River is the signposted West Point Lighthouse, 12 km return from the Arthur River Road.

There are numerous camping grounds by the Arthur River. They are well frequented due to the remote beach and river fishing available here.

When ready to leave continue south through even lonelier country. The sound of crashing waves and constant wind are your companions on this stretch south to Temma. There are numerous small tracks off to the right leading to relatively sheltered campsites by the water. The village of Temma is indeed a desolate place, being continually battered by the perpetual winds. The road deteriorates from here on. It turns inland and becomes sandy. Expert navigation and some local knowledge is needed to reach the abandoned remote mining township of Balfour near the Frankland River. Great opportunities exist for mountain bike pioneering here, although tracks are generally sandy even a few kilometres inland.

To the south is Norfolk Range, Tasmania's newest range in geological terms, with soils being remarkably fertile in contrast to the coastal heath and sedgelands around Temma.

This region, especially further upstream, is part of the huge north-west wilderness region, and believed to be one of the last possible refuges for the Tasmanian tiger.

Return to Marrawah and take the Bass Highway (A2) directly back to Smithton.

RIDE 74: NORTH-WEST FOREST RESERVES

FROM: Smithton
TO: Arthur River [RETURN]
VIA: Balfour Track Forest Reserve, Julius River Forest Reserve, Lake Chisholm Forest Reserve, Milkshake Hills Forest Reserve
LENGTH:
    Day 1: Smithton to Arthur River 63 km
    Day 2: Arthur River to Frankland River 37 km
    Day 3: Frankland River to Ḵanunnah Bridge 22 km
    Day 4: Kanunnah Bridge to Julius River 9 km
    Day 5: Julius River to Milkshake Hills 42 km
    Day 6: Milkshake Hills to Smithton 58 km
    Total distance is 231 km
TIME: 6–7 days
RIDE/TRACK GRADE: 8/8
WALKING: Short tourist walks in all reserves
HEIGHT VARIATION: 200 m
TRANSPORT: Redline coach service to and from Smithton
FACILITIES: Camping and picnic facilities, no supplies
SPECIAL GEAR: Self-sufficiency
MAPS: RACT Touring Map of Tasmania and Bluff, Sundown, Ordnance, Balfour, Dempster, Holder, Roger, Tayatea 1:25 000 topographicals. (See Map 10: *ARTHUR*)

On this ride the cyclist can tour the north-west coast and camp on the beautiful Arthur River in the large Protected Area and then head south and inland to visit a series of Forest Reserves on tributaries of the Arthur River supporting stands of cool temperate rainforest and mixed wet forests.

    Take the A2 and C214 to Arthur River. A cruise is available here aboard the licensed *MV George*

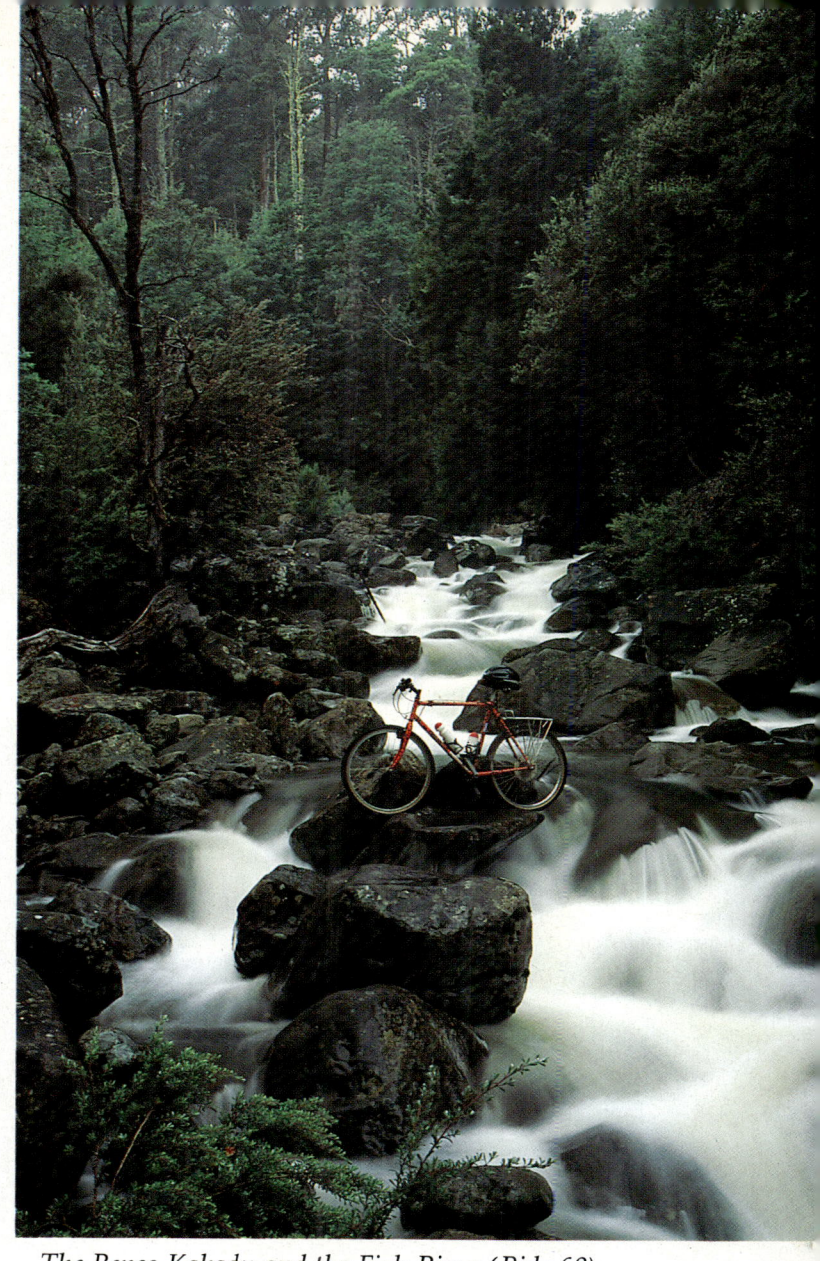

The Repco Kakadu and the Fish River (Ride 68)

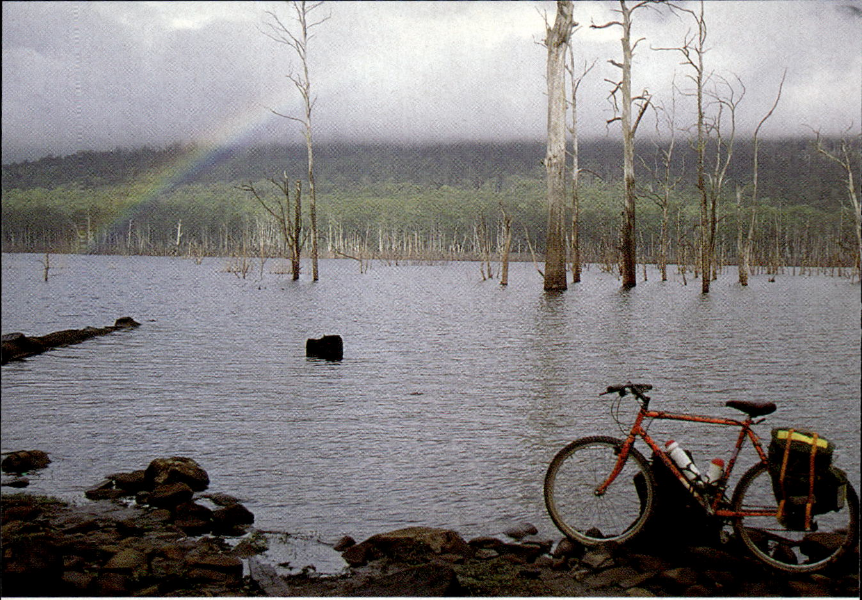

Lake Rowallan and the Walls of Jerusalem (Ride 69)

Arthur River from Kanunnah Bridge (Ride 73)

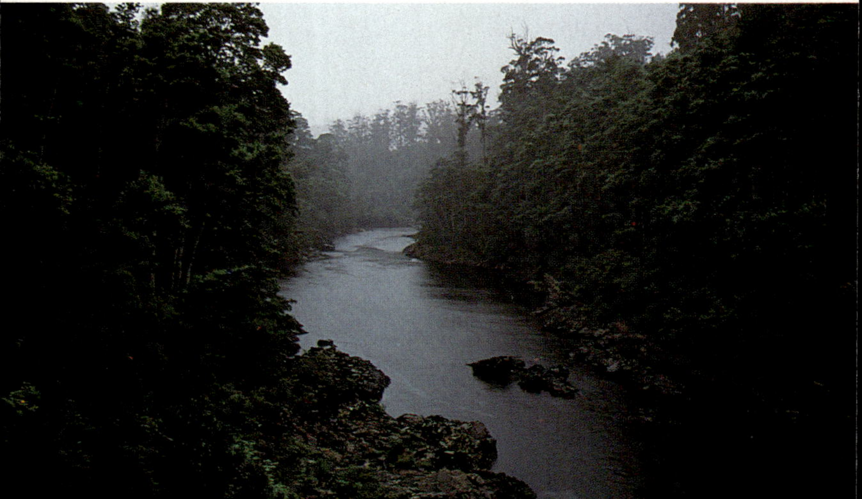

Robinson upstream to the confluence with the Frankland River. There are numerous camp grounds here, well frequented due to the remote beach and river fishing available here.

Leave early continuing south to Temma. 15 km along this road turn left onto Rebecca Road. You enter state forest dense due to heavy rainfall. Camping is permitted anywhere you find suitable. Fresh water is available from the Frankland River.

The next morning head north to the Kanunnah Bridge over the Arthur River peaking at 200 m. Along the way is the Balfour Track Forest Reserve (320 ha) featuring a walk along part of the pack-horse trail that accessed the remote mining township of Balfour.

When you've reached the Arthur River, cross the Kanunnah Bridge. On the other side is a picnic shelter with firewood. Camping is not officially allowed here but if it is raining I don't think you'll go to jail. Otherwise one can continue east up Sumac Road on the southern bank to a suitable spot.

This is a rest day with only a short scenic half-hour ride to the camping ground in the Julius River Forest Reserve (85 ha). Basic facilities and a walk to the Julius River are offered amidst the myrtle dominated forest.

Next day head to the Lake Chisholm Forest Reserve (76 ha). Have lunch by the lake and do the discovery walk. Then head back out to the C218 and north to the Milkshake Hills Forest Reserve (290 ha) via Rapid River Road. There are reasonable picnic/shelter facilities developed here, although no official camping ground.

Rise early for the final long day back to Smithton. The rainforests are left behind as you follow the C218 cross the Tayatea Bridge once again across the Arthur River and on to Roger River, Edith Creek, and Smithton.

RIDE 75: CORINNA

FROM: Cradle Valley
TO: Queenstown
VIA: Savage River, Pieman River, Granville Harbour, Zeehan
LENGTH:
    Day 1: Cradle Valley to Waratah 63 km
    Day 2: Waratah to Corinna 63 km
    Day 4: Pieman Heads to Granville Harbour 30 km
    Day 5: Granville Harbour to Zeehan 39 km
    Day 6: Zeehan to Queenstown 43 km
    Total distance is 238 km
TIME: 6–9 days
RIDE/TRACK GRADE: 9/8
HEIGHT VARIATION: 1 100 m
TRANSPORT: Wilderness Transport Network service to Cradle Valley and from Zeehan
FACILITIES: Camp ground at Corinna
SPECIAL GEAR: Complete self-sufficiency
MAPS: RACT Touring Map of Tasmania, Livingston, Stringer, Heemskirk 1:25 000 topographicals.
(See Map 3: *CRADLE MT*, Map 10: *ARTHUR*, and Map 11: *STRAHAN*)

Perhaps the most difficult ride in this guide, this incredibly varied extended tour covers the highlands of the Cradle Mountain area and the Black Bluff Range, the rich mining towns of Waratah and Savage River, the state reserve and rainforest of Corinna, a boat cruise down the Pieman River, the desolate windy west coast, rough four-wheel-drive tracks to lonely inlets, Zeehan, another mining town, and yet another, Queenstown, the largest of them all.
    Completing the ride is contingent upon the *Arcadia II* boat taking you from Corinna to Pieman Heads. It runs all year but bookings are necessary from June to October. Otherwise, it leaves daily

at 10.30 am. The one way trip is $12.50 and there is no charge for bicycles.

Spend *x* amount of days exploring Cradle Valley: see Ride 65 for features, walks, history, and facilities. Cycle north and left along the newly constructed C132 to the A10. Turn north, cross the Huskinson River and left on the road to Waratah (B23). Camping is available at Waratah.

Mt. Bischoff north of Waratah was once the world's largest tin mine. The alluvial deposits were discovered in 1871 and water-powered ore-crushing operations began five years later. Also at Waratah is a particularly large waterfall.

The next day head south-west though spectacular country to the mining township of Savage River (280 m). The Savage River mine is based on an iron ore deposit that was known for many years but has only relatively recently been economically viable due to the pelletising process. The treated ore is formed into a slurry and piped all the way to Port Latta on the north coast. Inspection times are Tuesday and Thursday at 9.00 am and 2.00 pm.

The C747 Long Plains Road replaces the B23 as you drop into the Pieman River Valley. One can spend a couple of days in Corinna (30 m) relaxing and exploring the gold mining ruins. The Pieman River has its steep rocky banks preserved in a state reserve of 3328 ha protecting an 800 m wide strip of rainforest which includes the most northerly limit of Huon Pine and a rare tree fern.

> *Corinna is a graveyard of hopes and houses. Once the home of a thousand . . . it is now as dead as Pompeii or Babylon . . . There was no need for the blackberries to get their stranglehold on Corinna for they are merely choking a corpse.*
>
> –E. T. Emmet, *Tasmania by Road and Track*

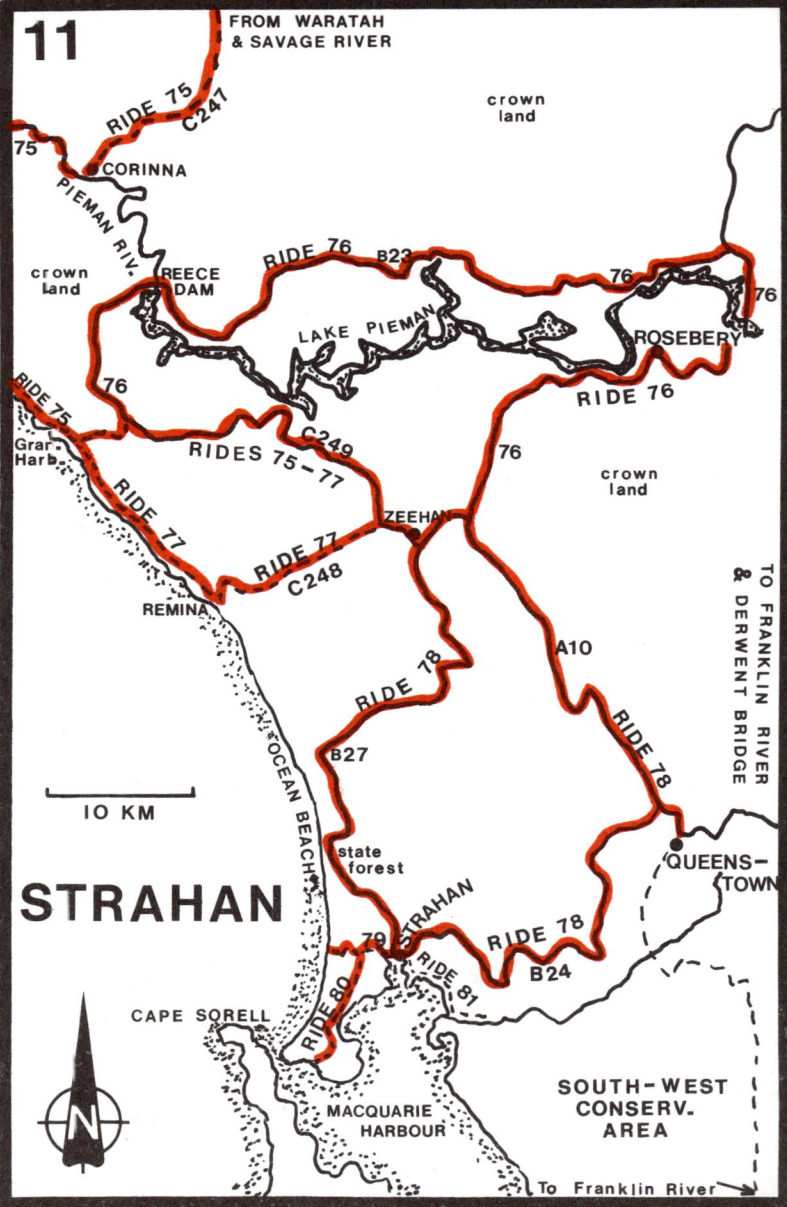

At Corinna one can stroll the Slender Tree Fern 5 minute walk along the Pieman starting west of the jetty. This leads to a very rare species of Tree Fern. A one hour track leads through rich rainforest along the Whyte River.

Take the *Arcadia II* (built in 1939) at 9 knots down the river to its mouth. Disembark at the southern bank and one can either camp here or head south along the four-wheel-drive track to Yarrana Hill to Ahrberg Bay. The next day take the rough coastal track south to Granville Harbour. This is a holiday resort for the mining communities of Zeehan, Savage River, and Waratah. The harbour was originally opened up as a soldier settlement in the 1920s. From here the C249, B71, and the A10 lead to Queenstown via Zeehan. A major tourist attraction of Zeehan is the West Coast Pioneers Memorial Museum, displaying the history of European development on the west coast as well as one of the most comprehensive mineral collections in the country.

This ride can be shortened in the future by the imminent construction of a road from the south bank of the Pieman at Corinna to the C249. This would be jointly funded by the National Parks and Wildlife Service and the Forestry Commission, leaving out the Pieman Head and coastal 4WD tracks.

RIDE 76: ROSEBERY LOOP

FROM: Rosebery
TO: Reece Dam [RETURN]
VIA: Zeehan
LENGTH:
   Day 1: Rosebery to Wilson River 46 km
   Day 2: Wilson River to Granville Harbour 53 km
   Day 3: Granville Harbour to Zeehan 39 km
   Day 4: Zeehan to Rosebery 29 km
   Total distance is 167 km
TIME: 4 days
RIDE/TRACK GRADE: 8/5
HEIGHT VARIATION: 400 m
TRANSPORT: Own to and from Rosebery
FACILITIES: None
SPECIAL GEAR: Self-sufficiency
MAPS: Stringer, Ahrberg, Heemskirk 1:25 000 topographicals, RACT Touring Map of Tasmania. (See Map 11: *STRAHAN*)

This town is based on the Electrolytic Zinc Company which conducts mining and milling operations. There is a quiet caravan park behind the plant with some vans available for reasonable rent if it is raining.

The central feature of this tour is the Pieman Hydro-Electric scheme and a relatively new road circumnavigates the Pieman crossing the dam wall itself. This is only one of a number of dams the HEC has built in the area after having the Gordon-Franklin scheme rejected by the historic 4–3 decision in the High Court. Start early and cycle up the steep A10 15 km through Tullah to the turn-off to the Eric Reece dam. Turn left and enter the bush peaking at 200 m. Several rivers are crossed on the 75 km to the dam and if the day is late one can make a camp on their shores where the access road crosses them. They are the Huskinson, the Wilson, and the Stanley. All are pure.

Another early start is required heading west before a great downhill takes you to the Pieman River and the dam constructed in 1987. The Pieman River was named after convict Alexander Pierce, nicknamed 'The Pieman'. He was a 19th century 'Hannibal the Cannibal' escaping from Sarah Island in the Macquarie Harbour penal settlement twice. He had an unusual way of carrying his food. He survived by killing and eating his accomplices. On the first attempt, he was apprehended at the river after eating seven people. After being sent back to Macquarie Harbour and again escaping and eating his companion, he was found and sent to the Hobart gallows.

Up the other side the road climbs to 200 m again and heads south. A turnoff on the right leads to Granville Harbour. This is a holiday resort for the mining communities of Zeehan, Savage River, and Waratah. The harbour was originally opened up as a soldier settlement in the 1920s. The C249, B71, and the A10 lead back to Rosebery via Zeehan.

A major tourist attraction of Zeehan is the West Coast Pioneers Memorial Museum, displaying the history of European development on the west coast as well as one of the most comprehensive mineral collections in the country.

RIDE 77: ZEEHAN LOOP

FROM: Zeehan
TO: Remine (Trial Harbour)
VIA: Granville Harbour
LENGTH:
    Day 1: Zeehan to Remine 22 km
    Day 2: Remine to Granville Harbour 30 km
    Day 3: Granville Harbour to Zeehan 39 km
    Total is 91 km
TIME: 3 days
RIDE/TRACK GRADE: 8/8
HEIGHT VARIATION: 200 m
TRANSPORT: Own to and from Zeehan
FACILITIES: None
SPECIAL GEAR: Water containers
MAPS: Stringer, Ahrberg, Heemskirk 1:25 000 topographicals, RACT Touring Map of Tasmania. (See Map 11: *STRAHAN*)

This route follows a triangle centred on Mt. Heemskirk and Mt. Agnew. The old ports of Granville and Remine (Trial Harbour) are featured as well as some great desolate coastal scenery. A degree of self-sufficiency is needed as some remote country separates the two harbours.

Access to Zeehan before 1932 existed solely by boat via Trial Harbour. It derived its name from Abel Tasman's ship. Its population was once 10 000 with 26 hotels, all seeking fortunes prospecting for silver and lead. A major attraction is the West Coast Pioneers Memorial Museum, displaying the history of European development on the west coast as well as one of the most comprehensive international mineral collections in Australia. Located on Main St, entry is free.

From Zeehan (population 7000) follow the rough C248 to Remine. Trial Harbour was used to ship Zeehan's steel before a road existed to Hobart or the north coast. Three kilometres of backtracking is needed before the turnoff north to Granville Harbour. This is a holiday resort for the mining communities of Zeehan, Savage River, and Waratah. The harbour was originally opened up as a soldier settlement in the 1920s. Alot of sand is encountered as well as some fierce cross winds as you cycle between the Heemskirk-Agnew plateau and the coast peaking at 200 m. The next day head south for 3 km before turning left to the C249 taking you back to Zeehan.

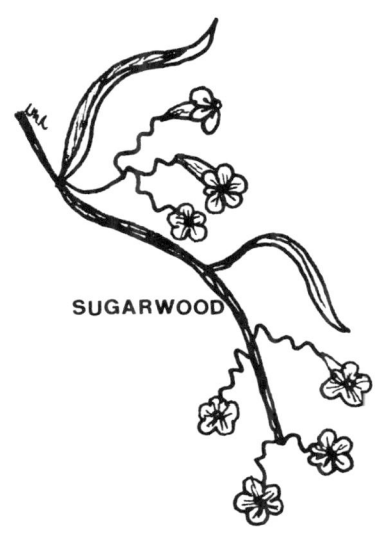

SUGARWOOD

RIDE 78: QUEENSTOWN LOOP

FROM: Queenstown
TO: Zeehan
VIA: Strahan
LENGTH:
   Day 1: Queenstown to Strahan 42 km
   Day 2: Strahan to Zeehan 48 km
   Day 3: Zeehan to Queenstown 43 km
   Total is 133 km
TIME: 3–4 days
RIDE/TRACK GRADE: 6/3
WALKING: 9 km return walk to Henty Dunes (Ocean Beach)
HEIGHT VARIATION: 300 m
TRANSPORT: Coach service to and from Queenstown
FACILITIES: Tourists catered for at Zeehan and Strahan. Camping ground at Strahan, caravan park at Zeehan
MAPS: RACT Touring Map of Tasmania. (See Map 11: *STRAHAN*)

The three most interesting towns on the west coast are included on this tour. Start at Queenstown (pop. 4400). If arriving too late to begin cycling one can spend some time on a tour of the Mt. Lyell mine. One of the most impressive sights is the big 50-tonne capacity trucks.

Exploring this town which owes its existence entirely to copper is quite fascinating. There is the gravel football ground, a few pubs, some old houses, and a symbolic Miners' Siding memorial park containing an old steam engine.

HISTORY: In 1883 two brothers, William and Michael McDonough, travelled from Heemskirk to the Queen River and marked out a claim on the ridge that joins Mount Owen and Mount Lyell.

266

A company was formed and smelting of the copper began in 1896, the outfall creating the famous barren 'lunar' landscape of Queenstown. The Mount Lyell Mining and Railway Company employs about 650 people and produces about 2 million tonnes of ore a year, from which is recovered 22 650 tonnes of copper, 500 kilograms of gold, and 4.2 tonnes of silver. There are actually several mines, the oldest being the Iron Blow, abandoned in 1922. Others in operation are the Prince Lyell, Cape Horn, and A Lens. The road to Queenstown was built in 1932 (it is said that there were only three sober men in town on the evening of the opening). Before then the only access to Hobart was by boat through the treacherous Hell's Gates. Direct access to the north wasn't completed until 1963, and at the time of writing there is still no direct access to the north-west coast.

Take the B24 to Strahan. You'll notice on the downhill through the ranges that there are no water-crossings. This was intentional as the road-builder couldn't be bothered building a bridge.

See Rides 79–81 for notes on seeing Strahan.

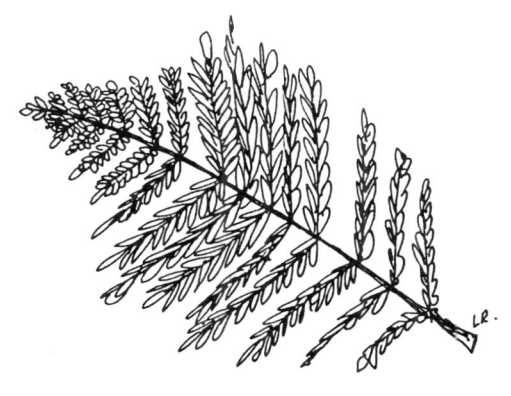

FERN

When ready to leave head up Andrew Street to Zeehan. On the way are pine plantations, the impressive Henty Dunes, and the Henty River. To see the 30 m high dunes, note the spot where the radiata state forests border both sides of the road about 14 km from Strahan. Take the unsealed trail on the left to a car-park and picnic area. A short distance further will get you to the dunes, but a full 45 minutes is needed to get to the ocean. You can split this day into two if you want to camp at one of the four lakes on the other side of the road a little further down.

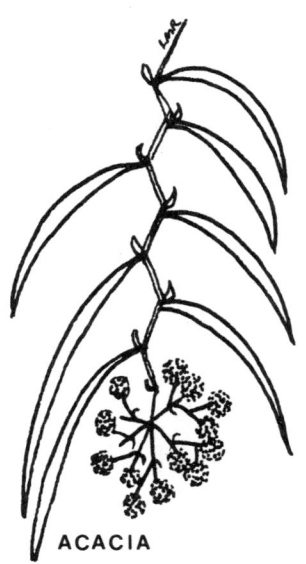

ACACIA

Continue cycling north (B27) crossing the Henty, Badger, and Little Henty Rivers. See Ride 77 for notes on Zeehan.

Next day head east along the B71 to the A10. It is relatively easy going south back to Queenstown with good views of the West Coast Range.

RIDE 79: STRAHAN

FROM: Strahan
TO: Ocean Beach
VIA: Town tour
LENGTH: 22 km
TIME: 1 day
RIDE/TRACK GRADE: 3/4
HEIGHT VARIATION: 30 m
TRANSPORT: Wilderness Transport Network to and from Strahan
FACILITIES: Camping ground and supplies at Strahan
MAPS: Strahan 1:25 000 topographical. (See Map 11: *STRAHAN*)

There is much to see in a comfortable day's cycling around the picturesque town of Strahan.

A. **Ocean Beach**: At 33 km, this is the longest beach in Tasmania. Take Harvey St west. Pass the turn-off to the aerodrome on the left and follow the C250 into strong headwinds (persistent westerlies known as the Roaring Forties). The return trip is 14 km
B. **West Strahan Beach**: Located in the sheltered waters of Long Bay, it's safe for swimming and has picnic tables and electric barbecues provided. This is an ideal spot for lunch after returning from Ocean Beach.
C. **Customs House**: This is located on the water in the central part of town. Built in 1900, the grand building has been used for law courts, post office, and as local headquarters for many other government utilities including the Department of Parks, Wildlife, and Heritage.
D. **Watertower Hill**: A lookout commanding reasonable views of the harbour, coast, and hinterland is located by following the shore

street from Customs House past the pub/hotel. The launching and booking place for the Gordon River cruises and scenic flights is on the right. During the early 1980s, Strahan was the campaign base for the hundreds of conservationists fighting to protect the Franklin River from damming. The wharves on the right were the site of their departure each morning as they made their way across Macquarie Harbour to take on the police and HEC. Turn left at Esk Road branching left at the cafe.

E. **Hogarth Falls:** Leave the bikes behind for a short scenic walk up Botanical Creek from the dirt track leading to the eastern side of People's Park.

F. **Regatta Point Railway Station:** Follow the shore road around Long Bay south to the old station (1899) disused since the 1960s. This was the terminus for a rail-line from the Mt. Lyell Copper Mine at Queenstown. See Ride 81 for more details.

G. **Strahan Cemetery:** Around the corner from the station is the cemetery with descriptive tombstones of the struggles of the miners and other early pioneers. From here it is about 2 km back around the town.

HISTORY: Strahan was founded by Frederick Henty in 1883 and named after Sir George Strahan who was Governor of Tasmania from 1881 to 1886. In 1821, Governor Sorell established a penal station at Macquarie Harbour on the basis of Kelly's reports, for criminals of the worst (7th) class. The *Prince Leopold* was despatched from Hobart with 74 convicts and their wardens. On Sarah Island a living hell was created. Conditions were atrocious, punishments severe, and murders common. And to escape was to exchange one hell for another and 71 perished trying to traverse the dense forests of horizontal scrub of what is now the Wild Rivers National Park without food and provisions. Many however made it; their dramatic accounts of negotiating the rugged terrain such as the Great Ravine of the Franklin River are worth reading.

The prison was abandoned in January 1834 due to high expense and inaccessibility. Whilst most of the work was Huon Pine extraction, other tasks were simply to dig holes and fill them up again in a desperate effort to keep the convicts busy. The last ship to leave, the *Frederick* was seized by the prisoners and taken to South America. There was a brief re-establishment in 1846 but the year after it was abandoned again.

Since then sawmills at Strahan treated the magnificent Huon Pines extracted from the Gordon River and floated across Macquarie Harbour. Dennis McCarthy was the first to extract Huon from the Gordon's banks in 1816. Very quickly thereafter the finest of the pines were removed by the pioneer-legends of the south-west such as Barnes Abel. Alarm at the rapid rate of disappearance was first raised in the 1870s, but of course was too late.

The cyclist-cum-tourist with a few dollars to spend can take one of the scenic river tours up the beautiful Gordon River via Sarah Island to Heritage Landing where a short stroll through Huon pine rainforest can be undertaken. For under $100 (for several people), a scenic flight takes you from Macquarie Harbour, west over Queenstown, Frenchman's Cap, south over the Franklin River gorges, and then *landing* on the Gordon River for tea and a bit of a walk! These have been popular since 1947.

RIDE 80: HELL'S GATES

FROM: Strahan
TO: Macquarie Head (Braddon Point) [RETURN]
LENGTH: 31 km
TIME: 1 day
RIDE/TRACK GRADE: 3/3
HEIGHT VARIATION: 30 m
TRANSPORT: Wilderness Transport Network service to Strahan
FACILITIES: Camping ground and supplies at Strahan. Camping ground also at Braddon Head
SPECIAL GEAR: Wind breaker
MAPS: Kelly 1:25 000 topographical. (See Map 11: *STRAHAN*)

Take the road to Harvey Beach (C250) then turn left to the aerodrome (C251) leading eventually to Braddon Point to view the notoriously dangerous passage known as Hell's Gates which sailing and steam vessels had to negotiate to enter Macquarie Harbour. Since those adventurous days, the Kelly Channel's sand bank was been deepened to allow relatively safer passage. Across the other side is the short stubby white lighthouse of Cape Sorell.

Macquarie Harbour was discovered in 1816 by Captain James Kelly when circumnavigating Van Diemen's Land and named after Governor Lachlan Macquarie. It is the drowned valley of the mighty Gordon River when waters rose after the last Ice Age about 4000 B.C.

RIDE 81: TEEPOOKANA

FROM: Strahan
TO: Teepookana [RETURN]
LENGTH: 29 km
TIME: 1 day
RIDE/TRACK GRADE: 4/5
HEIGHT VARIATION: 40 m
TRANSPORT: Wilderness Transport Network to and from Strahan
FACILITIES: Camping ground and supplies at Strahan
MAPS: Teepookana 1:25 000 topographical. (See Map 11: *STRAHAN*)

On this short ride, the cyclist can visit the ruins of the old rack-rail link from the Mount Lyell mine to the port at Teepookana which operated in the late nineteenth century. E. T. Emmett, the founder of the Hobart Walking Club, had this to say about the old track from to Strahan:

> *Easily the finest railway journey in Australia is that from Queenstown to Strahan. The engineer who laid down that track deserved a knighthood. Seeing this country from the rail it is easy to understand why there were no escapees from the region by land except when cannibalism was resorted to. The only way to get food was to have it walking alongside for use when you became hungry.*

From Strahan cycle around Long Bay and down to Bromley Street. This follows the route of the original railway. Where cars have to park, the cyclist on his all-terrain bike can continue for about 7 km past the old township of Teepookana to the iron Quarter-Mile Bridge over the King River. The track is not a disused firetrail, but the dismantled rail-line, overgrown with thick rainforest due to the wet climate. It was named the Abt railway, after the German designer. Closed in the 1960s, its terminus was the Regatta Point Railway Station which has lasted in Strahan since 1899.

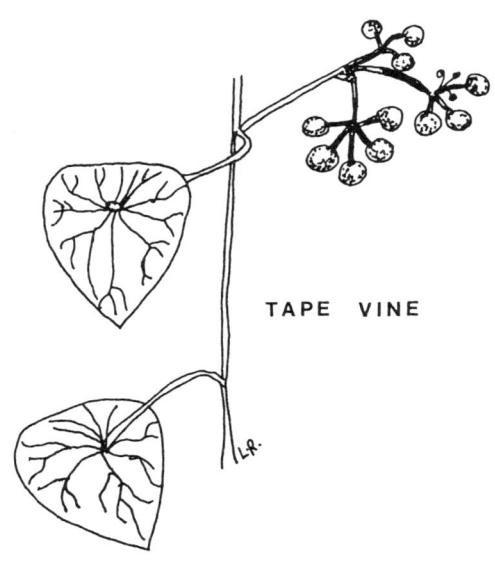

TAPE VINE

OTHER RIDES

Due to space constraints it is not possible to cover a great variety of areas that are directly accessible to the mountain cyclist from the north-west coast cities. This is one of the weaker points of this guide as a host of great rides in the hinterland behind Smithton are omitted. In particular is the Mawbanna Recreation Area between Rocky Cape National Park and Stanley and almost bordering the Bass Highway.

There are also a number of small Forest Reserves south of Burnie that would make interesting day rides. Although I've not cycled it, there is apparently a service track for the pipeline that extends all the way from Savage River to Port Latta. One would have to enquire as to the legality of cycling here, but it travels through some incredibly wild terrain.

Hydro-electric developments have also created a network of maintenance trails around the numerous schemes of the north-west. New detailed maps are needed for their location. The connecting road in between Marrawah and Savage River (under construction at time of writing) will also open up areas such as Balfour and the west coast.

9

THE SOUTH-WEST

The south-west is Australia's premier wilderness. There are no other similar landscapes in the world. Dozens of jagged quartzite ranges with spectacular peaks sharing ridgetops with glacial lakes, rainforest filled valleys, and button-grass plains make this ideal terrain for the hard-core adventurer.

For the mountain-biker there is little opportunity for extensive exploration as most of this area is primarily wild. Even if there were trails, their roller-coaster gradients and hard quartzite base-rock would make travelling very laborious for both bike and rider.

However, hydro-electric developments in the 1960s and 1970s have been responsible for the creation of roads penetrating into areas previously only accessible by air or foot. The two main roads to Strathgordon and Scotts Peak Dam have become tourist roads. However there are a number of maintenance trails around Lake Gordon and Lake Pedder, as well as a network of logging trails dating from 1932 throughout the Florentine River valley that offer excellent mountain cycling opportunities. Likewise, the park standing at the entrance to the south-west, Mt. Field National Park with its famous Russell Falls has its slopes riddled with logging tracks. The main tourist road from the plateau top has a 1200 m downhill.

For truly rewarding exploration of the south-west, overnight walking is mandatory. Detailed tracknotes are beyond the scope of this book but some one-day walks are outlined. For walking coverage, one needs a book like Tyrone Thomas's *100 Walks in Tasmania* (3rd edition) or a number of other field guides that deal exclusively with the south-west. Mapping coverage is limited and due to the rugged nature of the terrain, bushwalking, navigational, medicinal, and survival experience is crucial. Almost every year a few people venture into this huge wilderness never to be seen again.

How was it formed? One billion years ago, frequent crustal activity interrupted the deposition process in the low-lying areas. The quartzite that dominates the texture of the present ranges is made from silicon oxide deposits laid down and cemented over 200 million years. These Precambrian sedimentary layers became extremely tilted and folded and subject to high temperatures and consequently metamorphosed and fractured. Relatively recent events assisted in further turbulence: volcanic action injected molten rock up towards the surface displacing large planes of rock, glaciation, and erosion accelerated by the inclement weather—howling winds and three metres of rain a year.

The final Ice age, 24 000 years ago, saw the sea level 100 metres lower than at present allowing Aboriginals a 60 km wide corridor from the Australian mainland to Tasmania. Evidence of occupation remains in the form of middens, rock art sites, and cave deposits. The Aboriginals in the south-west, at the time the most southerly human habitat in the world, lived mainly on the coast overlooking a sea of icebergs and fed on a maritime diet: elephant seals, muttonbirds (short-tailed shearwaters), crayfish, shellfish, penguins, and their eggs. A common practice was firing (to aid hunting and travel) and the present coastal sedgelands are believed to be a product of this. The last of the native inhabitants left the south-west in the 1840s.

European history is one of exploitation. The unique huon pine trees were actively sought after and extracted, whaling and sealing were carried on from the bays along the coast such as Port Davey, mining leases dating back to 1890 for gold, coal, tin, copper, asbestos, limestone, lead, marble, nickel, osmiridium, antimony, and silica. Trout were introduced in the rivers, and convict road builders were starting to penetrate from the east and north. More recently, forestry operations, tourism, and above all hydro-electricity have all made a major impact on the south-west and management planning requires intense scrutiny and regulation of operations. For example, I myself am not permitted to detail certain rides that, while perfectly possible on the mountain bike, would violate the south-west's wilderness values.

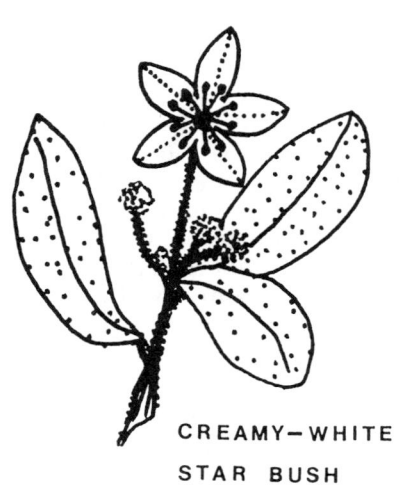

CREAMY—WHITE
STAR BUSH

RIDE 82: MT. FIELD NATIONAL PARK

FROM: Park Entrance
TO: Lake Dobson [RETURN]
VIA: Lake Dobson Road
LENGTH: 34 km
TIME: 3 days (2 days cycling, recommended 1 day walking)
RIDE/TRACK GRADE: 7/4
WALKING: Mt. Field West, Twilight Tarn, Lake Belton, Mt. Field East, Lake Belcher, Russell Falls
HEIGHT VARIATION: 750 m
TRANSPORT: Wilderness Transport Network to and from park entrance
FACILITIES: Developed camp ground at entrance. Huts on plateau top but bookings required, Youth Hostel at National Park
SPECIAL GEAR: Cold weather gear
MAPS: Mt. Field National Park 1:50 000. (See Map 1: *DERWENT*)

From National Park entrance head into the park. Chain your bikes up and see Russell Falls along the popular short stroll on the western bank of Russell Falls Creek. You've probably seen it in a million tourist brochures and post cards (and yes in this book as well), but seeing it for yourself is worthwhile. They're a photographer's paradise with just about every angle already being a cliché. The falls were discovered in 1856 and originally called Brownings Falls. Dropping 36 m, they were proclaimed a reserve in 1885.

Along the way are giant trees, *Eucalyptus regnans*, growing well over 100 m in height. They are also known as mountain ash, swamp gum, and Tasmanian oak.

If it is already afternoon, camp in the popular campground/caravan park at the park entrance.

Supplies and souvenirs can be purchased from the kiosk. One might have time to do a quick circuit of Lady Barron Falls and Horse-shoe Falls before dusk. This takes about two to three hours.

The camping ground here has 40 sites and provides full facilities: laundry, hot showers, toilets, and cooking shelter. It is often fully booked with firewood consumption close to 300 tonnes a year so prior arrangements might be necessary during holiday times. Otherwise arrive earlier and camp on the plateau tops.

HISTORY: Originally known simply as the National Park, the Mt. Field plateau was a popular weekend skiing venue for Hobart folk in the late 1920s and early '30s. The lack of facilities allowed cross-country skiers (langläufers) only and that's exactly what they did. Excursions into the south-west were not uncommon: the Hartz Mountains, Snowy Range, Mt. King William, over Newdegate Pass to the Florentine Valley, and even big Mt. Anne. The park was renamed after its highest peak in honour of Judge Barron Field of New South Wales who visited Hobart in 1819 and 1821. His achievements included writing Australia's first poetry and establishing the first bank.

The next morning begin the long grinding, painful cycle up to Sitzmark Lodge at 1220 m (you start at 180 m). The 18 km to the top following the C609 will take you most of the day. To break the monotony there is a short nature walk on the right about 7 km along through the towering eucalypts. As you ascend it'll get noticeably cooler. Boulder-strewn slopes contrast with icy lakes.

Just past Lake Fenton the going gets easier, there are some views and even a downhill! Along the way are the Government Huts. These were originally located at Lake Fenton in the 1930s. They provide wood heaters, water, bunks, and septic toilets. Public vehicles are barred from proceeding past Lake Dobson. Continue past the gate and around Eagle Tarn zig-zagging up the Mawson plateau. Leave the bikes at the lodge for a half-hour walk up the Mawson Tor to South West Lookout (1300 m). When not in the clouds, the scenery to Florentine Peak and Mt. Mueller is awesome.

The lodges in the area are for members only, the other huts are for emergency use. This requires tent camping in potentially arctic conditions. Choose either Lake Dobson or Eagle Tarn. Next day try some of the day walks detailed on the Mt. Field National Park 1:50 000 map.

From Lake Dobson:

Twisted Tarn	7 hours
Twilight Tarn	8 hours
Mt. Field West (1 434 m)	8 hours

The downhill of a lifetime awaits you when you're ready to leave the plateau. It takes less than 40 minutes to reach the bottom. Watch your brakes!

DATA TABLE: Mt. Field National Park

Size: 16 977 ha
Enactment: 1885: Scenic Reserve (2204 ha)
            1916: National Park (Tasmania's first)
Animals: Pademelons, wallabies, water rats, snakes, frogs, lizards, devils, wombats, potoroos, possums, robins.
Plants: Pandani, King Billy Pine, tanglefoot, pencil pines.
Attractions: Russell Falls, Mt. Field West (1 439 m). Most popular Tasmanian National Park.
Camping: Camp ground at base, accommodation huts on plateau
District Office: Westerway (002) 88-1148

RIDE 83: FLORENTINE RIVER

FROM: Maydena
TO: Florentine River [RETURN]
VIA: Florentine Road
LENGTH: 90-100 km depending on campsite preferred
TIME: 2-3 days
RIDE/TRACK GRADE: 7/6–7
HEIGHT VARIATION: 300 m
TRANSPORT: Wilderness Transport Network to and from Maydena
FACILITIES: None
SPECIAL GEAR: Self-sufficiency
MAPS: Maydena, Dobson, Tiger, Gordonvale 1:25 000 topographicals. (See Map 12: *GORDON*)

The Florentine River valley offers many outlets for the energies of enthusiastic mountain bikers. From the drop-off point at Maydena head west for 2 km along the road to Strathgordon. Turn right onto Florentine Road (300 m) where it's easy cycling across the upper catchment area of the Tyenna River close to the boundary of Mt. Field National Park. The road then climbs steadily to Florentine Gap (600 m) between the impressive guardians of Tim Shea (965 m) on the left and Wherrets Lookout (1000 m). This road was the main thoroughfare for loggers and miners in the Florentine Valley.

Keep on the Florentine Road. The topographical maps will come in handy in solving navigational queries as a multitude of major and minor tracks branch off on both sides. It is 31 km to the first crossing via Tiger Road. If you don't like this as a campsite head back up to the Florentine Road and north for 15 km to the next crossing at the confluence with Coles Creek.

The moderate to high rainfall here supports wet sclerophyll vegetation such as ferns and rainforest.

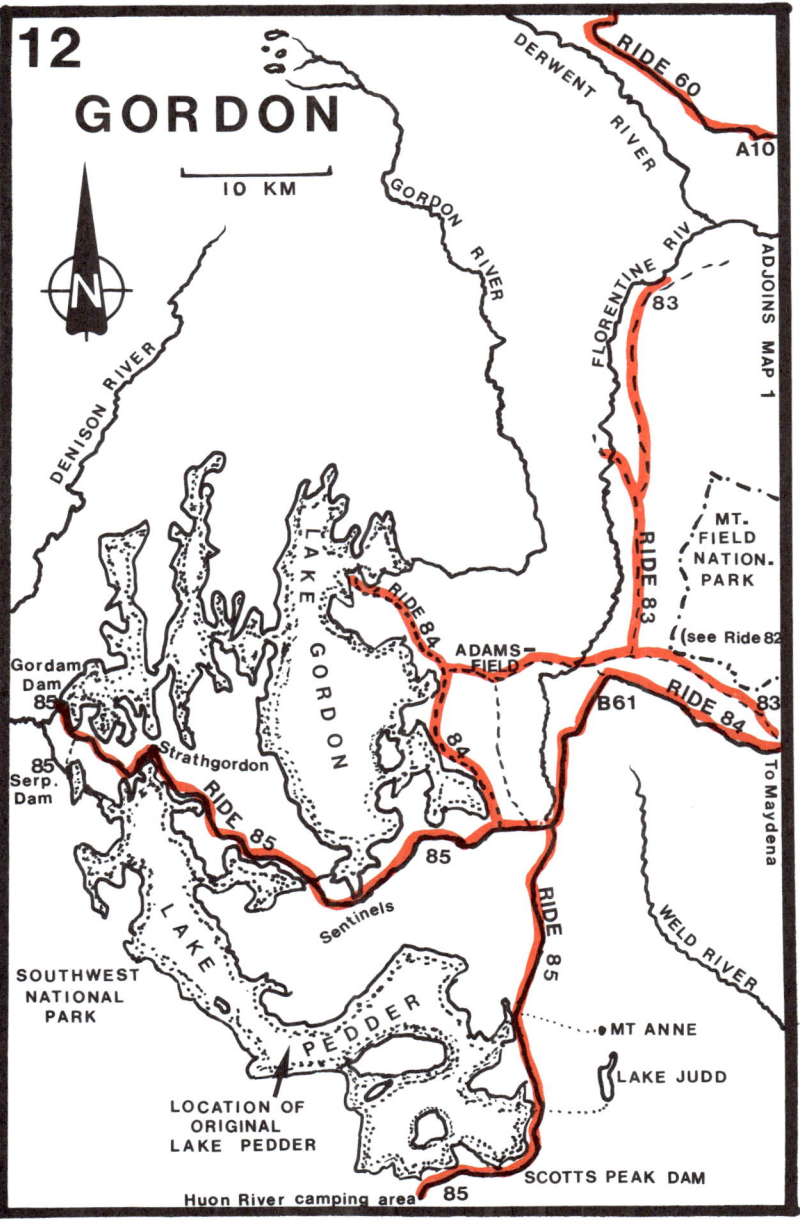

HISTORY: Artefacts such as burned bones from the Beginner's Luck cave in the valley have been dated at more than 12 000 years. Charcoal from the cave was dated at 30 000 years. During this time, known as the late Pleistocene period, man co-existed with *Macropus titan*, an unusually large kangaroo, and emus. This suggests that the climate was colder, drier and vegetation consequently more open. Other fossils found in the Florentine Valley paint a picture of the vicinity consisting of rolling grassy hills dotted with shrubs and isolated copses of eucalypt forest.

The area was extensively logged to the extent that part of the Mt. Field National Park had to be revoked. Some of the deepest caves in Australia became unprotected and now have thick sediment accumulation from accelerated erosion on the surface.

The river was named by Surveyor-General George Frankland in 1835, presumably after the Italian equivalent. It was here that the famous last Tasmanian Tiger was found in 1933. Many of the marsupial carnivores were found here in response to the £1 bounty paid by the Tasmanian government between 1888 and 1909.

Return via the same route.

RIDE 84: LAKE GORDON

FROM: Maydena
TO: Crossing Point [RETURN]
VIA: Florentine River, Adamsfield
LENGTH:
    Day 1: Maydena to Florentine River 37 km
    Day 2: Florentine River to Crossing Point 18 km
    Day 3: Crossing Point to Maydena 32 km
    Total is 87 km
TIME: 3–4 days
RIDE/TRACK GRADE: 8/9
HEIGHT VARIATION: 500 m
TRANSPORT: Wilderness Transport Network to and from Maydena
FACILITIES: None
SPECIAL GEAR: Complete self-sufficiency
MAPS: Adamsfield, Tiger, Wings 1:25 000 topographicals. (See Map 12: *GORDON*)

This ride details the only pure mountain bike ride one can do in the south-west wilderness region. It covers the base of Mt. Field National Park, the upper Florentine Valley, the abandoned overgrown town of Adamsfield and the shore of Lake Gordon Dam itself.

From Maydena head west for 2 km along the Gordon River Road. Turn right onto Florentine Road (300 m) where it's easy cycling across the upper catchment area of the Tyenna River close to the boundary of Mt. Field National Park. The road then climbs steadily to Florentine Gap (600 m) between the impressive guardians of Tim Shea (965 m) on the left and Wherrets Lookout (1000 m). This road was the main thoroughfare for loggers and miners in the Florentine Valley. The Adamsfield and Tiger 1:25 000 topographicals are needed to negotiate your way through the maze of old disused trails down to the Florentine River. Camp anywhere you find suitable.

Next morning cycle west to Adamsfield. Today little is left of the old township with melaleuca squarrosas and bracken ferns rehabilitating the site.

HISTORY: The township of Adamsfield was founded in 1925 supporting the workings of the osmiridium fields, first discovered by William Hope Twelvetrees in 1909. Its population quickly reached 2000, making it the biggest mining settlement in the south-west containing a hospital, school, police station, post office, bakery, and butcher. Osmiridium is a naturally occurring alloy of the platinum metal group with applications in dentistry, jewellery, and fountain pen nibs. Prospectors, using the sluicing method, were rewarded with about £25–£30 pounds per ounce, five times that of gold! Two years later, the small workable deposit was spent (2000 ounces were being extracted per month), the price declined, and the wet muddy conditions caused most to leave.

Head down into the Adams River valley by the northern end of Ragged Range. This will join up 5 km later with the Crossing Point Road. Turn right and head north rising to about 700 m before descending down to the water. This lake is characterised by the many dead trees that remained unfelled before the waters rose. Yet hundreds of thousands of Huon Pines (*Dacrydium franklinii*) *were* cut down before the dam was finished in 1974. They floated with the rising waters and were simply collected by boat. Some were dated at 2500-3000 years. Now, Lake Gordon's capacity is so great that if spread evenly over Tasmania's surface, it would drown the state in 18 cm of water!

After contouring round the base of Clear Hill (1198 m), there are three choices of potential campsites at Crossing Point. Once here, one can

286

cast a line in and relax. Just a few kilometres to the right the mighty Gordon River ends its natural flow, its headwaters to the north in the King William Range. The river's name is of interesting derivation. Captain James Kelly circumnavigated Tasmania, including Macquarie Harbour, in 1815. The bloke who lent him the whaleboat so he could do it was James Gordon.

When ready to leave head out to the Strathgordon Road following the lake shore south. It's 30 km to the road and then another 32 km to Maydena.

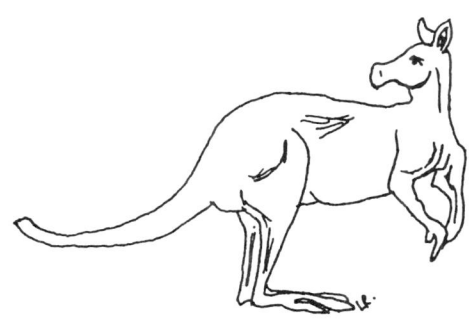

GREY KANGAROO

RIDE 85: LAKE PEDDER
(STRATHGORDON)
(GORDON DAM)

FROM: Scotts Peak Dam
TO: Maydena
VIA: Wedge River Rest Area, Strathgordon, Gordon Dam
LENGTH:
   Day 1: Scotts Peak Dam to Wedge River 57 km
   Day 2: Wedge River to Strathgordon 26 km
   Day 3: Strathgordon to dams return 36 km
   Day 4: Strathgordon to Maydena 61 km
   Total is 180 km
TIME: 4–9 days
RIDE/TRACK GRADE: 6/3
WALKING:
Short 'tourist' walks: Creepy Crawley, Jack's Track
Full day walks: Lake Judd, Mt. Anne, Sentinel Range
Overnight walks: Judd-Anne circuit, Truchanas Nature Reserve
HEIGHT VARIATION: 200 m cycling, up to 1100 m walking
TRANSPORT: Wilderness Transport Network to Scotts Peak Dam and pick-up rendezvous from Maydena
FACILITIES: Supplies at Strathgordon (prices slightly inflated), 2 camping grounds at Scotts Peak Dam, and rest area at Wedge River. Usual amenities, wood supplied.
SPECIAL GEAR: Cold, wet weather gear (fishing optional)
MAPS: RACT Touring Map if only cycling, relevant topographicals ESSENTIAL if walking. (See Map 12: *GORDON*)

This ride encompasses much of what the wild south-west is about. From the drop-off point at Scotts Peak Dam you are on your own. The mountain scenery on this ride is unsurpassed in Australia. Along the way, I've outlined some walks that can be done to get a greater feel of the essence of wilderness, essentially by a more intimate interaction between man and nature. For the inexperienced walker they are difficult involving vertical climbs of over a kilometre along extremely steep and rocky, or conversely wet and muddy, tracks. MAPS AND EMERGENCY PROVISIONS ARE ESSENTIAL. Furthermore, consideration must be given to the unpredictable weather changes. Snow can fall any time making difficult ledge and boulder descents treacherous.

At Scotts Peak Dam there are two camping areas. Invariably the anglers and general tourists go for the Edgar Camping Area close to Lake Pedder. The bushwalkers go for the more remote but beautiful Huon River Camping Area located off the road further west. Private campsites are provided with picnic tables, fireplaces, and wood. In your 'backyard', you'll have magnificent temperate rainforest comprising ancient Huon Pines and Myrtle Beeches. Watch your food as the possums are quite cheeky; less so are the many tame pademelons.

Upon arriving, spend the rest of the day looking around. Scotts Peak Dam is a kilometre long rock fill wall 43 m high that together with the Edgar and Serpentine walls, dams Lake Pedder so the total water impounded together with Lake Gordon is nearly 15 cubic kilometres (!) creating over a trillion watts per year for a population of well under 200 000.

HISTORY: Lake Pedder was originally labelled the 'jewel of the south-west'. Named after Sir John Pedder, Chief Justice of Van Diemen's Land Supreme Court when Wedge discovered it in 1835, it was lined by a famous white quartz beach 730 metres wide serving as the only landing strip and providing the only nonfoot access to the south-west. Winter rains in 1972 began flooding the lake and the unusually huge beach disappeared by 1973. The site of the original beach can only be reached by boat, lying under 15 m of water between the eastern rise of the Frankland Range and the Coronets.

The next day cycle north. The first option will soon confront you . . .

SIDE WALK 1: LAKE JUDD

For the fisherman, a one day side walk to Lake Judd (591 m) will be rewarded with perhaps the most scenic fishing lake in Tasmania, ranking with Shadow Lake. The huge 600 m vertical dolerite cliffs of the Mt. Anne complex, often covered in low cloud and snow, make a spectacular backdrop to this beautiful lake where thick wooded eucalypt and tea tree wet forest comes right to the shore.

The start of the 16 km return walking track is well signposted on the right hand side as you're cycling north 2 km from Edgar Dam. From the carpark, the track heads east, is well marked and relatively easy going as the height variation is only 250 m. However it is often swampy despite upgrading using duckboards. Before the Anne River is crossed for the second time, the trail branches right. Left (north) across the river will take you to the lake, while right takes you over the scenic route ascent of Mt. Anne.

Map needed for walk: Scotts 1:25 000 topographical.

About 4 km past the Lake Judd turnoff, another signpost and carpark marks the start of the walking track to Mt. Anne:

SIDE WALK 2: MT. ANNE

If you're fit, you can do this walk in a day. Others elect to stay at the High Camp Memorial Hut at 1050 m at the half way mark. The total return distance is 16 km with a vertical height variation of 1100 m. Follow the walking track straight up the steep ridge to the hut. This should take around 90–120 minutes. Continue straight up an even steeper slope to Mt. Eliza and thence along an undulating ridge following rock cairns to the summit itself. Some difficult rock scrambling over the frost-exploded dolerite is required and rope is required to protect the inexperienced. Views are superb as this is the highest peak in the south-west. However, quite often all that walkers get to see is the inside of a cloud.

Henry Judd walked from Huonville to Mt. Anne in 1880 but it wasn't until 1929 that the summit was first climbed by W. Crookall and G. Chapman. It was named after Surveyor-General Frankland's wife.

The north-east ridge, made of softer dolomite (limestone rich in magnesium) is the location of the entrance of Australia's deepest cave. Called the Anne-A-Kanada, it has its deepest survey point at 373 m and includes a vertical pitch of 118 m. So if abseiling dizzying heights and camping in total darkness appeals to you, this is the place to be. However it's not open to the public and a permit is required.

Map needed for walk: Anne 1:25 000 topographical.

Continue cycling north along C607, gradually moving away from Lake Pedder. Large poster-boards along the road tell of the geological history of the south-west. One in particular notes an interesting recent fault line, ensuring visitors that the process of change is perpetual. You'll also pass regular signs highlighting geographical features along the way. About two to three hours after passing the Mt. Anne turnoff, you'll come to . . .

SIDE WALK 3: CREEPY-CRAWLEY NATURE WALK

Located 26 km from Scotts Peak Dam, this 5 minute stroll is developed to the extent where you don't even touch the ground. The entire walk is done along a raised platform with regular information placards depicting a 'mystery-solving exercise' that insults your intelligence. Nevertheless the cyclist, who doesn't have time for the long side-walks listed in this ride, is given an insight into the nature of the temperate rainforest. Moss plays an important role here and photographers who'd like to catch the intense 'greenness' must carry a tripod for light conditions necessitate exposure speeds of 10 seconds or more.

Pedalling north once more you'll soon come to a T-intersection with the Strathgordon Road (B61) with views to Lake Gordon. Head left (west). The road you are cycling on here cost $5 000 000 and was paid for by a non-repayable loan from the federal government granted in 1963. Originally a permit was required to travel along it.

There are a number of camping options here. One can take one of the side roads to the shore of Lake Gordon or cycle all the way to the Wedge River Rest Area. This is located on the left about 57 km from Scotts Peak Dam. Facilities include a shelter, wood, and toilets. As a campground the rest area rates about 1 out of 10 because there's no grass. Self-supporting tents are a great benefit here as pegs are nearly impossible to drive in. As this is the only official camping ground along the Strathgordon Road, it is usually popular. The next day can be spent climbing the prominent range that dominates the western skyline of this area.

SIDE WALK 4: THE SENTINELS

This is a largely unmarked wilderness walk and only for experienced bushwalkers familiar with the practice of minimal impact walking. The Department of Parks, Wildlife, and Heritage classify their tracks on a scale of T1–T4 with the T1 being the easiest. This is a T4 which implies that the track is largely unmarked and visitor-use is less than 250 in a year.

From the Wedge River Rest Area cross the Wedge River to the south (fill up with plenty of water) and head straight up through thick low scrub. When looking ahead to the Sentinels, head for a sheltered 'chimney' to the right of a massive block of sheer grey rock (quartzite). It'll take about an hour to reach the foot but a track does eventually become apparent as the vegetation thins out. Look out for small white cloth markers. The track zig-zags up over rock and it'll provide a relief from the thick scrub. Diverge right off the track as it enters the gully as it is easier going over the rock. Watch out as foot and hand holds can become loose. Keep heading right around outcrops until you eventually reach the razor-ridge and views over the other side to Lake Pedder and the Frankland Range. Continue as close to the centre of the ridge as possible for 4–5 hours. Progress will be slow and occasionally scrubby. But the incredible vistas of Frenchman's Cap, Mt. Anne, and in fact a multitude of craggy peaks and saw-back ranges for 360 degrees with the gigantic lakes of Pedder and Gordon in the foreground make it worthwhile. Head down to the road when you've had enough. This could take two hours as once again thick scrub has to be negotiated. It's then a short walk back to the bikes at the rest area.

Map needed for walk: McPartlans 1:25 000 topographical

When ready to continue, head back up the Strathgordon Road and continue west. This section is the thin corridor of land between the two great lakes of Gordon and Pedder. You soon return to views of Lake Pedder as you cross a canal 6 km from Wedge River. This is the McPartlan Pass Canal opened in July 1974 connecting Lake Pedder to Lake Gordon (as the former is 61 cm higher). Occasionally flooding will cause the water to flow the other way as Lake Gordon has no orthodox spillway. Flow is controlled by a radial gate. It's named after the extraordinary bushman Francis McPartlan (1824-1888) who was a postman, policeman, prospector, miner, survey assistant, and track cutter.

You follow the northern shore of the beautiful Lake Pedder for 20 km with its dark waters reflecting the great Frankland Range on the far shore. The ever-present eyesore of the power lines is a reminder the wilderness here has been violated permanently. At Strathgordon you can restock on supplies, although prices are somewhat high. This village supported the construction workers peaking at 2000 inhabitants but today houses just the maintenance workers and visiting tourists.

SIDE WALK 5: JACK'S TRACK

Starting from the Gordon Dam road 200 m west of the Huon Pine log, this short track is maintained by the Public Relations Department of the Hydro-Electric Commission. It leads through mixed rainforest varying between 100 and 200 years old. Markers identify native species. At the end, cross the bridge and you're back on the Gordon Dam road. Return time is half an hour.

One can spend the night here as sheltered accommodation is provided. The next day jump back on your bike and head out to the dam through spectacular mountain scenery. At the end diverge right to the lookout before accessing the dam directly. It is just a short walk from the carpark. The concrete super-structure and steep narrow gorge are truly incredible feats of engineering from both man and nature. Built in 1974, the dam stands at 140 m, and has a crest length of 190 m.

Head back and down to the octagonal tourist shelter overlooking the dam. This was built in 1977 and contains a 3-D model of the power station. There are more great views of the bowl here and one is allowed to climb down via a steel cage ladder to the dam wall itself. The other side however is locked.

Tour guides will tell you the sheer pressure of the water behind the dam is actually pushing it down the gorge by fractions of a millimetre per year. Already there is a large crack in it (on the lower left) and surveyors check regularly with ultra-accurate laser instruments.

SIDE WALK 6: TRUCHANAS NATURE RESERVE

Permission is needed to walk up the steel ladder on the western side of the dam. Then it's a 30 km two-three day hike to the reserve which protects 400 ha of the largest remaining mature forests of the aromatic softwood, Huon Pine. Discovered in 1928, the reserve is named posthumously after Olegas Truchanas, a Lithuanian migrant, the first to canoe the Gordon and who fought for its preservation. He died in an accident in the south-west while taking photographs for the 'Save Lake Pedder' campaign in 1972. The reserve is on the Denison River, and there are no facilities. Phone (002) 30-8033 for details.

Map needed for walk: Olga 1:100 000 topographical

Head back to Strathgordon, but not before checking out the Serpentine Dam (8 km return). This inconspicuous looking rockwall is the one that flooded the original lake. There is a picnic area and lookout on the left-hand side as you cycle south.

After a night either here or at Strathgordon, make your way out of the wilderness by cycling back to Maydena 61 km to the east.

DATA TABLE: Southwest National Park

Size: 800 000 ha (20% of Tasmania)
Enactment: 16 October 1968
              Enlarged 1981
Aboriginal Sites: Middens along coast, little else
Animals: Platypus, pademelons, possums, wallabies
Plants: Huon Pines, King Billy Pines, Button grass, Cushion plants, pandani, laurel, sassafras, waratah, horizontal.
Attractions: Walking, rock climbing, fishing.
Camping: Scotts Peak Dam, Wedge River Forest Preserve
District Office: (002) 30-2620

OTHER RIDES

By catching a punt across Macquarie Harbour from Strahan, one of the remotest areas for mountain cycling in Australia is available to you. Old mining tracks totalling hundreds of kilometres lead through the South-West Conservation Area as far south as the Lewis River and Low Rocky Point. Experience and self-sufficiency would be of crucial importance due to the extreme isolation. Local information is essential from the Strahan Parks and Wildlife office and it is also possible that this area would be closed to cyclists if included in the South West National Park and World Heritage Area.

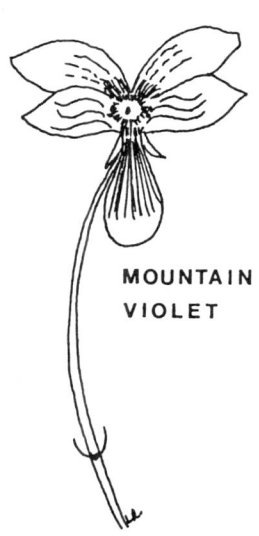

MOUNTAIN VIOLET

10
THE ISLANDS

Bass Strait has 120 islands. The two largest ones, King and Flinders, have been developed for tourists. However regulations are minimal and many areas, especially near the coast, are free for camping.

Cycling is the most efficient way of seeing these islands due to the great expense of importing or hiring a car. The islands are too large to walk, but small enough to cover in about a 10 day excursion.

There are plenty of natural and historical attractions but equally substantial is the unique tranquil atmosphere where one can truly 'get away from it all'. Bruny and Maria Island, while closer to Tasmania, are no exception. These two have the advantage of being easily accessible by ferry and indeed one-day trips based from the mainland are possible.

Please note that snakes are more concentrated on these islands than on the mainland so care is needed when walking in low scrub during summer.

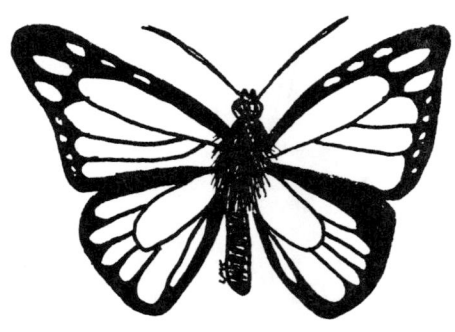

MARIA ISLAND
(The Ceylon of Australasia)

Named by Abel Janszoon Tasman in honour of the
wife of Anthony Van Diemen, Maria Van Aelst, the
island's European history dates from French
revolution times. In 1789, Captain Cox stepped
ashore at Shoal Bay. Contact with the resident
Aboriginals (who called the island 'Toarra Marra
Monah') was made, but unsuccessfully. Further
expeditions developed relations cautiously, but
when Hobart developed into a sealing and whaling
port and Maria Island was used as a base by ships
from all around the world, hostilities developed.
One attack by Aboriginals destroyed 2000 seal
skins. Whaling settlements were established at
Whalers Cove and Haunted Bay.

The convict colony was founded in 1825 by 50
Class 6 convicts. These were almost the worst of
them: convicted of offences in the colony and
sentenced to hard labour, one class away from the
hell-on-earth Sarah Island in Macquarie Harbour.
Conditions on Maria Island were luxurious in
comparison although there were continuous
escape attempts. Other convicts working for
settlers deliberately misbehaved so they could be
drafted to the island. The convicts produced a
variety of goods: cloth, shoes, blankets, mops,
wheelbarrows, tubs, stools, pots, and pans. These
were sold in Hobart.

However, escapees were repeatedly successful
and the settlement was closed in 1832, and most
of the remaining convicts were sent to Port Arthur.
For the next ten years it was leased by settlers,
then it became a probation station for about 800
convicts sent direct from England. A typical day
started at 4.45 am with punishment varying from
solitary confinement to lashings. By 1850, the flow

of prisoners from Britain had ceased and once again the settlement was abandoned.

The island was then leased for £300 a year until the 1880s when Angel Giulio Diego Bernacchi, an Italian silk merchant, arrived. He was granted a controversial lease for ten years paying just one shilling a year. Bernacchi prospered, spending and making thousand of pounds on wine and silk production. He hosted elaborate parties and Darlington became the thriving township of San Diego with 250 employees having their own school, bank, post office, and blacksmith. The Maria Island Company was floated in 1887 with capital of £250 000 establishing farms, quarrying limestone, fisheries, timber export, resort, etc. Orchards provided olives, oranges, cherries, and pears.

However all this prosperity came to a end. The company went into liquidation, profit projections were overestimated, and it was discovered that the wealth potential of the island was somewhat exaggerated by Bernacchi. Around the turn of the century, the island was open once again to selectors.

The population boomed again in the 1920s as Bernacchi made another attempt to exploit Maria for all it was worth. Annual production was 30 000 tons but economies of scale dictated that double that was needed in order to be viable. It went into debt and ceased business in 1930.

Another period ended, the island's population dwindled and it became known as the quiet place where it was 'always afternoon'.

It became a national park in 1971, principally as a reservation for fauna protection in dry sclerophyll forest. For example between 1968 and 1971, 45 of the endangered Cape Barren Geese were released which have now multiplied into many hundreds. The waters lining the island to the north are 1500 ha of marine reserve where no fishing is permitted. The convict ruins were restored and the island advertised as a tourist destination that is the highlight of any trip to Tasmania.

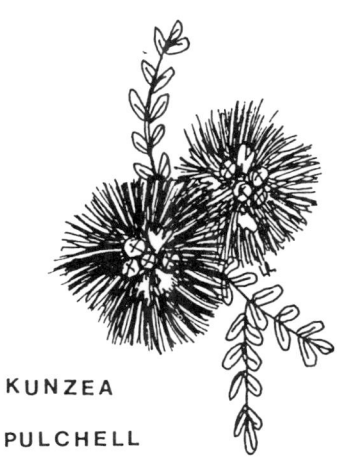

KUNZEA

PULCHELL

DATA TABLE: Maria Island National Park

Size: 9672 ha (20 km x 13 km)
Enactment: 14 June 1972
Animals: One of the last refuges for the 6000 remaining Cape Barren Geese, one of 130 species of birds found on the island.
Plants: Blue, white, and manna gums, stringybark, black & white peppermints.
Attractions: Darlington penal settlement, unique tranquil island atmosphere, and geologists' paradise as dolerite, sandstone, granite, and limestone formations are all represented.
Camping: Several campgrounds, two developed with standard facilities. There are also basic accommodation units in the penitentiary.
District Office: (002) 57-1420

RIDE 86: DARLINGTON

FROM: Ferry Wharf
TO: Bernacchis Creek reservoir
VIA: Darlington Penal Settlement, and various ruins
LENGTH: 12 km
TIME: 1 easy day
RIDE/TRACK GRADE: 3/4
HEIGHT VARIATION: 98 m
TRANSPORT: Ferry from Triabunna
FACILITIES: Camping ground at Darlington
MAPS: Maria Island National Park 1:50 000 (See Map 7: *TASMAN PENINSULA*)

The first buildings that are noticed as the ferry docks are the old granary, miller's cottage, and site of the old windmill to the north. The oldest building is the square stone one closest to the jetty. It's the commissariat store built in 1825, now an information centre. Pamphlets can be purchased via donation.

For a preliminary tour of Maria taking into account all the major historical ruins, head left to Cape Boulanger. This is the site of the landing ground and the location of the giant cement works built in the inter-war years. The sea here is home to giant kelp forests. The small flat island located off the tip is Ile du Nord, meaning north island. This was the proposed location of the female convict cloth-making factory. The smaller outcrop on the right is Bird Rock, a roosting place for the local sea-birds.

Next head into Darlington along a tree-lined avenue. All the noteworthy buildings are signposted: the penitentiary (built in 1830), Smith O'Brien's Cottage, the Coffee Palace (1888), chapel (1847), bakehouse and clothing store (1842), cookhouse and breadstore (1842), assistant superintendent's headquarters (1842), and school master's house (1922). The buildings that Bernacchi built to house the vineyard workers are now rubble to the south of Darlington.

Head east past the camping ground through pleasant forest. Ford a small creek and turn right at a signposted intersection. This track leads all the way to the old reservoir along Bernacchis Creek. The dam was originally built by the convicts but was cleared, deepened, and water carried to Darlington through cement pipes. It is still operational. It is a pleasant spot to 'do lunch'.

Next head back down to Darlington and south to Mrs Hunt's cottage, one of the last private residences. A fork to the left leads to the old hop fields and Oast House set amongst blue gums and blackwood. Along the way are views over the settlement. The rest of the day can be spent exploring the exhibits at Darlington, reliving the rich history of the island.

RIDE 87: FOSSIL CLIFFS

FROM: Darlington
TO: Fossil Cliffs [RETURN]
LENGTH: 4 km cycling, 7 km walking
TIME: 1 easy day
RIDE/TRACK GRADE: 4/3
WALKING: To summit of Bishop and Clerk
HEIGHT VARIATION: 620 m
TRANSPORT: Ferry from Triabunna
FACILITIES: Camping ground at Darlington
MAPS: Maria Island National Park 1: 50 000 (See Map 7: *TASMAN PENINSULA*)

Bishop and Clerk (630 m) is not the highest point on the island but certainly the most spectacular. The views over Fossil Bay to the Freycinet Peninsula are truly awe inspiring. This ride suggestion is an easy cycling/walking combination. The only difficulty encountered is some awkward boulder scrambling near the summit.

From the Darlington Penitentiary head east past the rubble and standing chimneys of the 12 Apostles. These cottages were used to house Bernacchi's vineyard workers and later moved to Maria Street, Hobart in the inter-war years. It's easy cycling as you pass through pleasant forest. Cross a creek and head left at an intersection. The land opens up into a huge upward sloping grassed area with the odd Forester roo. On the right is the site of the old cement works dating back to 1889.

Change into low gear and head up the steady slope. Leading up to the top of the cliffs, you will pass the site of the old carboniferous limestone quarry on the right. This is claimed to be the first Portland Cement quarry in Australia. It failed, however, to produce a uniform grade of cement.

At the end you are looking out over the fantastic fossil cliffs towering over turquoise waters. These contain many examples of marine fossils, the most common being mussel shells about 200 million years old. Turn right and try to cycle up the slope to a height of about 200 m. The forest closes in again but cycling is still possible. Resist the temptation to dump your bike as you'll appreciate it on the way down again. While it might be slower walking your bike up the slope, the total time saved by the flying return descent will result in an actual time saving.

Eventually however the track does become for walkers only and bikes must be hidden. Simply continue walking up the ridge. Some steep and tiring sections will be encountered. The track then comes out on an unusual boulder-strewn rectangle. There is no clear path. Just head straight up and eventually left. At the base of dolerite spires scramble up to the summit for the reward for your efforts.

The return simply involves backtracking. Watch out for walkers when freewheeling back down.

RIDE 88: CHINAMAN'S BAY

FROM: Darlington
TO: Encampment Cove
VIA: French's Farm
LENGTH: 37 km
TIME: 1 day (optional 2 day)
RIDE/TRACK GRADE: 4/3
WALKING: Optional walk to Mt. Maria (709 m)
HEIGHT VARIATION: 150 m
TRANSPORT: Ferry from Triabunna
FACILITIES: Camping grounds at Darlington, French's Farm, and Encampment Cove. There is usually reliable water at Chinaman's Bay but dry summer conditions can necessitate taking your own
SPECIAL GEAR: Self sufficiency
MAPS: Maria Island National Park 1:50 000. (See Map 7: *TASMAN PENINSULA*)

This is the most popular cycling tour on the island and is an activity encouraged by the national parks and wildlife service. Simply make your way south from Darlington turning left at Hopground Beach to take the high way. Climb rapidly to 100 m. This allows an 8 km return walk to the island's highest peak, Mt.Maria at 709 m. There are marvellous views of both parts of the island from the summit. The stunted shrubs at the top resemble alpine vegetation, but this is more due to the exposure to winds than altitude. Rejoining the bikes, continue south climbing up to 140 m before descending to Four Mile Creek. A short rideable uphill takes you alongside Ned Ryan's Hill before the final descent to French's Farm. This was named after Joseph French, one of the last residents. Head right to Encampment Cove on the Point Lesueur Peninsula. There are some historical ruins around here. The only remaining evidence of the probation station at Point Lesueur (formerly Long Point) are some dilapidated single cells. The camp site itself is near the old Edina Point Jetty.

The next day explore the peninsula and its evidence of industrial and penal periods. You also have time to relax on the beach but the surf is flat. One has to head down to the other side (east) of the isthmus for good waves. Then cycle back to the French's Farm camping ground and follow the coastal route back to Darlington. On the way are the Painted Cliffs, Triassic sandstone weather-eroded overhangs to the south of Hopground Beach producing some photogenic patterns when the light is bright.

RIDE 89: BEYOND THE ISTHMUS

FROM: Darlington
TO: Robeys Creek and Cape Maurouard
VIA: French's Farm and McRaes Isthmus
LENGTH:
   Day 1: Darlington to Robeys Creek (via Cape)
   29 km
   Day 2: Robeys Creek to Darlington 20 km
   Total: 49 km
TIME: 2 days
RIDE/TRACK GRADE: 4/5
HEIGHT VARIATION: 199 m
TRANSPORT: Ferry from Triabunna
FACILITIES: Camping grounds at Darlington, French's Farm, and Chinaman's Bay
SPECIAL GEAR: Self-sufficiency, water
MAPS: Maria Island National Park 1:50 000 (See Map 7: *TASMAN PENINSULA*)

Those wishing to explore the remote southern section of Maria must be self-sufficient with regards to food, water, and accommodation. Two trails exist south of the isthmus: one to Robeys Creek, the site of the former sheep property operated for 41 years by John Robey until 1965. The other trail leads to the Cape Maurouard Peninsula with great views south to the Tasman Peninsula. As these are the only trails, precise navigational skills are not necessary but it is still wise to have a copy of the Maria Island National Park 1:50 000 map.

Follow Ride 88's notes to French's Farm. Head south past the airstrip and old farms onto the sandy isthmus. Head left 5 km later following Riedle Bay and start climbing dramatically to a height of 205 m. This descends shortly and seascape photographers should exploit the emerald and turquoise waters.

Head back to the isthmus and take the left route

to Robeys Creek. One of the advantages of camping here is that the possums, being less used to humans, are slightly less cheeky in their food foraging. Here you are looking over Mercury Passage to Cockle Bay. The day's distance will have been 29 km. Darlington is 20 km away, slightly longer if choosing the highland way.

BRUNY ISLAND

The island was named after Admiral Bruni D'Entrecasteaux who in 1792 with Huon de Kermadec discovered the waterway separating the mainland and the island, now called D'Entrecasteaux Channel. It is the only place where the *Bounty* under William Bligh anchored in Australian waters (1788). It is said that the first apple trees in Tasmania were planted by Robert Brown, the *Bounty's* botanist. The last Tasmanian Aboriginal, Truganini came from here. In fact a who's who of maritime explorers landed here: Cook, Flinders, Bligh, Furneaux, Franklin, Bass, and Baudin.

Like Maria, it is actually two islands with the sea accounting for the construction of the connecting sand isthmus, called a tombolo, and named The Neck. The north is basically flat open pastoral land while the southern part in stark contrast is mountainous and heavily forested. The island's population totals 500.

The hostel at Lumeah is located at Quiet Corner, Main Road, Adventure Bay. There are 16 beds in 3 rooms costing $12.00 each.

BRUNY ISLAND FERRY

Mainland (Kettering)	Bruny Island (Roberts Point)
7:15*	7:35*
8:10**	8:35**
9:30	10:15
11:15	11:45
1:45	2:15
2:45	3:15
4:00	4:30
5:00	5:30
6:30	6:50

7:25pm   7:45pm

  * Does not run on Sundays
** 8:00 – 8:30 Sundays

There is no charge for cyclists!

Please note the ferry departure times are very punctual.

Kettering is 40 km south of Hobart via Kingston and Snug. From Roberts Point, it is 42 km to Adventure Bay. Motorists are charged about $17.00

The Bruny Island Parks Wildlife and Heritage ranger can be contacted on (002) 93-1108.

RIDE 90: BRUNY ISLAND NECK

FROM: Roberts Point
TO: Adventure Bay
VIA: Dennes Point and Cape Queen Elizabeth
LENGTH: 72 km (includes Dennes Point loop)
48 km (not including Dennes Point loop—this allows a 16 km optional walk to Cape Queen Elizabeth if time permits)
TIME: 1 full day
RIDE/TRACK GRADE: 4/4–6
WALKING: To Cape Queen Elizabeth and up stairs to Hammock Lookout
HEIGHT VARIATION: 177 m
TRANSPORT: Ferry to and from Kettering, see times above.
FACILITIES: Store at Dennes Point, camping area at The Neck. Water tank (not always full) and fireplaces. Caravan park, general store, and Lumeah Hostel at Adventure Bay
MAPS: Barnes Bay, Great Bay, Adventure Bay 1:25 000 topos. (See Map 8: *SOUTH COAST & BRUNY ISLAND*)

If you've caught an early ferry, you might like to cycle the 24 km C525 northern loop via Barnes Bay, Killora and Dennes Point. From here there are views up the Derwent to East Hobart and across the D'Entrecasteaux Channel to Tinderbox.

Head south along the Main Bruny Road through mundane grazing land where it meets with the sea at Great Bay. The tidal mud and lack of surf make this area rather ordinary. The turnoff to the Bruny Island Neck Game Reserve is on the right just north of the airfield. It is well signposted and a barrier bars entry to vehicles. A 4WD track leads to Big Lagoon (stocked with trout since 1982).

From here a walking track leads up to Mars Bluff (good views over The Neck) and down again to

Morina Beach. Here, for the first time, there is real surf. At the eastern end of the beach follow the dry creek-bed up to the headland of Cape Queen Elizabeth. One can make a round trip back to Mars Bluff north via the old Rookery Track momentarily entering private property before turning left past the ruins of St. Peter's Church (built by convicts in 1846) and over the 178 m trig at Church Hill (good 360 degree views) before rejoining the track at Mars Bluff.

Once back on the Main Road, head south along The Neck. You'll see an interesting sign: *BEWARE. PENGUINS CROSSING.* The Little Penguin breeding grounds are at Cape Queen Elizabeth in the Bruny Island Neck Game Reserve (1450 ha). Also along the way is Hammock Lookout. From the small carpark a walking track goes over to the surf beach and a million stairs lead up to the viewing platform. A plaque at the summit is dedicated to the Tasmanian Aborigines. Everywhere in the foreground are holes made by mutton birds, occupied from September to April. A sign down the bottom tells of their amazing migration around the Pacific circumference each year returning to same burrow.

The camping area is near the southern end of The Neck on the left. There are several sites, a shelter, fireplaces, and an informal supply of wood. A short track leads to the long surf beach. At dusk on the far left the tiny penguins can be seen returning from the ocean. From here it is 12 km to Adventure Bay (location of the hostel). This bay was commonly the first part of Australia set foot upon by European explorers travelling around Van Diemen's Land. Today the Bligh Museum, built from convict bricks, commemorates maritime exploration and the last of the Tasmanian natives who lived on the island.

RIDE 91: SOUTH BRUNY TOUR

FROM: Adventure Bay
TO: Lunawanna and Waterfall Creek State Reserve
VIA: Lockleys Road
LENGTH: 62 km
TIME: 1 full day
RIDE/TRACK GRADE: 5/5
WALKING: Short walk to see Mavista falls
HEIGHT VARIATION: 350 m
TRANSPORT: Ferry from Kettering to Roberts Point and a day's leisurely cycle to Adventure Bay. See ferry times above.
FACILITIES: Caravan park, general store, and Lumeah Hostel at Adventure Bay. Shop at Alonnah
MAPS: Adventure Bay and Fluted Cape 1:25 000 topographicals. (See Map 8: *SOUTH COAST & BRUNY ISLAND*)

This ride circumnavigates the southern part of the island taking in some sleepy villages, the odd waterfall, some temperate rainforest, and some rough mountain bike trails.

From Adventure Bay head north and then west for 20 km to Alonnah (80 m) following the B66. In starting from the camping area on The Neck head south and then to the right avoiding the turnoff at Simpsons Bay. Continue south to Lunawanna and head onto the Cloudy Bay Road (C644). Then follow Stanfords and the closed Lockleys Road back around Adventure Bay. As you're speeding down the Captain Cook Creek gully, watch out for the turnoff to the Waterfall Creek State Reserve 5 km before reaching Adventure Bay. The walking track starts from the left. It is well marked but unfortunately subject to minor flooding so your feet might get wet. If it has been raining recently, check your skin periodically for ol' Mr Leech. Return time is a little over an hour for the 4 km walk.

Once back on Lockleys Road, continue down crossing the creek and you're back at Adventure Bay. The Neck camping area is a further 12 km.

RIDE 92: LABILLARDIERE PENINSULA

FROM: Adventure Bay
TO: Hopwood and Butlers Beaches
VIA: Lunawanna
LENGTH: 78 km (39 km each day)
TIME: 2 days
RIDE/TRACK GRADE: 6/7
WALKING: Short walk to secluded Hopwood and Butlers Beaches
HEIGHT VARIATION: 500 m
TRANSPORT: Ferry from Kettering to Roberts Point and a day's leisurely cycle to Adventure Bay. See ferry times above.
FACILITIES: Caravan park, general store, and Lumeah Hostel at Adventure Bay. No facilities at Hopwood and Butlers Beaches. Developed camping area near Jetty Beach where water is sometimes available.
SPECIAL GEAR: Water
MAPS: Cloudy and Partridge 1:25 000 topographical maps. (See Map 8: *SOUTH COAST & BRUNY ISLAND*)

The south of Bruny is a mountain biker's paradise. The roads are sufficiently rough to be challenging, yet you can still keep your eye on the splendid island and coastal scenery. This route takes you to some lonely beaches at the most western point on the island. Public vehicles are barred from the peninsula so the track is exclusively yours.

From Adventure Bay cycle to Lunawanna (10 km) peaking at 440 m and then take Lighthouse Road (C629) left for 18 km until the turn-off to Labillardiere Peninsula State Reserve (proclaimed in 1975).

Follow Old Jetty Road leading to Jetty Beach. It is interesting to note that this was the first road built on the island (about 1860) supplying the lighthouse. There is a campsite here with standard facilities: pit toilets, BBQs, and shelters. About 300 m before the end of the road, you'll see the old 4WD track on the left. It follows the western shore high above Standaway Bay amidst low coastal heath stunted due to the salt winds. Almost all the way to Hopwood Point, there are great views across the D'Entrecasteaux Channel to Southport.

The peninsula was named after D'Entre-casteaux's naturalist who made the first detailed observations of Tasmania's flora and fauna along a 30 km stretch of the Derwent River.

The trail peaks at 142 m over Mt. Bleak and then it's a hair-raising downhill all the way to Hopwood Beach. Because of the protection of Bruny Island and the channel, there is not much surf.

Butlers Beach, opposite Partridge Island, makes the more pleasant campsite but the bikes have to be walked and this can be unpleasant due to the dense heath. The way to get around this is to carry all your provisions in a backpack and leave the bikes behind at the end of the trail. Water will have to be carried. BEWARE OF TIGER SNAKES.

RIDE 93: CAPE BRUNY LIGHTHOUSE

FROM: Adventure Bay
TO: Cape Bruny Lighthouse [RETURN]
VIA: Lunawanna
LENGTH: 56 km
TIME: 1 full day
RIDE/TRACK GRADE: 4/4
HEIGHT VARIATION: 440 m
WALKING: Short walk to summit of Mt.Mangana (571 m)
TRANSPORT: Ferry from Kettering to Roberts Point and a day's leisurely cycle to Adventure Bay. See ferry times above.
FACILITIES: Caravan park, general store, and Lumeah Hostel at Adventure Bay
MAPS: RACT Touring Map of Tasmania. (See Map 8: *SOUTH COAST & BRUNY ISLAND*)

Built by convicts in 1836, the Cape Bruny Lighthouse was the first to be erected in Tasmania, and the second in Australia. Over 100 m above sea level, it has walls almost a metre thick and its light is visible to ships entering the D'Entrecasteaux Channel 35 km away. Thirty years before the lighthouse was built, fire beacons built on Bruny were used to guide whalers into the Derwent. The ground is Commonwealth property and is open 10–12, 2–4 on Tuesdays and Thursdays.

As in Ride 92 cycle the Coolangatta Road over the South Bruny Range to Lunawanna and then 18 km south along the Lighthouse Road (C629) to the lighthouse. Return by the same route. For those wishing to make it a two day trip one can camp at the Labillardiere Peninsula campsite about 5 km from the lighthouse on Old Jetty Road. It has standard facilities: pit toilets, BBQs, and shelters.

Along either to and return routes one can take a walking detour up the highest peak on the island,

Mt.Mangana (571 m) with its telecommunications tower. The mountain was originally named by William Bligh in 1792 as 'Cove Hill' but was later changed in honour of the chief of the native tribe that inhabited the island. Mangana was the father of Truganini.

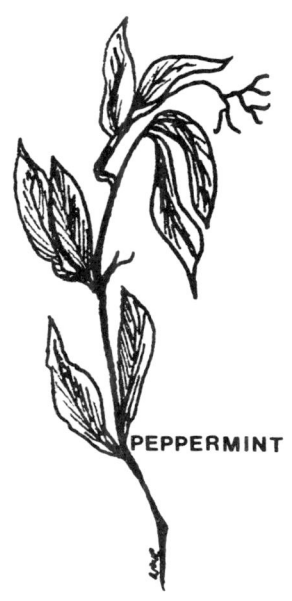

PEPPERMINT

The start of the 1.25 km footpad is 5 km from Adventure Bay and takes about 40 minutes each way. The amateur botanist will be impressed with the varieties of vegetation species observed from the summit, including sassafras, pine, laurel, waratahs, eucalypts, and myrtle. One can see all the way to the dolerite cliffs of Cape Raoul on the Tasman Peninsula. The height variation of the walk is 130 m.

RIDE 94: CLOUDY BAY

FROM: Adventure Bay
TO: Pine Log Bight
VIA: Cloudy Beach and East Cloudy Head
LENGTH:
　　Day 1: Adventure Bay to Cloudy Bay 42 km (via Bight)
　　Day 2: Cloudy Bay to Adventure Bay 36 km (via Lockleys)
　　Total distance is 78 km. (If leaving from and returning to The Neck Camping Ground, the round trip is 102 km)
TIME: 2 days
RIDE/TRACK GRADE: 9/8
WALKING: Short walk to muttonbird rookeries
HEIGHT VARIATION: 440 m
TRANSPORT: Ferry from Kettering to Roberts Point and a day's leisurely cycle to Adventure Bay. See ferry times above.
FACILITIES: Caravan park, general store, and Lumeah Hostel at Adventure Bay. No facilities at Cloudy Beach
MAPS: Cloudy 1:25 000 topographical. (See Map 8: *SOUTH COAST & BRUNY ISLAND*)

This ride is to the remotest area on the island, the Bruny Island Conservation Area centred on Mt.Bruny. At the end there are cliff-top views. To get there one must negotiate some disused trails that alternate between sandy and rocky. Also watch out for the two metre long jet black tiger snakes that are common in the south.

　　It is 29 km to Pine Log Bight and Tasman Head via Coolangatta Road and Cloudy Bay Road (C644) peaking at 440 m. The carpark which bars public vehicles from accessing the conservation area is 22 km from Adventure Bay. One has to follow Cloudy Beach to the southern end where a

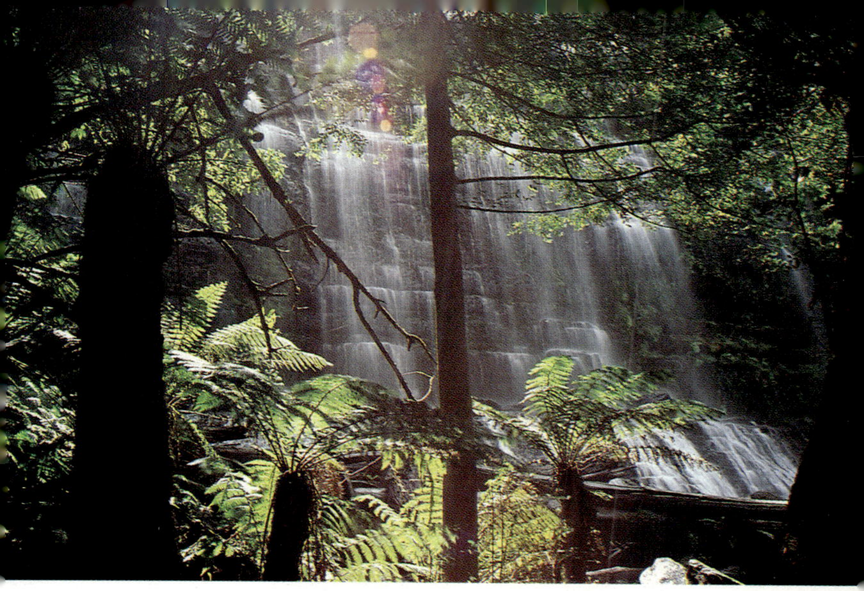

Russell Falls, Mt.Field National Park (Ride 82)

Lake Gordon (Ride 84)

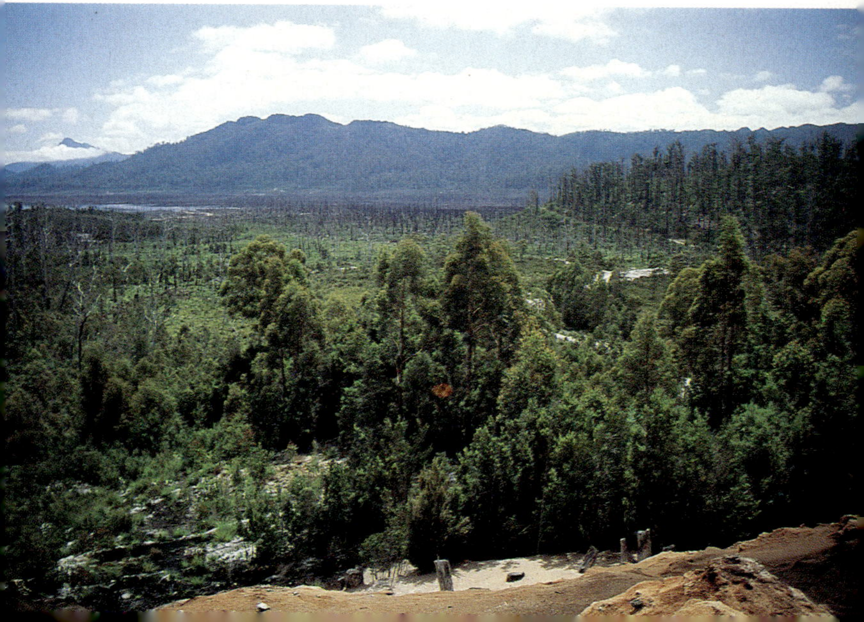

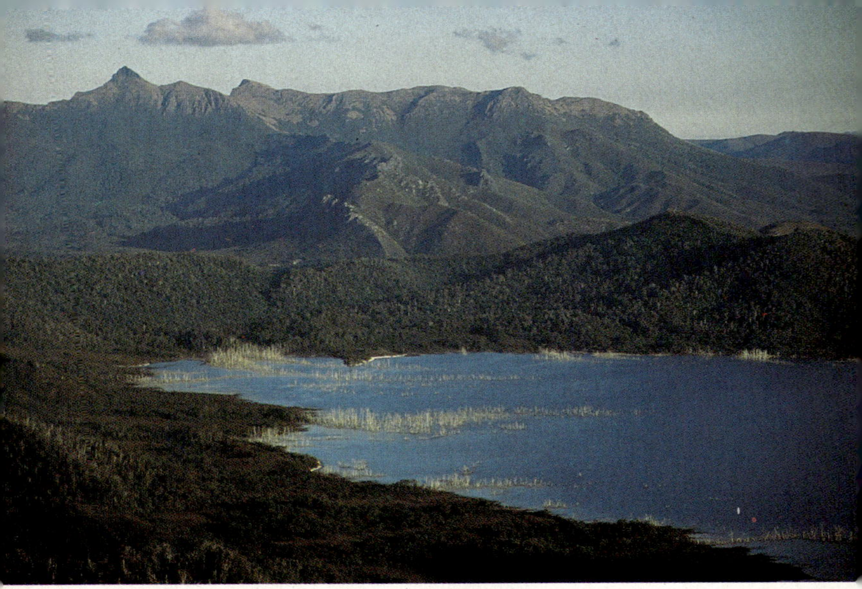

Mt. Anne and Lake Pedder (Ride 85)

Lake Gordon from the Sentinels

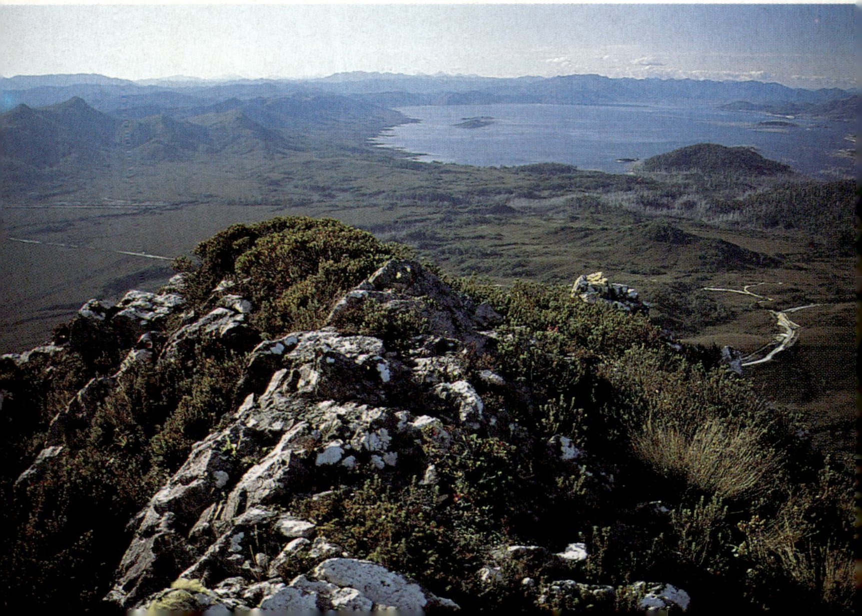

campsite is located. This is where you can camp on the first night when returning from Fine Log Bight. It is therefore recommended to dump all overnight gear here in order to save weight. A short distance inland from the end of the beach a 4WD track climbs to a height of 240 m before levelling out. There are terrific views across Cloudy Bay. There is a turnoff to East Cloudy Head (292 m) but the energetic will have to walk this side track. Continue across a creek and up again to the end of the track. From the boulder-strewn headland in the Fluted Cape State Reserve, there are good views to the Friars, a group of a dozen pointed rock outcrops to the south named by Furneaux in 1773. Backtrack to your gear at the Cloudy Beach campsite.

The next day return to Adventure Bay via Staffords Road (11 km), Lockleys Road (21 km) peaking at 400 m completing a loop. Along the way you cycle through patches of myrtle-dominated rainforest. If starting from The Neck camping area a further 24 km must be added, making the entire round trip 102 km, necessitating a 3 day camp to make it relaxing. If this is the case set up a sub-base at Cloudy Beach and use the second day to travel to Tasman Head and back. Carry your own water.

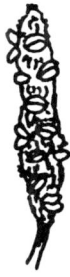

COAST

BANKSIA

FRUIT

WALKING

1. **Slide Track:** Allow a full day for this one. It starts at Adventure Bay and follows an abandoned wooden tramway south between the coast and Lockleys Road. There are education number markers along the walk detailing features. These were erected by the Bruny Island Historical Society.

2. **Fluted Cape:** The circuit track to Fluted Cape (274 m) (named by Furneaux) ends over columnar dolomite cliffs with impressive views over Adventure Bay. It also starts at Adventure Bay heading inland to the highest point of the peninsula then north to Grass Point and Penguin Island, before following the coast back to Adventure Bay.

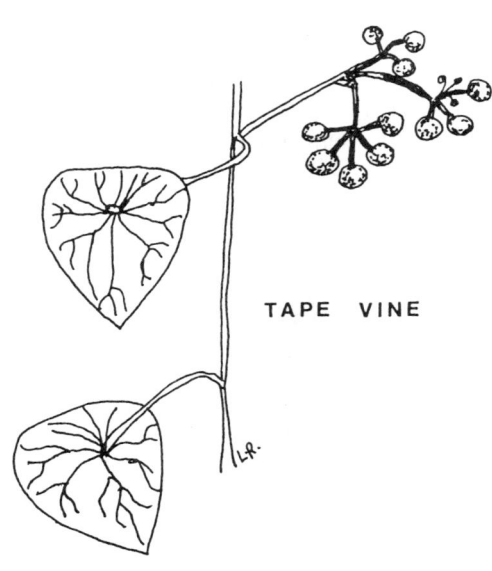

TAPE VINE

FLINDERS ISLAND

Flinders is the largest of a group of 46 granite islands named after Tobias Furneaux, captain of the *Adventure*, who first sighted them in 1773. Flinders itself is named after Matthew Flinders, who first charted it.

Like the other islands off the Tasmanian coast, it's a cyclist's paradise. The roads have little traffic, are of reasonably quality, and the whole place has a unique tranquil atmosphere. The islanders are friendly, but shy. Facilities outside of Whitemark and Lady Barron are limited, but regulations are relaxed and camping can be done at most coastal places. There are no unsightly telegraph poles as all communication cables are underground. There aren't any large trucks, or fast, ignorant drivers. In fact the only complaint that a cyclist might have is the sometimes harsh westerly winds, the notorious roaring forties.

A large contingent of the population are descended from the early sealers and their Tasmanian Aboriginal consorts, today engaging in agriculture, fishing, and mutton bird harvesting.

Flinders Island is the site of the settlement where several hundred Tasmanian Aboriginals were deported to in 1830. Wybalenna, about 20 km north of Whitemark, is where they died, in perhaps the darkest period of our history. The cyclist can explore the site as it stands today and see the grave yard where they were buried. The last, Truganini, died in 1876. A memorial to her, erected in 1972 was flooded together with Lake Pedder in the south-west.

All graves at Wybalenna are believed to be empty as universities and academic physicians around the world offered up to £100 for the skeleton of one of the most primitive races in the world.

It takes about a week to adequately explore the

island, and if staying for that long, one would want to combine the following rides into one so that all the highlights can be seen. Remember that rainfall is generally very low and if camping away from Whitemark and Lady Barron, you must carry your own water. There is also the opportunity to do sea or estuary fishing on some of the many beaches and inlets around the coast. Boats can be chartered for exploring the dozens of other islands in the vicinity, many having buildings and graves, reminders of the sealing heritage. With the exception of Cape Barren Island, all these are too small for mountain cycling. This is no loss— Chappell Island, for example, is infested with thousands of deadly Tiger Snakes measuring almost two metres.

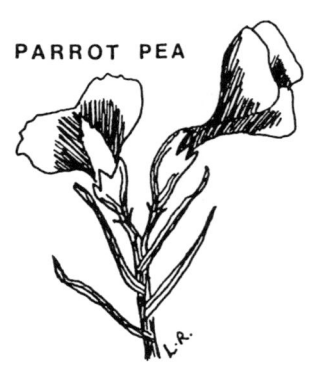

PARROT PEA

The airport at Pats River was opened in 1934 and is the main route by which visitors can access the island. There are regular flights from Launceston, and also from Melbourne and Welshpool. From the runway, a few minutes ride south to Whitemark will get you any supplies and information needed before starting off.

DATA TABLE: Flinders Island

Population: 1200
Settlement: Late nineteenth century
Capital: Whitemark: tidal port to trading vessels.
Area: 2000 km^2
Dimensions: 65 km long x 40 km wide
Animals: Mutton Birds *(Puffinus tenuirostris)*, Cape Barren Geese *(Cereopsis novaehollandiae)*, the second rarest goose in the world. The only two species of snakes are the Copperhead and Tiger, both venomous. Fossils have been found of the grey kangaroo.
Vegetation: The island includes both dry and wet sclerophyll forests containing species endemic to both the mainland and Tasmania. Mostly stunted on the west coast and exposed areas allow good visibility from any point a few metres above the ground.

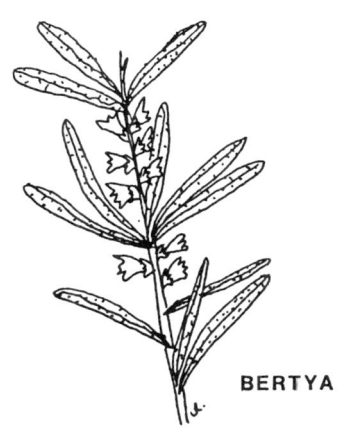

BERTYA

RIDE 95: STRZELECKI NATIONAL PARK

FROM: Pats River Airport (Whitemark)
TO: Strzelecki National Park
VIA: Trousers Point
LENGTH: 56 km (28 km each way)
TIME: 2 days
RIDE/TRACK GRADE: 3/3
WALKING: To summit of Strzelecki Peaks
HEIGHT VARIATION: 755 m (including walk)
TRANSPORT: Plane from Launceston, Welshpool, or Melbourne
FACILITIES: Supplies at Whitemark, Camping ground at Trousers Point
SPECIAL GEAR: Water containers
MAPS: Goose Island and Lady Barron 1:100 000 topographics from Flinders Island $6.50 package, or Flinders Island 1:100 000 land tenure (1985). (See Map 13: *FLINDERS*)

The return trip to Flinders Island's only national park is 56 km. There is a challenging but well developed walking track up to the summit with views over most of the island and the dozens of offshore outcrops in the Furneaux group. Of particular note is the 200 m bump on Chappell Island. Strzelecki National Park is named after the Polish explorer who visited Australia in 1845 and named Mt.Kosciusko. Scots say the peaks resemble the Hebrides. The park is 4200 hectares, mainly comprising only open eucalypt forest containing blue gums and peppermints, but also small patches of rainforest. There is a very scenic camping area at Trousers Point.

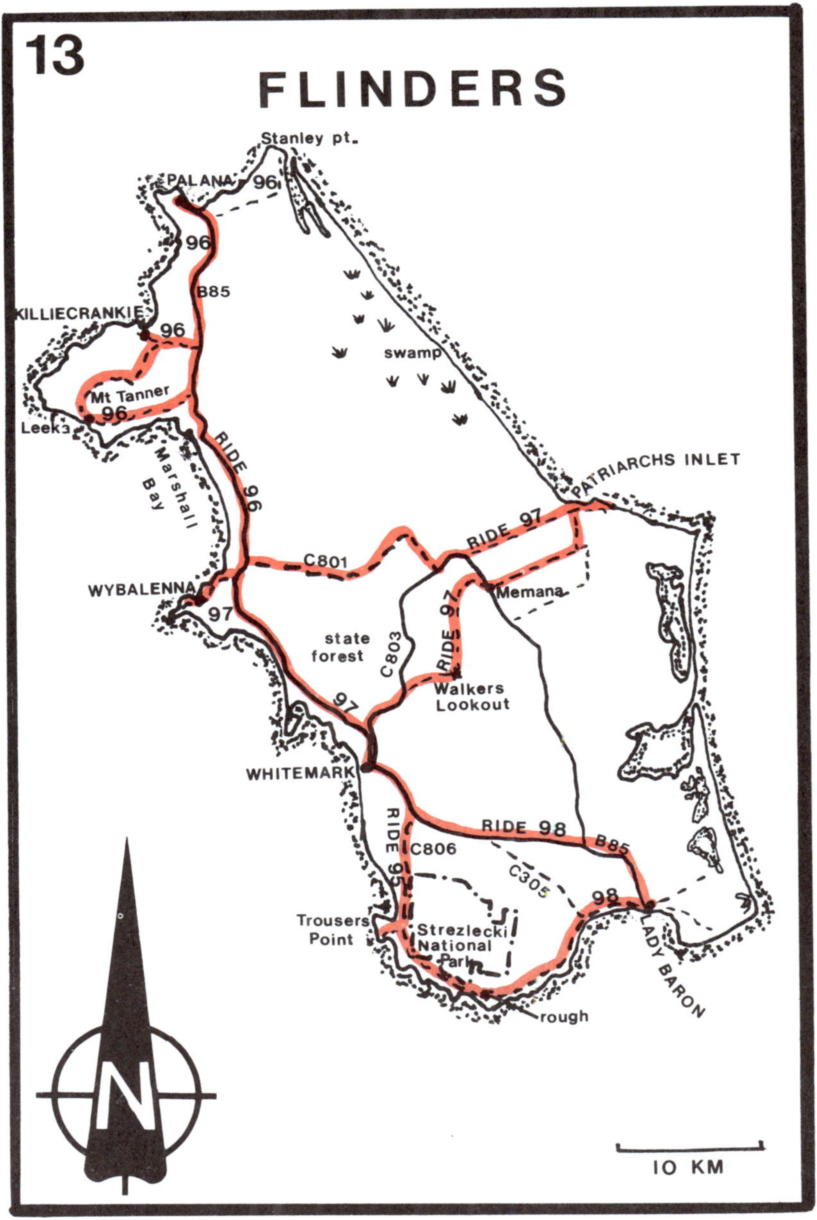

13

FLINDERS

Stanley pt.

PALANA 96

96

B85

KILLIECRANKIE

96

Mt Tanner

96

Leek

96

Marshall Bay

RIDE 96

swamp

PATRIARCHS INLET

C801

RIDE 97

WYBALENNA

Memana

97

state forest

C803

RIDE 97

97

Walkers Lookout

WHITEMARK

RIDE 98

B85

RIDE 98

C806

C305

98

Trousers Point

Strzelecki National Park

LADY BARON

rough

N

10 KM

RIDE 96: FLINDERS ISLAND (NORTH TOUR)
(KILLIECRANKIE)

FROM: Pats River Airport (Whitemark)
TO: Holloway Point
VIA: Mt.Killiecrankie
LENGTH:
    Day 1: Whitemark to Leeka 40 km
    Day 2: Leeka to Killiecrankie 23 km
    Day 3: Killiecrankie to Stanley Point 27 km
    Day 4: Stanley Point to Whitemark 64 km
    Total distance is 154 km
TIME: 4–5 days
RIDE/TRACK GRADE: 4/6
HEIGHT VARIATION: 315 m
TRANSPORT: Plane from Launceston, Welshpool, or Melbourne
FACILITIES: Whitemark
SPECIAL GEAR: Water containers
MAPS: Killiecrankie 100:000 topographical from Flinders Island $6.50 package or Flinders Island 100:000 land tenure (1985). (See Map 13: *FLINDERS*)

From Whitemark it is 40 km to Leeka, the first night's stop. The height variation along the B85 is 80 m. Camp anywhere along the coast at Tanners Bay. Marshall Bay, atypical of the northern shores, has a beautiful white beach which acts as an effective trap for debris washed up by currents through Bass Strait.

For thrills the next morning one can push up the steep slope to Mt.Tanner (331 m) with its telecommunications tower for reasonable views of Marshall Bay and the Pasco Islands. Head east to the Palana Road and then to Killiecrankie (the Stackhouse residence is located here).

The terrain is quite flat, usually level at 60 m.

Supplies at the township are very limited. It's 12 km from the township of Killiecrankie to Mt.Killiecrankie (316 m) via Quoin Road. One has to walk up the final slope. One can camp at Killiecrankie which provides reasonable facilities: cold shower, toilets, and water. Killiecrankie Bay is lined with large boulders, shipwrecks and deserted vessels, but of most interest are the run-off sediments from the peak of Mt.Killiecrankie which reveal a treasure of crystal pebbles, smoky quartz, beryl, and topaz. The cyclist beachcombing under boulders at low tide might be able to bring back an interesting souvenir.

The next day take the North East River Road which leads mainly downhill to Stanley Peninsula. Stop at Palana with its beautiful white beach, turquoise water, and dune hinterland. This is another place where one can camp. At Palana is a rare patch of pink belladonna lilies covering a grave. The final leg to Stanley Point is extremely rough. The only landmark is the conical 200 m Quoin Hill. Regardless of choice of tyre and tube pressure, the bike has to be walked for much of the way due to sand. The lighthouse is 27 km from Killiecrankie and 64 km from Whitemark.

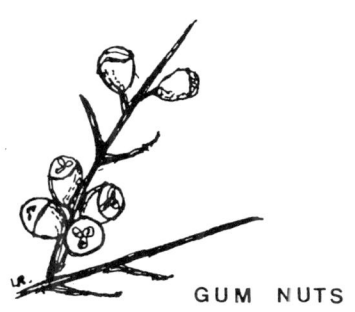

GUM NUTS

RIDE 97: FLINDERS ISLAND
(CENTRAL TOUR)

FROM: Pats River Airport (Whitemark)
TO: Patriarch Inlet
VIA: Settlement Point, Darling Range
LENGTH:
    Day 1: Whitemark to Patriarch Inlet 36 km
    Day 2: Patriarch Inlet to Wybalenna 35 km
    Day 3: Wybalenna to Whitemark 26 km
    Total is 97 km
TIME: 3-4 days
RIDE/TRACK GRADE: 6/7
HEIGHT VARIATION: 410 m
TRANSPORT: Plane from Launceston, Welshpool, or Melbourne
FACILITIES: Whitemark
SPECIAL GEAR: Water containers
MAPS: Lady Barron and Babel Island 1:100 000 topographicals from $6.50 package or Flinders Island 100:000. (See Map 13: *FLINDERS*)

From the airport, head south 2 km to Memana Road (C803). Nearly 6 km later turn right at Walkers Lookout Road which climbs over the Darling Range peaking at 411 m. A walking track leads from here along the range south to Mt. Leventhorpe taking an hour each way. There are good views of the island due to its central location. Especially significant are the Strzelecki peaks.
    From Walkers Lookout, head down the other side through treacherous sand patches to Memana (50 m) via Furneaux Lookout (180 m). Turn south along Lackrana Road and then soon left at Lees Road to the Patriarch Wildlife Sanctuary. The 30 hectare reserve was established from purchased farm and swampland in 1980 to assist the feeding and winter breeding of the unusual Cape Barren Goose, one of the largest Australian birds. There are camping

facilities here. The day's distance will have been 36 km. Another walk leads up to South Patriarch (192 m), the most distant of the three prominent granite peaks south of the sanctuary. Once again, walking is an hour each way although some of the initial distance can be cycled.

From Patriarch Inlet take Memana Road through the soldier-settler farms and then Lucks, Melrose, Fairhaven, Palana, Davies and Wybalenna Roads to Wybalenna. There is a camping area a short distance east at Allports Beach providing basic facilities.

The Wybalenna settlement (1833–1847) was organised by George Augustus Robinson who led the party of 18 who rounded up Aboriginals on the mainland and relocated them on Flinders Island. Another potential settlement was on King Island where the first lessee, Captain Malcolm Laing-Smith, offered to look after the Aboriginals in 1849 for £20 each per year. This offer, like a South Maria Island settlement proposal, was rejected. Across from the reconstructed chapel, under a tree, a grave's inscriptions tell of a wife who drowned when her crinoline got caught in the ship's rigging,

Another plaque reads: *Erected by the Junior Farmers of Flinders Island to commemorate approximately 100 Tasmanian Aboriginals buried in this vicinity.*

Other plaques also perpetuate the memory of the first white child born on the island, Robert Clark, and last of the Portland tribe chiefs, Mannalargenna.

The Furneaux Historical Association's Museum located at Emita houses relics from the island's wrecks and commemorates the island's natural, Aboriginal, and European history. It's open 2–5pm on weekends.

On a lighter note there is also supposedly the oldest outdoor dunny in Australia on display.

From Wybalenna it's 26 km back to Whitemark, completing the loop.

RIDE 98: FLINDERS ISLAND
(SOUTH TOUR)

FROM: Pats River Airport (Whitemark)
TO: Lady Barron
VIA: Strzelecki National Park, and south-east lagoons
LENGTH:
    Day 1: Whitemark to Lady Barron 32 km
    Day 2: Lady Barron to Trousers Point 32 km
    Day 3: Trousers Point to Whitemark 20 km
    Total distance is 84 km
    (With side-trip excursions- 112 km)
TIME: 3–4 days
RIDE/TRACK GRADE: 5/7
WALKING: Optional walking in Strzelecki National Park
HEIGHT VARIATION: 150 m (756 m with walk)
TRANSPORT: Plane from Launceston, Welshpool, or Melbourne
FACILITIES: Limited groceries at Lady Barron
SPECIAL GEAR: Water containers
MAPS: Goose Island and Lady Barron 1:100 000 topographics from Flinders Island $6.50 package, or Flinders Island 1:100 000 land tenure (1985). (See Map 13: *FLINDERS*)

From the airport, it is 32 km to Lady Barron, peaking at 100 m altitude. Lady Barron, named after the wife of Sir Harry Barron (Tasmanian Governor 1909-1913), is a deep sea port and home to the island's 50-60 fishing boats. These ships engage in cray fishing, scalloping, abalone diving, and shark hunting. Processing plants are been installed at Lady Barron. To the east is the granite rise of Vinegar Hill. Supplies are available here as well as a chance to meet the locals in the pub.

Camping is permitted near, not on, the tennis courts. If you wish to rough it or prefer not to stay at Lady Barron, you can cycle 12 km to Logan Lagoon Wildlife Sanctuary. The 2155 hectare reserve has a varied population of birds—sea birds, waders, Siberian, Antarctic, Alaskan migrants, and honeyeaters. In summer it can be dry due to the cutting of an illegal channel to the sea.

The return to Whitemark via the Coast Road is 26 km. The return via Trousers Point is twice as long but much rougher and more scenic encompassing the Strzelecki National Park (see Ride 95 for details). The break up is: 32 km to Trousers Point via Pigs Head Point, and a further 20 km to Whitemark.

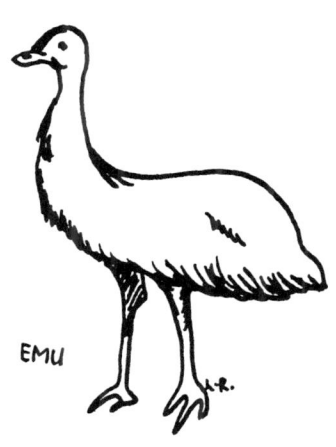

EMU

OTHER RIDES

CAPE BARREN ISLAND: Furneaux believed this 360 km² island was barren: so he named it precisely and simply that. And from this island, the unusual Cape Barren goose was named. A few kilometres to the south of Flinders, Cape Barren is dominated topographically by Mt.Munro (687 m), named after Jimmy Munro, a colourful character of colonial Bass Strait. There is only one tiny settlement, called the Corner (population about 60), and two cattle stations, where descendants from the sealers and Aboriginals engage in mutton bird harvesting from the 10 million birds that migrate to the Bass Strait islands every year. There is a schoolhouse, hall, post office, church, and graveyard. From here one can look across Franklin Sound and see the peaks of Strzelecki National Park. There are about 80 km of rough sandy trails over the island which make it possible to camp on the eastern or southern coasts. These include the 40 km Rooks River Road which follows the north coast to Puncheon Point peaking at 50 m, and Barrets Road to Battery Bay 25 km long which connects with Hardluck Road to the base of Mt.Munro. Apparently there is a 6 m cave, patches of rainforest, sculpted granite tors, and golden beaches. As I've not personally ridden on Cape Barren Island, I can't guarantee that there won't be more walking than cycling. There is also a considerable element of risk here. More so than any other place in Australia, the remoteness and abundance of tiger snakes make wild camping here very dangerous. But for the pioneering mountain cyclist, it is a comfort to know that there are still tracks out there yet to be explored. I'd be interested to hear from anyone who has cycled Cape Barren Island.

KING ISLAND

Like Flinders, King Island has a tragic history. Its western coast is one of the worst ship graveyards in the world, and hundreds of vessels, thousands of lives, came to grief between King Island and the Otway coast in Victoria. So spectacular were the shipwrecks that five lighthouses were built on the island, one of them the tallest in Australia.

There are no national parks and only one reserve of note but the aesthetic value is in the island as a whole. There is something about the character of the island and people and scenery and lifestyle that make it a unique experience. It is even flatter than Flinders and so makes for easy cycling along sealed roads, with fantastic isolated beaches, and a minimum of restrictions. Some of the smaller tracks however are quiet rough and the west coast especially is subject to ever-present on-shore winds.

Visiting cyclists will learn much of the rich maritime history of King Island ('Yeeroobin' in the native tongue): the commercial sealing, the shipwrecks, and its navigational role. The island also has a mining agricultural heritage. The former is evident with an open-cut scheelite mine at Grassy and sand mining by the Sea Elephant River estuary. When tungsten prices fell in the mid-1920s, dairy farming became an increasingly important contribution to the King Island economy. Although the population was only 1200 in 1927, there were 15 000 cattle, 3000 sheep, and 1500 pigs. Locals claim that their beef is regarded as the best in Australia due to a combination of the grasses and salt winds. Just before World War II, the mine re-opened and has continued to modern times. Today kelp is a major export.

Access is by cargo vessel from Stanley or air service from Wynyard or Melbourne. Kendell

Airlines provides a Bass Strait service connecting Devonport and Burnie to King Island via Melbourne. Return airfare is about $200. The island is relatively well set up for tourists and supplies and sheltered accommodation are available from Grassy and Currie.

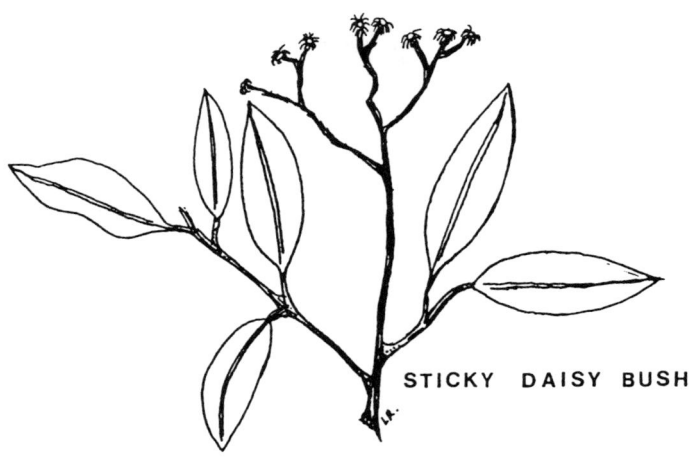

STICKY DAISY BUSH

DATA TABLE: King Island

Population: 1810
Capital: Currie
Area: 126 000 ha
Dimensions: 58 km long by 21 km wide
First settled: First lease granted to Captain Malcolm Laing-Smith in 1836, others arriving 1855. In 1861, land was slightly more reasonably priced than nowadays: £20 rent per annum could get the prospective pioneer 275 000 acres! In 1888, advertisements for selection started bringing in dozens of settlers and their families.

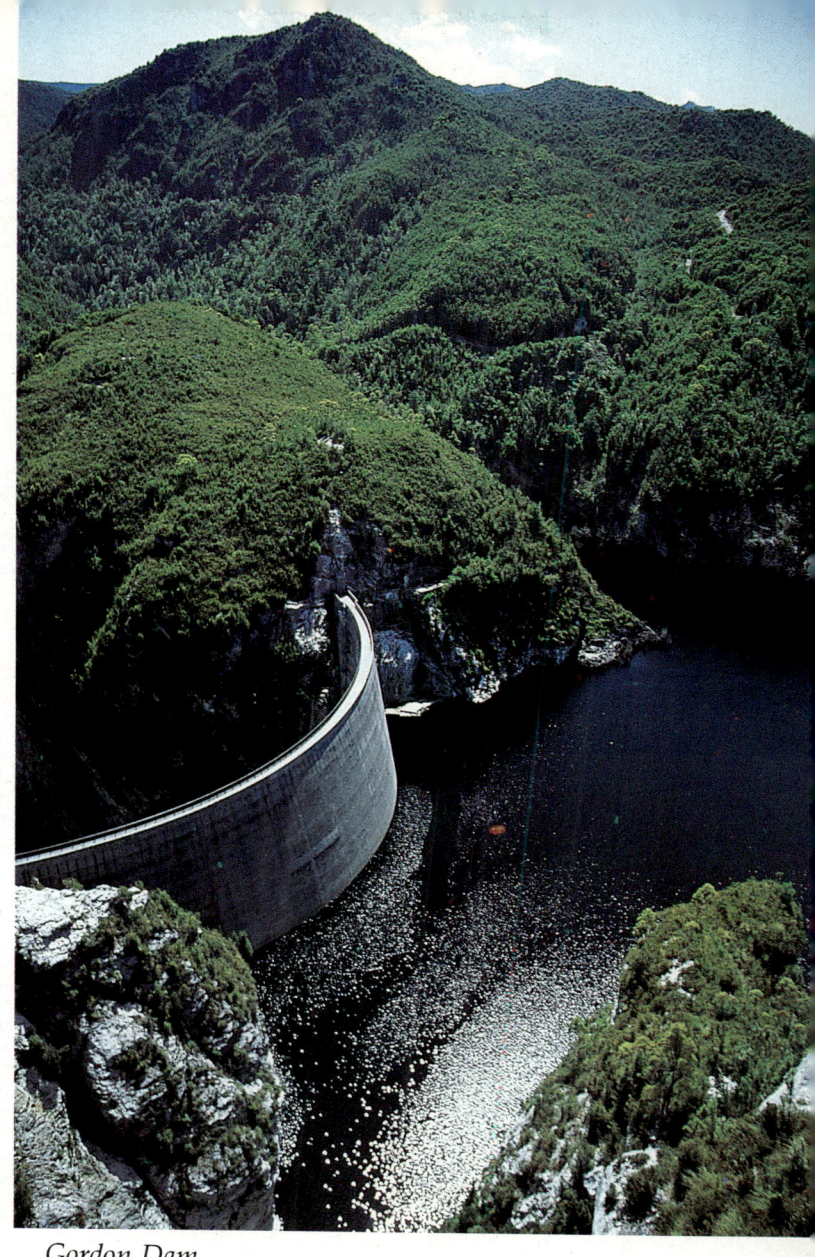

Gordon Dam

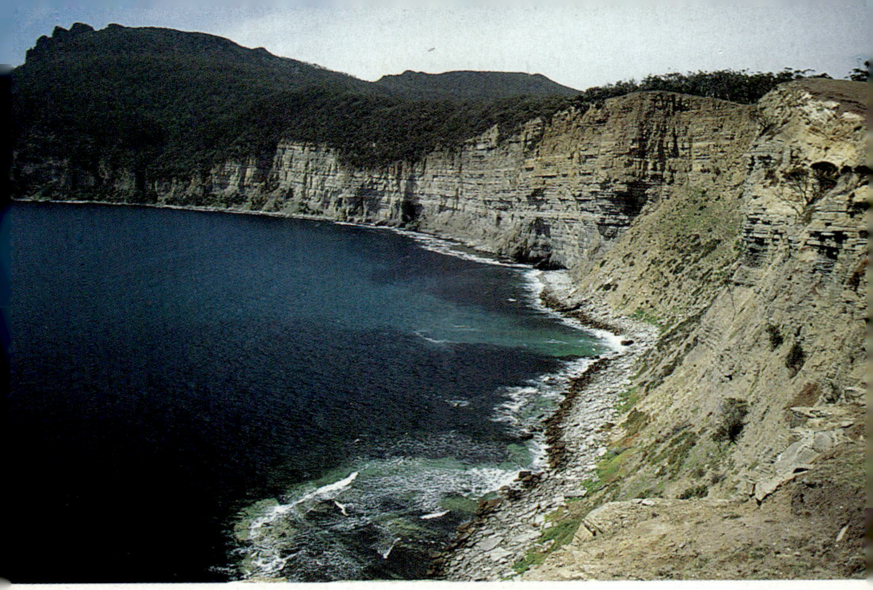

Fossil Cliffs, Maria Island (Ride 87)

The Neck, Bruny Island (Ride 90)

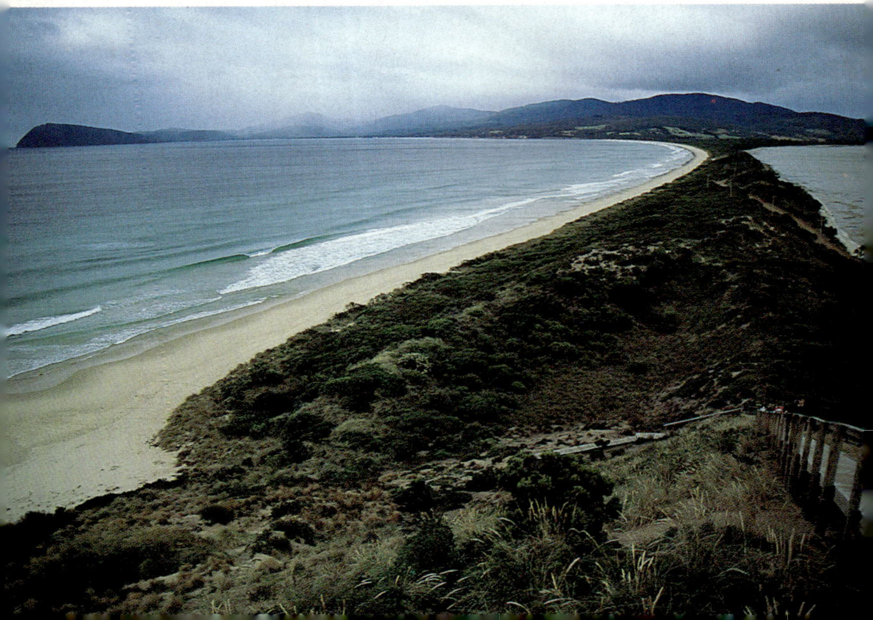

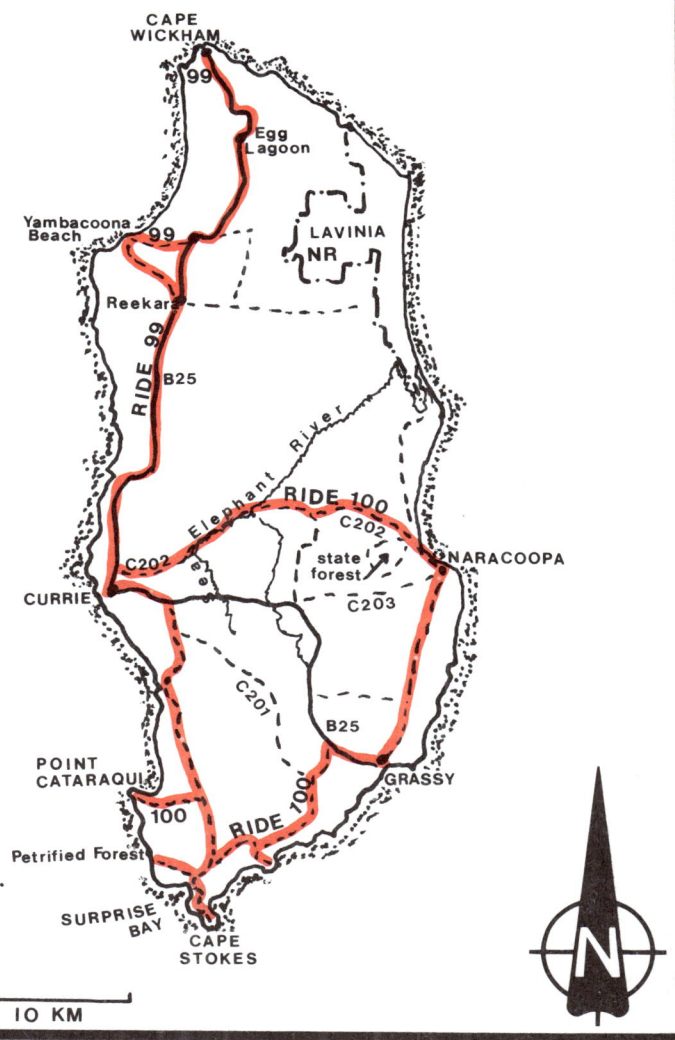

KING

14

CAPE WICKHAM

99

Egg Lagoon

LAVINIA NR

Yambacoona Beach

99

Reekara

RIDE 99

B25

Elephant River

RIDE 100

C202

state forest

NARACOOPA

C202

CURRIE

C203

C201

B25

POINT CATARAQUI

GRASSY

100

RIDE 100

Petrified Forest

SURPRISE BAY

CAPE STOKES

N

10 KM

RIDE 99: CAPE WICKHAM

FROM: Currie (11 km King Island Airport)
       27 km from Grassy Harbour
TO: Cape Wickham Lighthouse [RETURN]
VIA: Loorana and Egg Lagoon
LENGTH:
    Day 1: Currie to Yellow Rock Beach 27 km
    Day 2: Yellow Rock Beach to Cape Wickham
    return 42 km
    Day 3: Yellow Rock Beach to Currie 27 km
    Total is 96 km (With sidetrip excursions—142
    km)
TIME: 3–4 days
RIDE/TRACK GRADE: 3/3
HEIGHT VARIATION: 60 m
TRANSPORT: Cargo vessel from Stanley or flights from Wynyard and Melbourne
FACILITIES: Retail outlets at Currie
SPECIAL GEAR: Water containers
MAPS: King Island 1:100 000 topographical or 1:100 000 land tenure. (See Map 14: *KING*)

> *The light at Cape Wickham can only be*
> *regarded as a beacon warning navigators*
> *of danger, rather than a leading light to*
> *a great thoroughfare*
>   –Admiralty Sailing Directions

The tower is 44 m tall with mammoth granite walls over 3 m thick and standing on 10 m foundations, making this lighthouse a most interesting attraction. It was built in response to the frequency of ships slamming into the reefs off the island and off the Port Campbell coast in western Victoria. One of the most impressive stacks was the *Cataraqui* in which no fewer than 399 lives were lost. Even after the construction of the Cape Otway lighthouse in 1848, vessels still kept getting smashed on the reefs and cliffs and the slaughter of lives finally led to funds being allocated to King Island.

Cape Wickham, named after Captain Branscombe Wickham, who is buried on the island, began operation on November 1, 1861 with a relatively luxurious lightkeeper's residence. But still more ships, such as the *Netherby* carrying 500 people, came to grief and navigators were confusing the King Island lighthouse for the Victorian one, therefore turning south into more treacherous reefs.

Cycle north from Currie (20 m) to Porky Beach, a popular surfing beach. Spend time swimming here or at Yellow Rock Beach 24 km to the north. Access is via South Yellow Rock Road and a gate that must be kept shut. There is a 40 m downhill here. Although it's not an official camping area, conditions are relaxed. The paddle steamer *Shannon* was wrecked here.

In the morning make your way out via North Yellow Rock Road to Yambacoona, where one will see the homestead where the first Methodist service on the island was given in the cookhouse in 1910. There is also a bottle house and an old butter factory. Keep on the B25 to Cape Wickham. The road turns to dirt but reasonable averages can still be maintained. Follow the signs to Cape Wickham Lighthouse past a trout fishing venue at Lake Flanagan.

At Cape Wickham one has views over the desolate salt-hardy scrubs of Victoria Cove and Cape Farewell, where the sea is generally more sheltered and consequently calmer.

It is 51 km back to Currie. One can camp on the return at Yellow Rock Breach again, or one can take a diversion to Lake Martha Lavinia and Pennys Lagoon in the north or the rough Bicentennial Track which connects Reekara Road to Ridges Road. This is a short cycle from Lavinia Nature Reserve named after yet another wreck in 1871. Camping is permitted here.

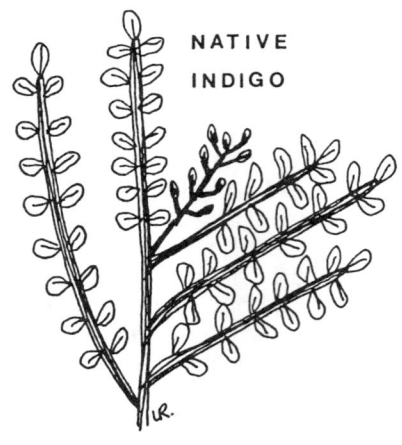

NATIVE INDIGO

RIDE 100: KING ISLAND
(SOUTH LOOP)

FROM: Grassy
TO: Currie [RETURN]
VIA: Naracoopa, Lavinia Nature Reserve, Seal Point
LENGTH:
    Day 1: Grassy to Surprise Bay 48 km
    Day 2: Surprise Bay to Cataraqui Point 32 km
    Day 3: Cataraqui Point to Currie 31 km
    Day 4: Currie to Naracoopa 29 km
    Day 5: Naracoopa to Grassy 21 km
    Total is 161 km (With sidetrip excursions 204 km)
TIME: 5–7 days
RIDE/TRACK GRADE: 5–6/6
WALKING: None
HEIGHT VARIATION: 135 m
TRANSPORT: Cargo vessel from Stanley or flights from Wynyard and Melbourne
FACILITIES: Groceries and amenities in Grassy and Currie. Basic camping in Lavinia Nature Reserve
SPECIAL GEAR: Water containers
MAPS: King Island 1:100 000 topographical or 1:100 000 land tenure. (See Map 14: *KING*)

From the jetty up to the township of Grassy is 3.5 km, involving a climb of 110 m. If the day is late upon arriving but you feel like some preliminary cycling to get acquainted with conditions, you can do a small 8 km loop to the south of Grassy visiting the 9-hole golf course and scheelite (tungsten) mine via Grassy Harbour and Port Roads. The deposit was discovered in 1911 and was mined in an open-cut quarry before operations continued underground in two locations.

    Next morning, stock up at Grassy and head out on Grassy Road (B25). Nearly 4 km later head left on the Mount Stanley Road passing Mt.Stanley, the highest peak on the island at 230 m, much lower than the peaks of Flinders due to being much older. Two kilometres later take the next left again (Red Hut Road) at 135 m altitude. The road leads down to Red Hut Point. Head right parallel to the coast (80 m) and then down a fast hill to Colliers Beach. Just off the coast here, the *Carnarvon Bay* was wrecked in 1910. One can either spend some time here swimming if the weather is nice or continue west and south to Seal Point. Backtrack to the Seal River Road, cross the river in between Big Lake and Colliers Swamp. These will sometimes be dry. Once on the South Road it's bumpy cycling down to Stokes Point (19 km from Seal Point). Remember to shut the gate behind you. The lighthouse is 3 km from the end on the left. Backtrack to Surprise Bay on the left for the first night's camp. The day's distance is 48 km.

The next morning head east to South Road again via the gate north and then immediately left again to the Calcified (or petrified) Forest and cliff-top views of the coast that has claimed many lives. Chances are you'll meet a frustrating headwind whenever travelling west. Spent the night in Fitzmaurice Bay near Cataraqui Point 9 km along Attrils Road. This was the place were 399 people lost their lives in 1845 aboard the *Cataraqui*. There is an unmarked mass grave somewhere to the north along the coast so don't go around digging deep holes. The day's distance is 32 km.

Currie, the capital, is 31 km to the north via Ettrick Beach. Along the way is another nice beach, British Admiral Beach, accessed by the road along Badger Box Creek. Here two ships were wrecked: the *British Admiral* in 1874 (79 lives gone), and the *Blencathra* a year later.

At Currie (20 m), resupplies can be bought. A good sea-food meal is recommended. King Island is renowned for its saltwater crayfish. Bass Caravan

Park has a few on site en suite vans for reasonable rates. In order to blend in with the locals one must walk and talk about half as fast as usual. Also located at Currie is the double-storeyed 100-year-old Clare Cottage, moved from Surprise Bay in the far south. The vegetation here on the west coast is very stunted, the harbour entrance formed by very low headlands that offer no protection to the eucalypts. Looking out west towards South America more often than not one will see the open Southern Ocean very uninviting—whipped up by the roaring forties into a frenzy of white-caps.

When ready to leave in the morning, head north for 2.5 km and then east onto Frasers Road (C202). This will take you all the way to the radiata pine state forest 4 km north-west of the quiet township of Naracoopa. For a drastic change in scenery the cyclist with energy to spare at this stage can complete an 11 km return loop of the forest before arriving at Naracoopa. Wildlife on King Island was decimated during the nineteenth century and many endemic species became extinct. However seal and sea bird colonies are re-establishing themselves with the aid of island reserves.

Out of the persistent westerlies, it is possible to spend several days at Naracoopa lazing on the beach. This day's distance without the forest loop will have been 29 km. Accommodation is available in units. For a 32 km (return distance) camping diversion to Sea Elephant and Lavinia Nature Reserve head north past the old rutile mine to the Sea Elephant River and Nine Mile Beach. The blow hole along the way is only operative during special wind, current, and tide conditions.

Where the Sea Elephant River flows into Nine Mile Beach, mining companies have extracted monazite (a phosphate mineral containing thorium and rare earth elements) and gold. These leases are now abandoned due to poor quantities making production economically unviable.

From Naracoopa it is 21 km back to Grassy.

For those flying into King Island, this ride can also be done starting at Currie and cycling to Grassy via the forest and back to Currie via Stokes Point.

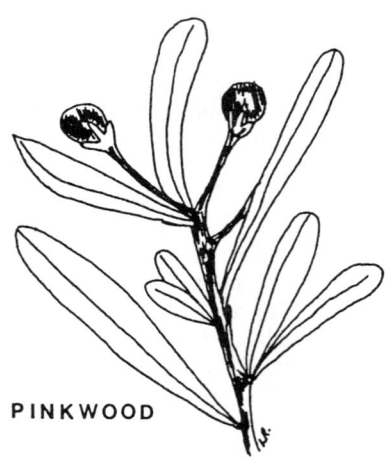

PINKWOOD

QUICK REFERENCE TO RIDES

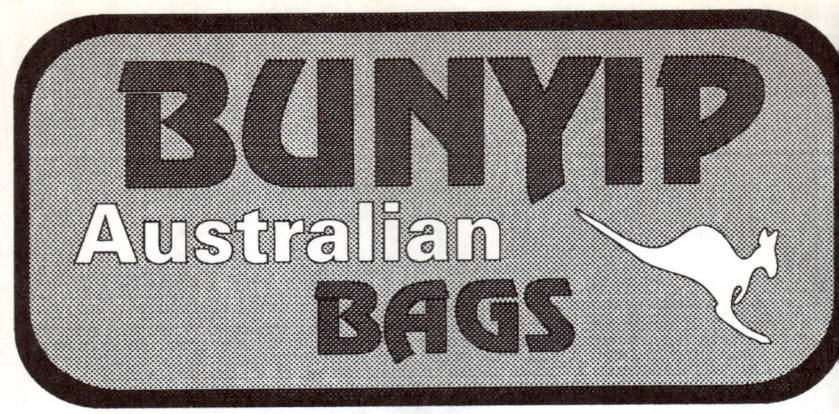

ENDURANCE EQUIPMENT

For mail order brochure and price list please contact:

Bunyip Bags,
PO Box 156
Summer Hill   NSW   2130

ph 02 797 8028
fax 02 797 9932

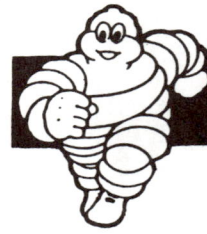

MICHELIN

Enjoyable cycle touring depends on good tyres!

Michelin make a range of high quality bicycle
tyres and tubes that include purpose designed
touring and mountain bike models that are
strong enough to handle the harshest conditions
in the world and still get you home!

Ask for them by name at your favourite speciality bicycle shop.